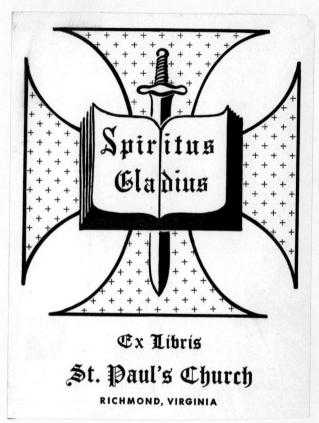

Spiritus Gladius

Ex Libris

St. Paul's Church

RICHMOND, VIRGINIA

THE PSALMS AND THEIR MEANING
FOR TODAY

THE
PSALMS
AND
THEIR MEANING FOR TODAY

by Samuel Terrien

THE BOBBS-MERRILL COMPANY, INC.
PUBLISHERS
INDIANAPOLIS   NEW YORK

538

FOREWORD

THIS book has been written not for scholars but for general readers. It grew out of informal lectures delivered to lay groups in New York and in the metropolitan area, and out of several summer conferences with ministers, Sunday-school teachers and superintendents. I wish to express my gratitude to these men and women who, by their devotion to Christian service, their interest in the Psalms, and their perspicacious discussions, have contributed not a little to the birth of these chapters.

More particularly, I acknowledge my debt to Dr. James Muilenburg and Dr. Paul Scherer for their friendly and keen remarks, to my wife Sara, who has read the typescript with critical acumen, and to others who have inspired me.

Mr. Julius Birge of The Bobbs-Merrill Company deserves special mention, for it is he who suggested the writing of this book. I wish to thank him here for his patience and unfailing help.

S. T.

Preface

THE PSALMS IN THE
LIFE OF THE WESTERN WORLD

THE vitality of the Hebrew Psalms in the worship life of the Western world is a noteworthy and almost enigmatic fact. No other book of hymns and prayers has been used for so long a time and by so many diverse men and women. Here is an anthology of religious poems composed and collected in a remote land many centuries ago. The Temple of Jerusalem, in whose shadow most of their poets lived, has remained destroyed for more than fifty generations. Its cultic pageantry and ritual, of which the Psalms were the theological expression and lyrical adornment, have gone the way of ancient Babel and Memphis. Yet this archaic hymnal has survived the cult for which it was created.

Today the Hebrew Psalms are read, chanted, or sung by countless people, every day of the year and everywhere on the face of the earth. They constitute the core of personal prayer and corporate adoration for all forms of Judaism—Orthodox, Conservative, Reformed—and for all churches of Christendom—Greek, Roman, Protestant. Such an enduring and widespread power of survival may be claimed for no other book of poetry and song.[1]

---

[1] Many of the illustrations mentioned in the following pages are found in Rowland E. Prothero, *The Psalms in Human Life* (London: Thomas Nelson and Sons, 1903). See also John Ker, *The Psalms in History and Biography* (Edinburgh: Andrew Elliot, 1888), and Jane T. Stoddart, *The Psalms for Every Day; with a Thousand Illustrations from Life and Literature* (London: Hodder and Stoughton, 1939).

I

First of all, the Hebrew Psalms were the liturgical food of the inner life of Jesus. He was born and reared to their strains. As a Jewish boy in a pious home, he probably learned them by heart at his mother's knee. When he was baptized as a man conscious of his solidarity with the human race, it was a psalm, according to the Gospels, which crystallized in his mind the goal and scope of his mission; and when he hung on a cross, in his naked solitude and destitution, preyed upon by physical and spiritual torture, it was a psalm which his voice uttered, and it was with a psalm that he gave up the ghost. Christians without number, after the example of their Lord, have praised, prayed, suffered, and died with their spirits attuned to the virile melodies of the same lines.

In prison at Philippi, Paul and Silas chanted psalms at midnight (Acts 16:25). In the Roman catacombs wretched craftsmen and slaves who had found in Christianity the secret of a new life recited Ps. 73 before dawn and Ps. 141 after dusk. With the sentence, "Idols are only silver and gold" (Ps. 115:4), they defied the imperial orders to sacrifice in honor of a human ruler. Young and old faced the arena singing, "I will bless the Lord at all times; his praise shall ever be in my mouth" (Ps. 34:1), or, "Lighten mine eyes that I sleep not in death" (Ps. 13:3).

During the Middle Ages many men and women retired to the wilderness in order to devote their lives to the adoration of God, and the Psalter became the basis of their spiritual exercises.[2] Francis of Assisi modeled his *Canticle of the Sun* on the lines of Ps. 148. The author of *The Imitation of Christ* was strongly influenced by the Psalter, taking as a motto for Book III, "I will hearken to what the Lord God will say concerning me; for he shall speak peace unto his people and to his saints that they turn not

---

[2] Through the Divine Office or breviary the 150 Psalms are read every week by all priests and nuns of the Eastern Orthodox and Roman churches. Likewise, the Book of Common Prayer prescribes the reading or chanting of the entire Psalter every month.

again to folly" (Ps. 85:8; the Latin version translated here differs from the Hebrew text).

The precursors as well as the preachers of the Reformation found in the manly passion with which the psalmists sought the presence of God and salvation a comfort and a spur in the struggle they waged for the defense of their faith. In 1415 John Huss was condemned to death by the Council of Constance, and he ascended the stake reciting Ps. 31. A year later at the same place Jerome of Prague perished while pronouncing the same words of hope and certainty. In 1498 Savonarola lay in a cell, mutilated in body; with the right hand that had been left him so that he might write a confession of conformity to ecclesiastical authority, he composed a meditation on Pss. 31 and 41.

During the whole of his life, Martin Luther expounded with great relish and power the spiritual substance of the Psalms. He translated them into rhythmic prose or adapted them for the hymnal of the evangelical church. After him, many Christians under stress have asked with the poet of Ps. 42, "Why art thou cast down, O my soul?" and affirmed in triumph, "A mighty stronghold is our God!" (Ps. 46.) It is mostly on account of the Psalms that the German chorals, especially those of Johann Sebastian Bach, offer an unsurpassed blending of musical beauty with religious truth.

The Huguenots sang the Psalms in the metrical translations of Marot, Beza, and Calvin, set to the melodies of Bourgeois and Goudimel. "To sing the Psalms" is still today in several countries of Europe a popular way of saying "to be a Protestant." Tormented by ill-health and harassed by news of the persecutions which befell his disciples, Calvin used to submit to the will of God by repeating the words of Ps. 39:9, "I became dumb and opened not my mouth; for it was thy doing." One of the many artists who embraced the reformed faith, Bernard Palissy, rediscovered after frightful labors the secret of producing enameled pottery; in the hour of success, he only cried, "Not unto us, O Lord, not unto us, but unto thy name give praise!" (Ps. 115:1.)

Spanish, French. Italian, Bohemian, Polish, and Hungarian

Protestants were hunted for one century or more, and they perished by the hundreds of thousands for the sake of their fidelity to scriptural Christianity. On the scaffold or at the stake they met death singing, "This is the day which the Lord hath made; we will rejoice and be glad in it" (Ps. 118:24).

Likewise, England and Scotland passed through the throes of religious reform and civil wars, and the Psalms inspired martyrs on both sides. While awaiting decapitation the Catholic Thomas More simply repeated his favorite penitential prayer, "Have mercy upon me, O God!" (Ps. 51:1.)

Many psalms were translated for English singing by Thomas Sternhold during the reigns of Henry VIII and Edward VI. Another version was made by Matthew Parker, who later became Archbishop of Canterbury and wrote in 1587, "I persist in the same constancy, upholden by the grace and goodness of my Lord and Saviour, Jesus Christ, by whose inspiration I have finished the Book of Psalms turned into popular verse." The Old Hundredth, translated by William Kethe and set to one of the Genevan tunes, is still used in most services conducted in the English language throughout the world. In Scotland the metrical paraphrases of the Psalms became the hymnbook of John Knox and of the Presbyterian churches.

The Puritans of the seventeenth century sang psalms as they crossed the seas in order to worship in the freedom of the new world, and it was after a verse of Ps. 76, "At Salem is his tabernacle," that pioneers named the first settlement of the Massachusetts Bay Colony. The Bay Psalm Book was the third volume ever printed in America (1639-40).

When the convention for the framing of the Constitution of the United States met at Philadelphia in 1787, some delegates reminded their colleagues of the religious significance of their undertaking by quoting Ps. 127, "Except the Lord build the house, they labor in vain that build it."

As a new Philosophy Hall was being erected recently on the campus of a famous Eastern university, it was proposed for a time to inscribe over the main entrance the aphorism of Protagoras, "Man is the measure of all things," but the phrase which may be read there today is the quest of the psalmist: "What is man that thou art mindful of him?" (Ps. 8:4.)

Why do the Psalms offer in all ages and climes a wisdom and a consolation for living and for dying?

II

The secret of the vitality of the Psalms lies first of all in the sense of *worship* which animated their poets. As the derivation of the word indicates, worship is "worth-ship," namely, the acknowledgment made by finite man of God's infinite worth, and also the aesthetic representation or dramatic expression, by symbolic acts, attitudes, and words, of this recognition. A service of adoration does not primarily aim at edifying, elevating, purifying, or consecrating the worshipers. To be sure, it should bring about all these results, but they are only its by-products. The purpose of worship is to ascribe glory to God. The psalmists placed God at the center of their existence, not themselves: in other words, their conception of worship was "theocentric" and not "anthropocentric." Man was not their main concern, but the service of God was the goal of their life.

In the potent formula of the catechism, they knew that "man's chief and highest end is to glorify God." They held that nothing on earth is "worth while" unless it be properly related to the creator of the universe, the giver of life, the master of nature, man and beast, the judge and saviour of history. But they did not lose themselves in the godhead, and their preoccupations with things divine and eternal did not prevent them from remaining men of flesh and bones, living on earth, and concerned with the world of human life and its manifold realities. There was no trace of Hindu pantheism in them, no deluding mysticism of the type which seeks to evade the self and the responsibilities of social existence. And thus they not only offered "in a right manner the sacrifice of praise," but they also prayed for and obtained the heavenly benefits and rewards which make earthly living, in spite of its trials and madness, a wise, sound, and eminently "worth-while" experience. Again, in the words of the catechism, they realized that "man's chief and highest end is" not only "to glorify God," but also "fully to enjoy him forever."

In the second place, therefore, the secret of the vitality of the Psalms lies in their poets' *boldness in prayer*. As Calvin put it, they have "opened up to us familiar access to God." Like the widow of the parable they may have begged unashamed, but in their eagerness to obtain from God the grace and power to live aright, they analyzed themselves; their emotions, sentiments, and passions; their thoughts, doubts, and prejudices; their instincts, tendencies, and determinations, with the sharpest kind of lucidity. They brought to light, from the recesses of their subconscious minds, the loves and hatreds that our hypocrisy usually conceals, even from ourselves. They expressed their sorrows and their despairs, their anguish and their hopes, in the most persuasive display of introspection. And they did not investigate the murky corners of their personalities as if—Narcissus-like—they looked in the mirror of a pond or lay on a psychoanalyst's couch. They examined themselves in the presence of God, borrowing for a time the cold glare of eternity, and their preoccupation with self grew from the true motivation of their existence: an unshakable belief in a God who is truly God, who reigns on high, and yet who cares for each man.

Thus, in the third place, the reason for the survival of the Psalms may be found in their poets' *theological certainty*. Out of the abysses of despondency and skepticism the psalmists climbed on rocks of faith. And when they proclaim to us the ultimate victory of God in the world, we are enabled to listen, precisely because we sense the sincerity and realism which permeates their psychological outlook. An unadulterated awareness of man's weakness and folly is the prerequisite to any affirmation of God's goodness and power. The psalmists had the right to claim that "the Lord reigneth" because they never closed their eyes to the rule of evil within themselves and without. In addition they thought out their faith. In a sense only music can do justice to the ineffable surge of the human spirit, facing with awe and wonder-

ment the magnitude of the "grand design" of salvation. But, as
Paul said, "I will sing with the spirit, and I will sing with the
understanding also" (I Cor. 14:15). Man's intellect, by reflecting
on his emotions, refines them, enlightens them, and, most important of all, confers on them a principle of stability, a quality of
duration, and a capacity for transmission. What happens to a
faith which remains intellectually unexpressed, untranslated, un-
transmuted into beliefs? To be sure, it is impossible to shackle
the fullness of life within the words of a dogma, and even the
right doctrine may for a time stifle religion. Yet, whenever theological search is despised, man's response to the demands of God
ends in sterile sentimentalism. The "sweet singers of Israel" lyrically and critically applied their minds to the mystery of their people's mission and failure, and by doing this they described so
graphically the work and the word of God in nature and in history—the *opus dei*—that Luther rightly called the Psalter "a
Bible in miniature."

In the fourth place, then, the Psalms appeal to modern man
because their poets had a sense of *historical and social responsibility*. They were not only individuals who stood naked before
their maker, they were also members of a closely knit community,
which extended itself in time as well as in space. They belonged
to the people-elect, the true Israel, the church of the promise, the
corporate agency of judgment and salvation in the world, the spiritual body which has a mission to fulfill among all the nations of
the earth. They were the sons of fathers who claimed to have
been set apart for a purpose, and they were determined to show
that history is not a meaningless and incoherent meeting of material forces, "a merry-go-round run by a madman," but that it
unfolds itself to its appointed end, which is the triumph of good
over evil. Even the most lonely sufferers among them, emerging
from the labors of their soul-searching agonies, went out to preach
and to proclaim, like the prophets, the deeds of God to the fathers
and to the sons. They wrote their poems as a testimony. Their
literary activity itself reveals their social concern and sense of
duty toward posterity. They were possessed by a missionary zeal
that, far from leading them to separate themselves from society

like some mystics and saints, prompted them on the contrary to share their faith with the community and to build an edifice for generations yet unborn. They looked forward to a kingdom where justice and peace shall dwell, and they lived already, in poetic and liturgical fashion, at the moment of that kingdom's advent.

Finally, the Psalms have survived the test of time on account of the *aesthetic form* in which their poets couched the religious truths they had apprehended. Today poetry and theology are not often associated together. Indeed, theologians are not popularly supposed to have poetic minds, and many poets repudiate any theological inclination or intent; but a true poet deals with matters of theological import: love and death, estrangement and despair, life and eternity. The psalmists acknowledged the claims of God on man and they responded in adoration, but they formulated that response with a sublimity of diction that still forces itself on the modern mind in spite of the strangeness of metaphor, the archaism of idiom, the awkwardness and betrayal of translation. Their language was that of poetry and thus it was able, as John Donne once said, "to contract the immensities" within the scope of human words. Their treasure was not carried in earthen vessels and it could survive the injuries of age. The poetic form and structure of their strophes (or stanzas), which adequately espoused the movements of their moods, the tortuous detours of their travails, and the ascents of their triumphs, remain the channel by which their message, over the barriers of time and tongue, still offers itself to us, and produces, in the words of Keats, "the instantaneous conviction." We never truly appropriate the Psalms to ourselves. It is the poetry of the psalmists that compels our assent just as the power of inspiration compelled them to write. Whenever their faith reaches our spirits, some spark of the original fire is rekindled. For some of us, at least, their wisdom and their consolation influence our decision to live and to die as responsible creatures.

Before we turn to the study of the Psalms themselves, it will be necessary to consider the milieu and circumstances in which they were composed.

CONTENTS

1

The Origin of the Psalms

THE ORIGIN OF THE PSALMS

ACCORDING to modern scholarship, the Psalter is an anthology of hymns and prayers which were composed from the tenth to the third or second centuries B.C. It grew from the aspirations, vicissitudes, humiliations, and hopes of a people who adored God with music and song even in time of distress. It is therefore a poetic expression of that people's religious history during a period of seven or eight hundred years.

The ancient Hebrews worshiped their God in a manner unique among the populations of the classical Orient, and the Psalter is the mirror of their worship. In order to determine the origin and growth of the Psalms one needs to consider the distinctive characteristics of Hebrew worship, and these may be analyzed under five dominant motifs: (1) deliverance in warfare; (2) cultic presence; (3) harvest thanksgiving; (4) holy history; and (5) personal communion with the divine.

I

The motif of *deliverance in warfare* is not peculiar to Israel's religious poetry, but it received in the Bible an unparalleled coloration or stamp from the faith of the people. Hebrew worship began when a group of frightened slaves, under the leadership of Moses, left their Egyptian taskmasters and despite pursuit escaped across the northern tip of the Gulf of Suez. All had seemed lost. As the powerful frontier detachments of the Pharaoh's army were about to overtake the fugitives, a most unexpected deliverance occurred, and with that event the nation was born and the religion of the Old Testament received its historical seal and foundation.

In that historical occurrence the Hebrews recognized the evidence of Yahweh's grace and power;[1] indeed, they concluded that the God of their fathers was more powerful than the most powerful nation on earth. This theological interpretation of a fact which, through the celebration of the Jewish Passover and of the Christian Easter,[2] remains at the very center of Western civilization, found its immediate expression in a psalm. The tradition was remembered that "Miriam the prophetess . . . took a timbrel in her hand; and all the women went out after her with timbrel and dances; and Miriam answered them [antiphonally]:

> "Sing ye to Yahweh!
> For he hath exalted his majesty.
> The horses and their riders
> He hath thrown into the sea."[3]

In spite of its brevity this psalm is a complete hymn of praise in thanksgiving. Salvation came at the imminence of death. Release from fear led to an acknowledgment of gratitude for the victory received, not to self-congratulation. A full act of worship is here described as joy pours forth collectively in dancing and music with a meaningful song which at once ascribes deliverance, not to man's efforts and cunning or to natural coincidences, but to the sheer grace of the deity. An undercurrent of vindictiveness directed against the defeated enemy is implied in the poem; but let no modern mind glibly condemn this feeling. Israel's survival depended on war against oppression.

---

[1] "Yahweh" is the personal name of Israel's God as revealed to Moses (Exod. 3:13-14). The form of "Jehovah" represents a mistaken reading of the sacred consonants (Tetragrammaton) with the vowels of "Adonay" (the Lord) that the scribes inserted in the manuscripts of the Hebrew Bible during the early Middle Ages.

[2] There exists profound unity as well as historical continuity between the two feasts: the former celebrates deliverance from political oppression and the latter commemorates salvation from the enslavement of sin and death.

[3] Exod. 15:21-22. The poetic perfection and the archaic abruptness of the diction may be sensed quite clearly in the sounds of the Hebrew original:

> *Shîrû layyahweh*
> *kî gaoh gaah*
> *Sûs werokebhô*
> *ramah bhayyam.*

The point which requires emphasis is that Hebrew worship—and the Psalter—originated in a dramatic and musical exteriorization of the inward emotion of thankfulness at the issue of a mortal situation. Victory, which is "by nature insolent and haughty," led not to the glorification of man but to the exaltation of God.

For centuries thereafter struggle for life was almost the daily concern of the tribes wandering in the wilderness and entering the land of Canaan. Fragments of archaic battle prayers which have been preserved in the tradition reveal that the nation was conscious of fighting, not so much for its own existence, as for vindicating the honor of its God:

"A hand on the banner of Yah!
    War for Yahweh!
Against Amalek from generation to generation" (Exod. 17:16).

Yet the Hebrews knew at the same time that it was Yahweh himself who was fighting their battle for them. This clearly appears in the Song of Deborah:

"I, even I, will sing unto Yahweh!
    I will sing praise to Yahweh, the God of Israel!
Yahweh, when thou wentest forth out of Seir,
When thou marchedst out of the field of Edom . . ."
                    (Judg. 5:3-4).

And perhaps at the same early date they discerned an intimate connection between divine guidance in war and the soldier's inward attitude of devotion toward his God:

"So let all thine enemies perish, O Yahweh!
    But let them that love him be as the sun
When it goeth forth in its might" (Judg. 5:31).

It is in the light of these emotions of gratitude for liberation from deadly peril that many of the psalms must be viewed, and one will then more easily withhold the severe judgment which might otherwise be pronounced on the passion of hatred that animates some of them.

II

The second factor which determined the origin of the Psalter is to be found in the motif of the *cultic presence* of God. Inasmuch as the Hebrews, alone in the ancient world, refused to represent the godhead through the means of man-made images (see the prohibition of the Second Commandment in Exod. 20:4), they were profoundly aware of the fact that the deity whom they adored was beyond all human encompassing, and was not limited to a fixed and localized abode, as were the gods of pagan shrines. From the earliest days they knew that Yahweh could say, "All the earth is mine" (Exod. 19:5). They were sure that Yahweh was not a god who sat in a sanctuary. At the same time they were certain that in a very real sense he "sojourned among them" or, more literally speaking, "tabernacled" in their midst[4] and "walked with" his people (II Sam. 7:6 ff.).

The traditions vary with regard to the forms in which this real presence of God was described. Beneath the diversity of expressions, however, the same conviction remains. The theme of the deliverance from Egypt was linked with the motif of real presence. The very purpose of the Exodus was to bring the slaves to the proximity of their God. "Ye have seen what I did to the Egyptians, and how I bare you on eagles' wings, and brought you unto myself" (Exod. 19:4). Likewise, other traditions described how Moses "drew near unto the thick-darkness [*araphel*], where God was" (Exod. 20:21). At other times the divine presence was made visible as "a pillar of cloud . . . and a pillar of fire" (Exod. 13:21; etc.), and in a more concrete and material fashion, when the ark was carried into battle, Moses used to say:

"Rise up, O Yahweh!
Let thine enemies be scattered
And let those who hate thee flee away from thy presence"
(Num. 10:35).

---

[4] See the New Testament echo of this potent formula in John 1:14, "The Word . . . tabernacled among us."

Later on, after the conquest of the land, it was again the ark which gave to the temple of Shiloh its justification and meaning: there the people felt that "they worshiped before the face of Yahweh" (I Sam. 1:19). When the ark was taken by the Philistines, the people realized that "the glory [was] departed from Israel" (I Sam. 4:21-22). Still later, when the ark was brought to Jerusalem, "David and all the house of Israel played before the face of Yahweh on all kinds of" musical instruments (II Sam. 6:5). David himself "danced before the face of Yahweh with all his might" (II Sam. 6:14). Finally, when Solomon erected the Temple, "the ark was brought in" (I Kings 8:4) with the result that "the cloud . . . and the glory of Yahweh filled the house. . . ." (I Kings 8:10-11). In order to prevent in the mind of the people any confusion between the Temple of Yahweh and the sanctuaries of the pagan gods, which were personifications of natural forces, especially the sun, Solomon opened the dedication of the new edifice with this significant formula:

> "The sun, Yahweh has set in the heavens;
> But he, himself, has resolved to dwell in thick-darkness:
> Therefore, have I built for thee a lofty mansion,
> A place for thee to dwell in for all ages."[5]

According to this amazing statement, probably inspired by the king's theological advisers, God is not a part of the universe: he is the creator of the heavens, and especially of the sun, the natural source of light and life, which the ancient Semites and Egyptians alike turned quite understandably into the most attractive deity. Although the God of the Hebrews transcends the created cosmos, he has decided, as an act of pure grace and love, to manifest his presence in the midst of his worshiping people. The Old Testament grasped these mutually excluding aspects of the deity— "cosmic transcendence and cultic immanence." Israel held that proximity and remoteness are inseparable in the true being of God. Whenever Biblical man was encountered by the divine person, he

---

5 I Kings 8:12-13. This liturgical poem is quoted from the complete text, which has been preserved not in the Hebrew Bible but in the Greek version of the Septuagint. Note the use of the word "thick-darkness" [*araphel*] as in the Mosaic tradition.

sensed, obscurely perhaps, but also with profound certainty, that God the creator was at once distant and close, hidden and revealed, absent and present. And when the Temple of Jerusalem became in the course of the centuries the focus of Hebrew worship, Yahweh was not only adored as the ruler of nature and the master of history, but also as the lord of Zion.

Many of the psalms were created for the purpose of celebrating the divine presence at the moment of the cultic drama. But the tension between the cosmic transcendence and the cultic immanence of God was never resolved in Hebrew worship. The great prophets (eighth—sixth centuries B.C.) fought the popular superstitions which found in the presence of Yahweh in Zion an argument for shallow optimism. Jeremiah scoffed at his contemporaries who in time of dire danger sang intoxicatedly, "The temple of Yahweh, the temple of Yahweh, the temple of Yahweh!" (Jer. 7:4.) The prophet predicted the imminent ruin of the sanctuary (Jer. 26:4-6). Worship without a shrine became a necessity during the Babylonian Exile (586-538 B.C.), and while some Jews returned to Jerusalem and rebuilt a temple on the burned remains of the old (about 516 B.C.), some disciples of the great prophets proclaimed the inadequacy of such a form of cult:

> "Thus, saith Yahweh, the heaven is my throne,
>   And the earth is my footstool:
> What kind of house could you build for me?" (Is. 66:1).

Nevertheless, the faith of the scattered Hebrews could not separate itself from Zion:

> "I will bring them to my holy hill,
>   And I will make them joyful in my house of prayer . . .
>   For my house shall be called
>   A house of prayer for all peoples" (Is. 56:7).

Thus the hymns of praise as well as the national and individual prayers which are now included in the Psalter are to be understood in the light of the Hebrew grasp of this paradox: God is really present in the act of worship, but he is not "contained" by an earthly temple. He is not possessed by man; he is not the property of a people; he is not at the disposal of man's will; he does not come to man as a result of priestly technique; he is not captured by a fulfillment of ritual acts or the pronouncement of sacerdotal words.

Although the Psalms were collected presumably with the approval of the priests of the Second Temple, the ideas which were developed therein are remarkably antiritualistic. At least they reflect a religion which cannot take ritualism as an end in itself without utterly corrupting the adoration of Yahweh.

III

The third factor which determined the origin and growth of the Psalter is closely related to the feeling of gratitude after deliverance in warfare and to the belief in God's tabernacling presence in the cultic act. It may be called the motif of *thanksgiving for harvest*. Like other nomads who gradually settled in fertile lands and became prosperous farmers, the Hebrews had to learn how to till the soil and to breed cattle. They lived in a religious environment which was largely conditioned by the fear of hunger and thirst, and which was consequently dominated by an elemental concern for the powers of fertility in nature. Peoples of the ancient Near East had deified these powers, and their religious beliefs and activities were centered around the mystery of sexual reproduction and procreation. The Semitic paganism which surrounded Israel may be described as a perennial attempt to secure the necessary staples of life from the powers which were supposed to produce them.

While the Hebrews borrowed from their predecessors and neighbors the habit of celebrating the cycle of the seasons in agricultural festivals, they adapted those practices thoroughly to the specific requirements of their faith. They knew that their God was the free master of nature, and they did not believe that by some kind of semimagical rite they could ensure the coming of rain and sunshine or induce the continuation of plant and animal life. They felt themselves to be entirely in the hands of their maker, and they ascribed the increase of the land to his gracious generosity. They asked for divine blessings on field, barn, and home, to be sure, but primarily they sang the praises of the creator of heaven and earth, seed and fruit, and they thanked him for dispensing with liberality his gifts for the sustenance of man. At the same time they never separated their economic existence from the historical consciousness of their mission as a people.

IV

The fourth element which thus played a part in the origins and growth of the Psalter is the motif of *holy history*. One of the earliest liturgies of harvest thanksgiving shows the connection which existed in the Biblical mind between the life of the individual man on earth and the destiny of the elected people in the context of world-wide history. When the newly settled Hebrew peasant, still aware of his ancestors' nomadic insecurity, presented to Yahweh the first fruits of his fields, he repeated the following prayer (Deut. 26:5-10):

"My father was a nomad Aramaean, exhausted from wandering and ready to perish[6]; and he went down to Egypt and sojourned there—but he became there a great nation, powerful and populous; and the Egyptians dealt with us in an evil way, and they afflicted us and laid upon us hard bondage: and we cried unto Yahweh, the God of our fathers, and Yahweh heard our voice, and he saw our affliction, and our toil and our oppression; and Yahweh brought us forth out of Egypt with a mighty hand, and with an outstretched arm, and with great terribleness, and with signs, and with wonders; and he hath brought us into this place, and hath

---

[6] Strictly translated, the Hebrew words are "my father was a perishing Aramaean," but it is perhaps permissible to paraphrase in order to bring out the fullness of the meaning implied by the text.

given us this land, a land flowing with milk and honey. And now, behold, I have brought the first fruit of the ground, which thou, O Yahweh, hast given me."

This archaic liturgy reveals in astounding fashion the unique character of Hebrew worship. Here is an individual farmer who at the time of his prosperity is united with the past of his nation. He feels again the horrors of famine and of slavery (notice the abrupt shift in the use of the personal pronouns from "they" to "we" and "us"), and in his hour of plenty remembers the destitution and oppression of a distant past as an experience which is liturgically made present. He communes with generations gone long ago and responds with them, as it were, to the mighty act of God's redemption and re-creation by which the people was brought into historical existence and maintained over the centuries.

For the ancient pagans of the Near East an agricultural festivity was primarily intended, through the performance of an appropriate ritual, to induce the gods and goddesses of fertility to promote life on the earth. For the Hebrews, on the contrary, a harvest festival was the occasion for commemorating the grace of a sovereign God who elected and saved a people.

The Psalter is filled with poetic expressions of that faith in which a sense of gratitude for the gifts of nature is intimately bound with a will to dedicate the nation anew to its historical purpose and mission. Thus, some of the psalms hail the feast of the Passover, originally an early-spring festival, as the memorial of God's deliverance of the people from economic want and political oppression. Other psalms are associated with the Feast of Weeks (Pentecost), originally a late-spring harvest festival, ultimately the solemn recollection of the covenant which on Mount Sinai (Horeb) sealed the destiny of the people as the instrument of God's intentions toward mankind. Still other psalms are related to the celebration of the Feast of Tabernacles, originally an autumn festival connected with the gathering of grapes and olives and the making of new wine and oil, ultimately a remembrance of the years of sojourn in the wilderness when the fathers dwelt in tents under the skies.

The motif of history, which dominated the worship of the Hebrews and conferred on the Psalter its main characteristic, is related to the theme of the *election* of Israel, as it is expressed by the memory of the promises made to Abraham and of the *covenant* which united the people to the God of their fathers and at the same time obligated them to follow a certain way of life. Hebrew worship received in the ancient world its distinctive quality because each generation remembered that Abraham had separated himself from his fatherland in obedience to the divine command, and had received the promise that his posterity might become a nation through which all the nations of the earth would be blessed and would bless one another (Gen. 12:2 ff.; 18:18 ff.; etc.). The memory of these promises gave to the covenant made in the wilderness its historical anchor and its hope for the future:

"Ye have seen what I did unto the Egyptians,
And how I bare you on eagles' wings,
And brought you unto myself.
Now, therefore, if ye will obey my voice indeed
And keep my covenant,
Then ye shall be a peculiar treasure unto me above all peoples,
For all the earth is mine:
And ye shall be unto me a kingdom of priests
And a holy nation" (Exod. 19:4-6).

The word "covenant," which has been translated "testament," is the key to the whole Bible. If they kept the covenant, the Hebrews felt themselves to be on earth a "holy nation," a nation separated from the others, set aside for the purpose of communicating God's will to the world. By their own obedience, they thought they could become "a priestly commonwealth" which would bear the solemn and perhaps crushing honor of revealing, like a priest, the fullness of God to man. This was an almost incredible idea in a world of powerful empires more than a thousand years before the gospel of Jesus. No wonder many Hebrews themselves remembered only the glory of the mission and forgot the responsibility of its obligation.

The prophets of the eighth and seventh centuries, such as Amos, Hosea, Isaiah, and Jeremiah, proclaimed that the covenant had been abrogated through the tolerance of social injustice and moral corruption. "You only have I known of all the families of the earth: therefore I will punish you for all your iniquities" (Amos 3:2). And the people passed into the throes of agony and death. A nation born to be king, prophet, and priest of mankind, "the servant of the Lord" (Is. 42:1; 49:3; etc.), was now thrown down and trampled underfoot. The Temple was burned, the land was conquered, the royal line was brought to exile and annihilation, the sons were scattered on the face of the earth. But they were still singing.

The psalmists understood the meaning of the covenant. They had been impressed by the stern judgment of the prophets. They had learned that the Lord's demands on man are forever true, "to do justly, and to love mercy, and to walk humbly with [one's] God" (Mic. 6:8). Thus, when a handful of priestly families were allowed by the Persian emperors to come back to Zion in the sixth and fifth centuries and to erect a new temple on the ruins of the old one, the psalmists, imbued with the prophetic spirit, still insisted that worship must be the expression of the whole of man. They prayed for the integrity of religion. They yearned for the moral decency of the individual in the midst of the community. They grasped the meaning of *shalôm* (peace), not as a negative reality, the cessation of strife brought about by the forceful exclusion of some men, but as a total, inclusive, wholesome, healthy *(shalem)*, ongoing communion with God and solidarity with all men. They conceived religion not only as a temple service but also as a complete and sustained attitude of life—in the home, at the shop, at the market place, and on the highways of trade and culture.

Still, the psalmists had no illusion about the discrepancy which appeared between the evils of the present and the goodness of God's rule. Like Jeremiah, who was waiting for a "new testament" (Jer. 31:31 ff.), they were looking forward to that kingdom when God's law would be written on the hearts of man, when religion and morality would become an integrated oneness, when wars would cease and God be exalted on the earth. History for them was not a meaningless chaos, a cycle of growth and decay, or an endless consummation of iniquity. Just as they lived liturgically in the past and brought to their cultic present the promises made to the fathers and the deliverance from Egyptian bondage, so also they brought into their act of worship the future manifestation of God's rule over injustice as a liturgically realized and accomplished victory. History for them moved toward its appointed end, and they contemplated it already as the fulfillment of creation, singing, "The Lord reigneth!" They could not have entertained, however, this cosmic vision had they not been personally and individually engaged in a face-to-face encounter with the God they adored collectively.

V

Thus, the fifth and final element which prepared the origin of the Psalter and oriented its distinctive development is the motif of *personal communion with the divine*. Hebrew worship was characterized from the earliest times by a naïve, unhampered, direct, and intimate dialogue between God and man. The traditions of the fathers are sparkling with gems of individual prayer. "Enoch walked with God" (Gen. 5:24) is more than a picturesque figure of speech. "Walking with God" is a comprehensive expression that describes the fundamentals and the summits of religion. It represents a kind of mysticism which is neither Greek nor Hindu but peculiarly Hebraic; there is in it no possibility of losing the self into infinity, for man remains man and God truly God—a mysticism which respects both godhead and manhood. It is because Enoch walked *with* God that the psalmists could declare, "Nevertheless, I am continually *with* thee" (Ps. 73:23). It is because Abraham "stood before the Lord, and ... drew near, ... and

said, 'Wilt thou also destroy the righteous with the wicked?' "
(Gen. 18:23) that the psalmists could boldly and almost blas-
phemously pour out their doubts and ask, "How long,...O Lord?"
(Ps. 13:1.) It is because Jacob fought in the night and said to the
mysterious wrestler as the day was breaking, "I will not let thee go
except thou bless me" (Gen. 32:26), that the psalmists could
strive in the depth of their loneliness and sing, "Thy face, O Lord,
will I seek!" (Ps. 27:8.) It is because the same Jacob, pursued by
his brother whom he had wronged, begged abjectly, "O God of my
father, . . . I am not worthy of the least of all thy mercies . . ."
(Gen. 32:9-10), that the psalmists could shout, "Out of the depths
have I cried unto thee, O Lord!" (Ps. 130:1.) It is because Moses
cried on behalf of the people, "If thou wilt forgive their sin—; and
if not, blot me out, I pray thee, of thy book" (Exod. 32:32 f.),
that the psalmists could declare, "Not unto us, O Lord, not unto
us, but unto thy name give glory!" (Ps. 115:1.) It is because
Nathan said to David, "Thou art the man!" (II Sam. 12:7) that
the psalmists could whisper, "Have mercy upon me, O God, according to thy lovingkindness!" (Ps. 51:1.)

It is on account of this long habit of coming to God ashamed
and yet unashamed, desperate and yet full of hope, a habit which
was ingrained in generation after generation of destitute or guilty
men and women, that the psalmists could affirm, "The Lord is the
strength of my life: of whom shall I be afraid?" (Ps. 27:1.) A
long inheritance of a people's spirituality constitutes the human
secret of the Psalter.

Some scholars have maintained that the poets who composed
the Psalms could not have laid this emphasis on individual communion with the divine before the time of Jeremiah, the first writer
of religious confessions (20:7 ff.; etc.). As a matter of record,
however, Hebrew worship from the first was different from any
other religious form precisely because it was not the prerogative
of monarchs or members of a professional hierarchy but was fully
accessible to the rank and file of the community—a peasant's wife
like Hannah (I Sam. 1:10-11) or a landless herdsman like Amos

(Amos 7:14). The psalmists represented an anonymous elite, the folk-aristocracy of immediate religion.

VI

The present collection of one hundred and fifty psalms may be quite correctly called "the hymnal of the Second Temple" (*ca.* 516 B.C.-A.D. 70), that is to say, the sanctuary which was built on the ruins of the Temple of Solomon (*ca.* 952-587 B.C.). 365 yrs.

In New Testament times Judaism attributed the whole Psalter to David, and this fact explains the Davidic references made by Jesus and the early Christians with regard to several psalms quoted in the Gospels and in the New Testament generally. In the book of Psalms itself many poems are not attributed to David's authorship, and one of them is even explicitly ascribed to "Moses, the man of God" (Ps. 90). The familiar superscription, "A Psalm of David," comes from the collectors of the hymnal and probably means "Psalm dedicated to David" or "Psalm written in the name of David." Like most ancient peoples, the Hebrews had not conceived the notion of a strict, "copyrighted" authorship. During those years when the psalms were collected together and for centuries thereafter, Judaism published most of its literary productions under the sponsorship of great names of the past, like Enoch, Abraham, Jacob, Moses, David, Solomon, and even Adam and Eve!

Modern scholarship, after several decades of intensive study, tends to admit that the core of several pieces comes from David himself (1002-962 B.C.) or even from pre-Hebraic poets. Archaeological research of the nineteenth and twentieth centuries has brought to light a considerable number of cultic poems which were used in the third and second millennia B.C. by the ancient populations of Mesopotamia, Syria, Palestine, and Egypt. Many of these hymns and prayers offer a number of stylistic patterns, rhythmic and strophic structures, and even trains of thought which may be recognized also in the Hebrew Psalms. From careful comparative study[7] it appears that not a few of these have been composed according to the poetic form of earlier hymns and prayers which were sung by the Akkadians, the Canaanites, and the Egyptians for centuries before the birth of Israel as a nation. However, while the Hebrew psalmists were undoubtedly influenced by their predecessors, they recast the old formulas and adapted them in such a radical fashion that the crass paganism of their models was completely transfigured by their own monotheistic faith in Yahweh, the creator of the universe, the master of history, and especially the lord of Zion.

The name of David imposed itself on the collectors of the hymnal in a quite natural manner: Not only had tradition associated the king with musical talents of unusual fame (I Sam. 16:14 ff.; Amos 6:5), but it had also represented him as having created the various guilds of musicians (I Chron. 15:16 ff.) led by such men as Heman, Asaph, and Ethan, whose names were also preserved in the Psalter.

VII

One of the major difficulties hindering modern enjoyment of the Psalms is due to the lack of order with which the various hymns and prayers have been placed together. A careful analysis of each piece reveals that several smaller collections were made separately and then added side by side, probably in different groups and in different ages, with the result that there are some instances of duplication (cf. Pss. 14 and 53). Modern scholars have given considerable attention to the "types" of the various

---

[7] See for instance *The Psalmists,* ed. by D. C. Simpson (London: Oxford University Press, 1926), especially the essays of H. Gressmann, "The Development of Hebrew Psalmody," pp. 1-22; G. R. Driver, "The Psalmists in the Light of Babylonian Research," pp. 109-176; A. M. Blackman, "The Psalms in the Light of Egyptian Research," pp. 177-197. Also, W. O. E. Oesterley, "The Psalms as Part of a World-Literature," in *A Fresh Approach to the Psalms* (New York: Charles Scribner's Sons, 1937), pp. 11-35; J. H. Patton, *Canaanite Parallels in the Book of Psalms* (Baltimore: The Johns Hopkins Press, 1944); *Ancient Near Eastern Texts Relating to the Old Testament,* ed. by J. B. Pritchard (Princeton: Princeton University Press, 1950), pp. 365-401; A. R. Johnson, "The Psalms," in *The Old Testament and Modern Study,* edited by H. H. Rowley (Oxford: Clarendon Press, 1951), pp. 162-209.

hymns and prayers. Hermann Gunkel, who is perhaps the greatest exponent of the Psalter in the twentieth century so far, has proposed a classification based on literary form and strophic structure and has listed among others the following *Gattungen,* or genres: Hymns, Collective Laments, Individual Laments, Pilgrim Psalms, Royal Psalms, Wisdom Psalms, etc. No single classification will prove to be adequate, for the simple reason that many of the pieces now preserved in the Psalter have been amplified, edited, or conflated from two or more smaller units which belonged originally to different types; see Ps. 19, for example. The classification adopted here, similar to that of Gunkel, is based on the form analysis as well as on the dominant theme of each poem. It is proposed only in a provisional way, for the mere purpose of study.

The "Hymns of Praise" contemplate God as he reveals his glory and his will through the world of nature, the events of history, and the tabernacling of his presence in the Temple. The "Prayers in Time of Crisis" are offered by the community or the individual in time of straits when man is at his wits' end. The "Songs of Faith" confront life in its tragic depths, but they ultimately move toward the heights of certitude and serenity.

2

Hymns of Praise

I | WORSHIP OF THE LORD OF NATURE

ONLY two poems of the Psalter bear the title "Psalm of Praise" (Pss. 100 and 145), but the whole hymnal is called in Hebrew *Tehillim*, "Praises." Yet the psalmists on the whole prayed and begged much more than they praised. They lamented and confessed more often than they thanked. They queried and complained and even cursed more violently than they blessed. They argued and meditated more obstinately than they adored. Why is it then that such a title imposed itself on tradition for designating all the poems now included in the Psalter?

The answer lies in the fact that all the prayers of the hymnal, whatever may have been the tortures in the midst of which they were at first whispered or sobbed, came to be used in the services of public worship, first in the Temple of Jerusalem, then in the synagogues of the Dispersion. Thus they received the new meaning of a liturgical context which always represents the triumphant faith of the community.

The highest level of Biblical worship is reached when man, overcoming the obsession of his guilt or of his needs, places himself resolutely before his creator, judge, and saviour, and responds in lyrical contemplation to the grace of life that sustains him in his distress. The name "Praises" may not be comprehensive enough as a title for the Psalter, but its use reveals that the psalmists succeeded in transmuting all their moods and attitudes into an act of adoration. Even in their sorrow and despair they sensed that God sought them. And in reply to that divine search they turned their regrets into aspirations, and their failures into resolves. Even the agonies of their abandon could ultimately make room for dedication.

Nevertheless, there are a number of psalms that belong in the strictest sense to the type of "Hymn of Praise," in which the poet contemplates the deity and does not allow his feelings or passions to sway the objectivity of his lyricism in the direction of psychological introspection. In such poems the ancient Hebrew steps aside and merely adores his God; and when he does, he is generally moved by three themes which in many cases overlap one another and only seldom are kept fairly separate: he worships Yahweh as the sovereign of nature, as the ruler of history, and as the lord of Zion.

Both ancient and modern paganism—as amply shown by the allusions of the classical writers and the undertones of our culture—have deified or at least personified nature as a whole or the main forces thereof. The gods and goddesses of the ancient mythologies are not wholly different from the unnamed deities of modern science or the deified nature of the romantic poets. They are essentially projections of man's elemental fears and needs.

For the psalmists, on the contrary, as well as for all the Biblical poets and writers, nature is never conceived as a power or as a group of forces endowed with autonomous existence and activity. God is omnipotent. The creator of the world is and remains in complete control of his masterpiece. No hymn of nature ever suggests the view made familiar by the deists of the eighteenth century, according to whom, to be sure, there is a creator—"by hearing the clock ticking, I know," said Voltaire, "that once upon a time there was a clockmaker"—but "natural" laws are now taking care of the orderly functioning of the world's existence. Such a thought lies completely outside the psalmists' minds. At grave philosophical risks which they did not surmise, they showed God at work, comparing him to the artist who never lets his creation go forth out of his hand. They did not suspect any problem of injustice arising from the occurrence of "natural" catastrophes. God is always and everywhere the sovereign master of the universe.

Such a faith appears whenever the psalmists contemplate the continuous activity of God. They interpret events of nature only as manifestations of God's judgment and providence. At times they face the terrors of thunderstorms, as in Ps. 29. At other times they meditate on the serenity of night and day, as in Pss. 8 and 19. Or again they embrace within their poetic grasp the whole range of the cosmic picture, as in Ps. 104. In any one of these poems they never think of nature as benign or adverse to man. They merely discern behind its manifold displays the gracious or righteous touch of the giver of life, and they seize the occasion to sing his glory.

I

The Lord of the Seven Thunders
(Psalm 29)

(Gloria in excelsis)   PRELUDE

1.   Give unto Yahweh, O ye sons of the gods,
            Give unto Yahweh glory and power;
2.   Give unto Yahweh the glory of his name:
            O worship Yahweh in the beauty of holiness!

(Gathering)   I

3. The roaring of Yahweh is upon the waters;
        The God of glory thundereth;
        Yahweh thundereth upon many waters;
4. The roaring of Yahweh cometh in force;
        The roaring of Yahweh is swelling in splendor!

(Bursting-forth)   II

5. The roaring of Yahweh is breaking cedars;
        Yea, Yahweh breaketh the cedars of Lebanon!
6. He maketh even Lebanon skip like a calf,
        And Sirion like the young of wild bulls!
7. The roaring of Yahweh is hewing out flames of fire!

(Dying-away)   III
  8. The roaring of Yahweh causeth the wilderness to writhe;
        Yahweh causeth the desest of Kadesh to writhe in anguish!
  9. The roaring of Yahweh maketh the hinds bring forth,
        And he strippeth the forests bare . . .
        But in his temple all say, Glory!

(Pax in terris)   POSTLUDE
10.   Yahweh was enthroned at the flood;
                Yea, Yahweh sitteth as king for ever.
12.   Yahweh give power unto his people!
                Yahweh bless his people with peace!

Recent studies have shown that the literary origins of this poem
are to be found in the archaic liturgies of the Phoenicians. The
psalmist, however, was a triumphant monotheist. Pagan as the
roots of the hymn may have been, as revealed for instance by
the invitation issued to the "sons of the gods" (vs. 1*a*), the whole
tone is one of faith in an omnipotent God, who forever is in complete control of his world. Before one of nature's most awesome
phenomena the Hebrew poet does not beg for protection. He does
not even display the elemental fear which most probably shakes
his frame. Whatever his terror may be, he conquers it and he
uses the thunderstorm as an occasion not for hysteria but for
praise and contemplation.

Franz Delitzsch called this hymn "the Psalm of the Seven
Thunders" because the expression *qôl Yahweh*, "the voice of the
Lord," recurs seven times as the theme is unfolded. Thus the
book of Revelation (10:3), centuries later, alluded probably to
this expression: "And he cried with a great voice, as a lion roar-
eth, and when he had cried, seven thunders uttered their voices."

The body of the hymn is constituted by *three strophes* of five
lines each; these are preceded by a *prelude* or *call to worship* and
followed by a *postlude* or *confession of faith* and *benediction*. The
strophic pattern suits admirably the development of the theme.

The prelude and postlude, of four lines each, form a distant prefiguration of the angels' chorus in the Christmas gospel according to St. Luke (2:14):

> "Glory to God in the highest,
> Peace on earth to men of his delight!"

The *Gloria in excelsis* (vss. 1-2) begins with a threefold call to adoration, perhaps sung antiphonally by three different choirs converging in stately procession on the Temple's esplanade. The triple repetition of the first hemistich, "Give unto Yahweh," makes the invitation more and more pressing and forceful, while the second hemistich of each line adds one idea at a time; the structural device of repetition and catenary addition may have coincided with the climbing of steps by the various groups of singers and officiating priests. However, that which takes place on earth is but a mirror of the drama which is enacted in the heavens. The "sons of the gods" are the members of the divine court. They are bidden to "give" or "render" to Yahweh "glory and power." The verb translated "give" is unusual—*yahabh,* a cognate of *ahabh,* "love." Thus the first word of the hymn is in itself a commentary on the nature of Biblical worship. The members of the heavenly court and, by liturgical participation, the congregation in the earthly temple as well, are bidden to "ascribe lovingly" and to "render" to Yahweh "glory and power." They are invited to recognize symbolically his distinctive qualities. Men and heavenly beings should not let themselves be intoxicated by their own glory and power. Remembering the frailty of their condition, they should submit themselves to the only "powerful" God and express with loving gratitude their dependence on his grace. More especially should they "render unto Yahweh the glory of his name." The God worshiped by the psalmist manifests his glory in supreme fashion by revealing his name: he consents to communicate his will toward men and his intention toward his people. The God of the universe, even in a pure hymn of nature such as this, is in a very special sense the God of the covenanted people. His name and activity within mankind's history are known to the church of the promise and of the covenant. It was perhaps the officiating priest who summed up the threefold call in a climactic invitation addressed again to the heavenly beings and by implication to the mighty of the earth: "Prostrate yourselves before Yahweh in the beauty of holiness!"

The verb "prostrate yourselves" is ordinarily translated "worship" but it suggests the elaborate gestures, the bows, genuflections, and several postures which depict concretely for the Oriental mind the complete humiliation of self and the acknowledgment of total dedication to the service of the deity. This liturgical act is accomplished by the priests, singers, and various sacerdotal attendants, properly purified and attired in holy vestments. The traditional expression "in the beauty of holiness" attempts to render in English two difficult Hebrew words which seem to mean more than the idea of "sacred attire" or "holy array." They ring some undertones of religious as well as aesthetic "increase" or "swelling, going-beyond process," a spiritual as well as artistic experience of suprahuman beauty which invades the worshiper's being at the time of corporate adoration. The self-deprecating act of the prostrating attitude leads to the perception of "the beauty of holiness," within and without. Men are hallowed by ritual and also by inward transformation when in the sanctuary they find themselves corporately in the presence of the holy God.

The geographical setting of the psalm fits the pattern of a typical electric storm in Palestine. In the first strophe (vss. 3-4), distant rumblings are heard from the western horizon of the Mediterranean Sea. Very soon the roaring of thunder, which represents for the ancient mind the very voice of deity, comes across "the waters" (vs. 3*a*), the "many waters" (vs. 3*b*), and then explodes "in force" (vs. 4*a*). The sounds of the tempest are "swelling" (a word related to that used for "beauty" at the end of the prelude) and convey to man the sense of divine "splendor" or "majesty." The choice and location of this term, at the end of the first strophe, is most fortunate. It links the contemplation of God's mighty acts in nature to the act of worship in the Temple.

The second strophe (vss. 5-7) depicts in a graphic way the moment when the storm, having advanced from the west across the sea, at last hits the coastal mountain range. The poetic technique is here unexcelled. Every detail is placed in close parallelism or succession so as to lead to the natural climax, "fire!" (Vs. 7.) The cedars of Lebanon, symbols of perennial solidity, are not only broken (vs. 5*a*) but also shattered to pieces (vs. 5*b*). More enduring than the cedars, the mountains themselves shake, quiver, and leap, like the newborn of the heifer (vs. 6*a*). Not only the Lebanon range, but Sirion, the snowy, towering peak of Mount Hermon, which may be seen from the whole Palestinian chain, skips and jumps like the young of wild animals (vs. 6*b*). All the elements of nature respond with fear to the might of their master. The flashes of lightning strike the earth like the axes of the lumberman (vs. 7). The storm has reached its "deep, dread-bolted" moment.

After the crescendo of the first and second strophes there is a corresponding decrescendo in the third (vss. 8-9), while the tempest swiftly flees from north to south and dies away in the wilderness of Kadesh. Nature lies wounded and exhausted in its fright, but, with sharp contrast, "in his temple all say, Glory!" This last word is the key to the psalm. It offers the response of worship to the appeal of the prelude. The sons of the gods in heaven and the congregation on earth are united in a single shout of adoration. The poet does not give to man's reactions any direct or elaborate attention. Psychology is conspicuously absent. No suggestion is explicitly made either of fear or of faith. While natural man, under the threat of death, would beg, promise, or gamble, for the sake of his carnal security, man in worship, united with the heavenly world, merely adores and sings, "Glory!"

The postlude is inevitable. As the storm is now gone, *Pax in terris!* The aftercalm, as in the last movement of Beethoven's *Pastoral Symphony,* offers the poet an opportunity to meditate on the meaning of his recent contemplation. Reminded of the primeval Flood by the downpour of rain which has been unleashed by the storm, he makes the congregation recite a creed (vs. 10) and the officiating priest offer a benediction (vs. 11). The king who sat enthroned at the Flood is ruling the world still and for-ever. The thunderstorm produces the life-giving showers which in the autumn renew the face of the earth and the hope of its in-habitants. But the cataclysm will be kept within beneficent limits, for Yahweh remains in control. May he offer to his people the blessing of his strength. May he communicate to them the stored energy and the sustaining potentiality they need in order to endure without failing or faltering the storms and the catastrophes of ex-istence. May they receive a goodly measure of the power which in the prelude is ascribed to God himself. May peace and social harmony be granted for the health of the whole community of worshipers.

Before the spectacle of nature in torment and under the threat of her own destruction, the church militant glorifies in this psalm the creator and lord of nature, and is blessed with peace.

II

The Lord of Man's World
(Psalm 8)

PRELUDE

1.
    O Yahweh, our sovereign,
    How magnificent is thy name
    In the whole of the earth!

I

  Thou, whose majesty is set upon the heavens,
2.
    Out of the mouth of babes and sucklings
  Hast thou ordained strength, on account of thy foes,
    In order to still the enemy and the revengeful.

II

3.
  When I consider thy heavens, the work of thy fingers,
    The moon and the stars, which thou hast ordained,
4.
  What is man, that thou art mindful of him?
    And the son of man, that thou visitest him?

III

5. Yet thou hast made him lack almost nothing divine,
   And hast crowned him with glory and honor;
6. Thou hast given him rule over thy handiwork;
   Thou hast put all things under his feet;

IV

7. All sheep and oxen, yea, all of them,
   Even the beasts of the open fields,
8. The birds of the heavens and the fish of the sea,
   Whatsoever passeth through the path of the seas!

POSTLUDE

9.   O Yahweh, our sovereign,
          How magnificent is thy name
          In the whole of the earth!

This hymn has often been misunderstood as a poem on the splendor of nature and the dignity of man. The poet was not concerned, however, with these themes; he used them only as means toward a higher end: praise of a God who created the world for the sake of man and conferred on him the honor and responsibility of its dominion.

To be sure, the psalmist was sensitive to the beauty of nature around him, and he admired in awe-struck silence

> "Heaven's ebon vault,
> Studded with stars unutterably bright,
> Through which the moon's unclouded grandeur rolls. . . ."

But even had he lived in another age he would not, like Shelley, have yielded to the temptation of sentimentalism. He would not have written that the darkened firmament

> "Seems like a canopy which love has spread
> To curtain her sleeping world."

He would not have composed a "Hymn to the Night." He would not have been a romanticist, whose imagination loses itself in natural wonders, and takes the night for a confidant or a lover. The psalmist adored God, the creator of heaven and earth, and he indicated plainly his intention in the identical prelude and postlude of his hymn.

He did not try either to bolster faith or to prove God's existence by the contemplation of an orderly universe. The contemplation of the world of nature is in itself sterile or at least completely ambiguous. Man does not receive anything from such an exercise. He brings to it what he already possesses. There are of course some people, like Baron von Hügel walking at night on the Wiltshire Downs, who look up into the sky and, seeing those boundless heights and depths, cry out, "God, God, God!" There are also those who receive no comfort whatever from the observation of the cosmos, and who find on the contrary in its enigma a source of dismay and even despair. They exclaim with Blaise Pascal, "The silence of those infinite spaces terrifies me." The psalmist was not attempting to prove the existence of a creator by observing the regular course of planetary movements. He was worshiping a God whom he already knew, a God whom he had learned to revere from the example of his fathers and from the living creed of the church to which he belonged. Notice the plural possessive in the invocation, "Yahweh, *our* sovereign!" The poet is not speaking here as an individual thinker or scientist. He does not sing as a lonely musician or as a dilettante artist, buffeted by society and playing the part of the nonconformist. On the contrary he feels himself to be a member of this holy company of men and women who, from distant ages, are bound together across the limitations of time and space, beyond the barriers of official institutions, and above the arrogance of a particular tradition or hierarchy.

"Yahweh!" This is the first word, the personal name of the deity. Not a name common to all tongues and religions, a name which may be translated from one language to another, like Elohim, Deus, or God, but the intimate, peculiarly Hebraic name which Moses learned while "the bush was burned with fire and the bush was not consumed." The name of the God who said, "Now, behold, the cry of the sons of Israel is come unto me; I

have surely seen the affliction of my people that are in Egypt . . ."
(Exod. 3:7); the name which is in itself the sign of creative
power—"I cause to be whatever I cause to be" (Exod. 3:14);
the symbol of the tireless worker whose activity keeps the cosmos
in order and preserves man; the name which designates a God
who enters into the history of mankind and declares through the
prophet:

> "When Israel was a child, then I loved him
> And I called my son out of Egypt" (Hos. 11:1).

The invocation therefore is addressed to that God who has revealed his intention and purpose to his people, and the first strophe
immediately develops the theme of the poem. The creator who
displays his majesty in the heavens has also uncovered to his
church the true character of his power. The poet discerns here
the central mystery of Biblical religion. Divine strength is to be
found not primarily in the equilibrium of cosmic forces which both
attract and repel the galaxies compared to which the planet earth
is a mere speck, but in the praise and trust of the children of men.
There is a divine strength at work in the sweet patter of an infant.
Jesus, also, when he defines the requirements for entry into the
kingdom or proposes to his disciples a model of greatness among
them, turns to childhood with its directness, its humility, its utter
dependence on love, its trust without calculation, and at the same
time its uncanny shrewdness at detecting deceit and its refusal to
be encumbered by mundane conventions. When scholars and dig-
nitaries want to silence the children who shout hosannas in the
Temple, Jesus merely quotes from this psalm, "Out of the mouth
of babes and sucklings hast thou perfected praise" (Mt. 21:16).
With complete disregard for the wisdom of men Christianity knows
that God reveals the most sublime thoughts of him and of his ways
to those humble men who consider their earthly course and achievements and yet, comparing themselves with the creator and upholder of their lives, exclaim like Tennyson:

"But what am I?
An infant crying in the night:
An infant crying for the light,
And with no language but a cry."

There lies in this weakness a kind of inward strength which is able to still God's enemies and to silence those who avenge themselves and snatch the law from the judge into their own hands. Biblical religion testifies to the terrible power of the meek.

After having stated his main proposition in the first strophe, the psalmist considers the paradoxical situation of man in the universe. This mortal creature is not worth God's care and attention, but to him has been delegated dominion over the world of things and beasts. The poet holds equally fast to the two opposite poles of man's lowness and of man's height. He does not look at man's conferred greatness without remembering at first man's native insignificance. Moreover, he believes that man's kingship of the earth is in fact a vice-regency, a trust, and a stewardship, for which alone the creator may be praised. And thus the psalmist wonders at the vastness of the divine appointment—"Thou hast placed all things under his feet!"

A modern reader might draw the line somewhat as follows: "Yes, all things—the control of floods and erosion; the making of rain and the conquest of the atmosphere, of the stratosphere, perhaps tomorrow of the interplanetary spaces; the forcing of distance, the successful eradication of many epidemic diseases; and now the splitting of what is called the 'atom,' i.e., the 'unsplittable.' Yes, thou hast made him lack almost nothing divine. Man has over nature the power of a God. But he does not behave like one." Thus appears today the irony of man's situation in the universe. The psalmist did not pursue his meditation to its expected end. He did not wish to introduce the factor of inward evil and of corrupting pride which grows in earthly men in proportion to their exercise of power. But the impact of the thought he expressed in the first strophe should not be forgotten. He was aware of the abuse perpetrated by "the enemy and the revengeful." From the whole poem perhaps may be drawn the implication that man is master of the world only in so far as he recognizes his utmost dependence on the creator of the world. Failing to make this recognition, man intoxicates himself with the thought of his supremacy over the created order, and the viceroy of creation is thrown back into subhuman impotence.

Pascal grasped clearly the tension in which man on earth finds himself when he wrote, "What a mystery, then, is man! What a novelty, what a monster; what a chaos, what a subject of contradiction; what a prodigy! A judge of all things, stupid worm of the earth; depositary of truth, cloaca of uncertainty and error; glory and refuse of the universe!" It is against the horrors of modern man's achievements that his greatness must be observed and appraised. The conqueror of the forces of nature has not been capable of overcoming evil within himself. Created in the image of God, man is sufficiently like God to believe that he is a god and thus becomes an idolater of himself. He no longer asks in wonder and humility, "What is man that thou art mindful of him?" He does not even acknowledge any more that his dominion over nature is a responsibility entrusted to him by the lord of nature. He courts self-destruction by indulging in self-congratulation.

The irony of human "greatness" is dissolved only when the psalmist's picture of perfect manhood is viewed in the light of the man on the cross and in the hope for the coming of God's new world. After having quoted the central part of this hymn, the author of the Epistle to the Hebrews is compelled to remark, "Now we see not yet all things subjected to [man]. But we see Jesus, who for a little while was made lower than the angels, crowned with glory and honor by the suffering of death . . ." (2:8-9). The psalmist certainly did not intend to write a prophetic description of Christ, but his clear vision of a regal humanity is mirrored in the man from Nazareth. Where is modern man's crown of glory as he crawls into his own fears and graves? But in the man "crowned with thorns" the image of God may be quite plainly discerned. His meekness has a devastating power and his obedience can "still the enemy and the revengeful."

III

The Lord of Nature and Law
(Psalm 19)

I

1. The heavens declare the glory of God
    And the firmament proclaimeth his handiwork.
2. Day unto day poureth forth speech
    And night unto night revealeth knowledge.

3. There is no speech and there are no words,
    None can hear the sound of them;
4. Yet in the whole earth their echo goeth forth
    And their utterance reacheth the extremities of the world.

There he hath set up a home for the sun,
5.   Who goeth as a bridegroom out of his chamber
    And rejoiceth as a champion in a race.

6. His starting point is at one end of the heavens
    And his circuit is completed at the other end:
    Thus from his ardor nothing remaineth hid.

II

7.   The law of Yahweh is perfect,
            Restoring life.
        The witness of Yahweh is truthful,
            Making wise the simple.
8.   The precepts of Yahweh are straight,
            Giving joy to the mind.
        The commandment of Yahweh shineth **brightly**,
            Enlightening the eyes.
9.   The fear of Yahweh is pure,
            Enduring forever.
        The judgments of Yahweh are right,
            They are altogether just.
10.   They are more desirable than gold,
            Even much refined gold.
        They are sweeter than honey,
            Even the droppings of the honeycomb.

III

11. Now, thy servant is warned by them:
    In their observance there is great reward.
12. Who can discern errors of ignorance?
    From hidden faults make me innocent!

13. Also, from presumptuous thoughts hold back thy servant:
    Let them not rule over me!
    Then I shall be steady and faithful
    And free from grave transgression.

14. Let the words of my mouth be acceptable,
    And the meditation of my heart, in thy presence,
    O Yahweh, my rock and my redeemer!

The composite character of this psalm readily appears at first reading, for the language, style, meter, strophic structure, and ideas of the first part (vss. 1-6) have little in common with those of the second (vss. 7-10) and third (vss. 11-14). The first part is a pure hymn of praise for the God of nature, the second part is an antiphonal canticle in honor of the law of Yahweh, and the third part is a prayer of supplication.

However, the psalmist who was responsible for the poem in its final form may have brought together those various parts, not in a haphazard way as it is commonly assumed, but for the specific purpose of intimating a subtle message. One may even venture to suggest that this psalmist, discovering an ancient hymn on the glory of God as it may be seen in the wonders of sky and sun (vss. 1-6), was inspired to compose as a sequence and as a counterpart, perhaps as an implied corrective, a poetic meditation on the glory of the Lord as it is revealed in the Hebrew law (vss. 7-10); and that this meditation, in its turn, led him to offer a prayer of dedicating and searching supplication (vss. 11-14).

While men like Carlyle call the sky "a sad sicht," the poet of the initial hymn was moved to aesthetic and religious awe by contemplating the never-ending succession of nights and days, the movement of the stars and of the planets, and especially the faithful rising and setting of the sun. He may have been influenced by ancient liturgies of the proto-Phoenicians, for he designated the deity by the name of "El," an appellation which appeared in the literature of Ugarit long before the Hebrews emerged in the realm of history as the covenanted people of "Yahweh." His monotheism, however, is not to be doubted, for, although he described the sun as "a bridegroom" and a "champion" in the fashion of the pagans, he was careful to point out that the sun itself, far from being a god, was the created instrument of "El" in the same way as the heavens and the firmament, the days and the nights.

It is easy to understand how such a poem may have thrilled the thinkers of the eighteenth century and inspired, for instance, a man like Joseph Addison to compose his hymn on creation:

> The unwearied Sun, from day to day,
> Does his Creator's power display. . . .
> What though nor real voice nor sound
> Amidst their radiant orbs be found?
> In Reason's ear they all rejoice,
> And utter forth a glorious voice;
> For ever singing as they shine,
> "The Hand that made us is divine."

The ancient psalmist would not have understood that this hymn of creation reached "reason's ear." No one can hear the voice of the heavens, and it is faith, answering God's word to man, and not reason by itself, which can discern their language. The poet was living in the presence of his God and he was therefore able to interpret the silent speech of day and night. It was his faith, and not his reason, that prompted him to sing, "The heavens declare the glory of El." Those who find here a basis for erecting a "natural theology" and who believe that one can prove the existence of the creator by the observation of the cosmos forget that Biblical man knew his God in an immediate fashion and then proceeded from this knowledge to interpret the world around him.

The psalmist who preserved the hymn of nature may easily have subscribed to the thought that the heavens and the sun celebrate the majesty of the creator. In addition he may have wished to suggest that they are impotent to reveal the will of God toward men and to teach them how to live. This may have been the impulse which moved him to compose his poem in praise of the Hebrew law.

Thus the second part of this psalm passes swiftly and without transition from the "glory of El" to the "torah of Yahweh." The God of Israel is of course the same "El" who created the world, but he is also the guide and saviour of his people and he has disclosed to the men of his covenant a way of life which is more glorious than his display of power and order in the universe.

Like the sun the law of Yahweh is perfect, *temîmah,* that is to say, sound, round, and complete, for it restores life to the inward man. Like the sun the law is sure and faithful, for it provides a sense of security at the right moment and it gives joy to the man who obeys its prescriptions. Like the sun the law is bright, and its light enables man to walk ahead on his way in full knowledge of his goal. Like the rays of the sun, falling sharply at high noon, the judgments of Yahweh are straight, dividing good from evil; "they are altogether just."

This psalmist did not suffer from "the yoke of the law." His devotion was genuine, for it was based on a deep love of the will of God. Yet, as he continued to meditate on God's demands, he began to question the adequacy of his obedience and he begged for the grace of perfect fidelity. Then he became aware of a new danger. Is there not a temptation of presumptuousness and arrogance in the very success with which a man of integrity fulfills the law? Is not the righteousness of the law involving a perfect man in the sin of pride? The praise of the torah of Yahweh led to critical self-examination and the fear of hidden faults or even of the grave transgression. Praise therefore made room for prayers, for, as Milton noted, "Law can discover sin, but not remove."

Thus the psalm ends with a supplication for grace. A song of nature becomes the inspiration for a praise of the law which in turn leads to a simple and anxious prayer of petition. "The sun will not transgress his measures," said Heraclitus, but man is a complex creature, at once immersed in the realm of nature and rising above it. His moral achievements and even his religious obedience may be corrupted by a sense of self-satisfaction. He therefore must fall on his knees and supplicate the God of his fathers, the author of his strength, and the perfecter of his salvation, to receive his whole being, not only the words of his mouth but also the meditation of his heart, as a total sacrifice of praise and adoration.

IV

The Lord of the Seven Wonders
(Psalm 104)

1.   Bless Yahweh, O my soul!
     O Yahweh, my God, thou art exceedingly great!
         Thou are clothed with majesty and magnificence!

(Sky)   I
2. He is wrapping himself with light as with a garment;
     He spreadeth out the heavens as a curtain;
3. He layeth the beams of his chambers in the waters;
     He ordereth the clouds as a chariot;
     He walketh upon the wings of the wind;
4. He useth the winds as his messengers;
     He sendeth the flames of fire as his ministers.

(Earth)   II
5. He hath established the earth upon its foundations
     That it should not be moved for ever and ever;
6. Thou didst cover it with the deep as with a vestment;
     Above the mountains were standing the waters;
7. At thy rebuke, they fled;
     At the sound of thy thunder, they hastened away;
8. They went up toward the mountains, they went down in the valleys,
     Unto the place which thou hadst founded for them.
9. A boundary thou didst set that they would not trespass,
     So that they would not return to cover the earth.

(Water)   III
10. He sendeth forth the springs into the river beds;
     Between the mountains they run along;

11. They give drink to all the animals of the fields,
     And even the wild asses quench their thirst.
12. Above them the fowl of the heavens have their home,
     Among the branches they send forth their song.
13. He watereth the mountains from his upper chambers;
     From the fruit of thy works the earth is satisfied!

(Vegetation)   IV
14. He causeth the grass to grow for the cattle,
     And the fodder for the beasts which serve man
     So that food may be brought out of the earth,
15. And wine to rejoice the heart of mortal man,
     And oil to make his face to shine,
     And bread to sustain his mortal heart.
16. The trees of Yahweh are satisfied;
     The cedars of Lebanon which he hath planted,
17. Where the birds build their nests,
     The stork whose dwelling place is on the cypresses.
18. The high mountain ranges are for the wild goats;
     The crags are the refuge of the rock badgers.

(Moon and Sun)   V
19. He hath appointed the moon for the seasons;
     The sun knoweth its going down.
20. Thou makest darkness, and it is night.
     Then all the beasts of the forest creep forth;
21. The young lions roar after their prey,
     And they seek their food from God.
22. When the sun ariseth, they retreat
     And lie down in their dens.
23. Man goeth forth unto his work
     And to his labor until eventide.

(Sea)   VI
24. How manifold are thy works, O Yahweh!
     In wisdom hast thou made them all.
     The earth is filled with thy creations.
25. There is the sea, great and wide,
     Wherein creeping things are without number,
     The small ones together with the big ones!
26. There go the ships,
     Leviathan which thou didst make to play with him!

(The Gift of Life)   VII

27. All of them wait for thee
      To give them their food at the right time.
28. Thou givest to them, they gather;
      Thou openest thy hand, they are sated with good.
29. Thou hidest thy face, they are seized with fright.
      Thou takest away their breath, they expire
      And they return to their dust.
30. Thou sendest forth thy spirit, they are created,
      And thou renewest the life of the soil.

(The Glory of Yahweh)   VIII

31. Let the glory of Yahweh be for ever!
      Let Yahweh rejoice in his works!
32. He looketh upon the earth and it trembleth;
      He toucheth the mountains and they smoke.
33. Let me sing unto Yahweh as long as I live;
      Let me sing a psalm to my God as long as I have my being;
34. Let my meditation be acceptable unto him!
      I shall rejoice in Yahweh.
35. Let sinners be consumed out of the earth,
      And let the wicked be no more!

Bless Yahweh, O my soul!
Praise ye Yahweh!

Nowhere in the Psalter can one find a hymn comparable to Ps. 104, in which the whole universe is encompassed within a single sweep of religious vision. The poet worships Yahweh, "the faithful creator" (I Pet. 4:19), and he contemplates in turn seven realms of God's activity. The order which he follows is similar to the sequence of the creative works in the first chapter of Genesis. Some scholars therefore believe that the singing of this hymn accompanied the celebration of the New Year festival during which the drama of creation was commemorated.

The first strophe (vss. 2-4) is directed toward the phenomena of the sky and atmosphere: primeval light, the blue ether yonder, the vault of the firmament, the clouds, the winds, and the bolt of lightning. Every object of contemplation is lyrically related to God, the ever-present and wonder-making creator. We moderns may easily sneer at the naïveté of ancient man,

> "whose untutored mind
> Sees God in clouds, or hears him in the wind."[1]

But to the Hebrew psalmist the spectacle of universal harmony, which of course was not explained in any way by the intermingling of natural laws, merely suggested the power and gracious purpose of an active God.

Most of the verbs are used in participle form, and the poet may suggest thereby the continuity of God's support and endeavor. Creation is not a moment at the beginning of time, but the ever-renewed manifestation of God's will. The choice of words in the first line, "He is wrapping himself with light as with a garment" (vs. 2), is felicitous and shows a profound understanding of God's mode of revelation. The upholder of nature at once conceals his true being and discloses his presence through the light which can be seen and yet is too dazzling for human sight. The verb translated "wrapping himself" or "enveloping himself" is related to an Akkadian root meaning "to be darkened," and the poet may have attempted to express the ineffable when he said that God "darkens himself with light." As Calvin has well noted, "The knowledge of this truth is of the greatest importance. If men attempt to reach the infinite height to which God is exalted, although they fly above the clouds, they must fail in the midst of their course. Those who seek to see him in his naked majesty are certainly very foolish."

The second strophe (vss. 5-9) betrays the influence of pagan myths according to which the creator God had to fight the monsters of chaos and of the primeval ocean in order to secure a dry earth. There is no intimation, however, of the pre-existence of a demonic abyss which would have had to be conquered by the architect of the terrestrial mansion. The thought of an uncreated power of evil, coexistent with God and therefore independent of him, is utterly incompatible with the absolute character of Hebrew monotheism.

---

[1] Alexander Pope, *Essay on Man*.

It is Yahweh who "covered the earth with the deep as with a vestment" (vs. 6*a*). The image of a cosmic combat which dominated the creation stories of the Babylonians and other ancient Semites has been transfigured by the Hebrew poet. The waters of chaos do not represent here an uncreated and personified force, hostile forever to the God of law and order. They were not overcome in battle by the divine champion of life. Yahweh merely spoke the word, and they retreated in fear. "At thy rebuke, they fled" (vs. 7) and they now remain within their boundaries. The danger of a cosmic cataclysm, to be sure, is still in the back of the poet's mind. But he believes without question that God is and remains in control of his universe. Through the never-failing vigilance of Yahweh, creator and preserver, the forces of destruction that surround the theater of man's existence will never "return to cover the earth" (vs. 9).

In the third strophe (vss. 10-13) the poet turns his gaze to the marvels of springs, streams, and rain. Like all the inhabitants of the Near East, ancient and modern, he knows that plant and animal life depends on fresh water, but his concern is not simply of a utilitarian character. He is deeply sensitive to what others might call superfluous beauty. "Even the wild asses quench their thirst" (vs. 11*b*), and the birds send forth their song (vs. 12). All living beings lie within the realm of providence. "From the fruits of thy works the earth is satisfied!" (Vs. 13*b*.) Rain is the gift of heaven to which the soil makes its response.

No transition is needed for introducing the fourth strophe (vss. 14-18), which describes the miracle of vegetation. The bounties of the ground are destined for man's sustenance and enjoyment. The Hebrews did not know any antagonism between body and soul, and consequently their religion was free from the aberrations of asceticism. The psalmist appreciated to the full the simple pleasures of earthly life and he praised the creator not only for the necessities of existence but also for joy-giving wine and for the oil of anointment and perfume. He probably did not even consider wine and oil as luxuries. The expression "carnal living" would have been meaningless to him. Unlike the prophets he did not polemize against the pleasures of the senses, perhaps because in his time pagan worship with its sensuous rites did not present any serious threat against his monotheistic faith. He would not have understood any sermon on the excesses or the corruption of the flesh. He may have been aware of the problems presented by the presence of evil forces in nature and in human society, but he refused to consider them at this particular moment in the unfolding of his act of adoration. Other psalmists were oppressed by the enigma of suffering and the tensions of social existence. This poet, on the contrary, chose to adore his God, the provider of life, and his naïve gladness has its legitimate place in a hymnal which otherwise is not lacking in cries of agony and despair. There are moments in worship when it is sound to declare with God himself that the world is "good, very good indeed" (Gen. 1:31). Even the cedars of Lebanon, which produce no fruit, and such seemingly useless creatures as the storks on their cypresses and the rock badgers on their high cliffs are beneficiaries of the benevolent master. They play their respective tunes in the vast symphony of creation.

It is quite characteristic of a Hebrew poet to mention in merely an incidental fashion the moon and the sun, at the beginning of the fifth strophe (vss. 19-23). While the ancient world worshiped the moon and the sun as the most important deities, the psalmist took subtle care to give them credit as the obedient servants of Yahweh. The moon is an appointee in charge of the calendar. The sun marks the alternance of day and night. It is not even the absence of the sun which brings the night about. "Thou makest darkness, and it is night." Far from being a god, the sun is a subservient tool and "he knows when to get off the stage." The psalmist looks at the jungle animals without fear—an unusual note in the Bible. Lastly, man works as long as there is daylight. His labors are also a part of the order of creation.

The sixth strophe (vss. 24-26) considers the sea. Obviously, sea travel lies outside the poet's experience. He does not belong to a nation of sailors, like the Egyptians or the Phoenicians. Ships are for him a foreign wonder (cf. Is. 2:16; Prov. 30:19), almost as awesome as the mythological Leviathan which haunted the imagination of his fellow countrymen (cf. Ps. 74:14; Job 41:1; Is. 27:1). However, he would not like to suggest for a single moment that the famous monster presents a problem to his God. With a daring touch of theological humor, he maintains that Yahweh made Leviathan merely "to play with him" (vs. 26). This is another illustration of his triumphant faith. No shady allusion to pagan mythology can shatter his monotheism.

In the seventh strophe (vss. 27-30) the poet is now ready to focus his attention on the most amazing wonder of all: life itself, this ever-renewed gift which is not the possession of man and beast, but results from the constant action of God. Life continues on earth only because Yahweh in his grace wills it so. The poet is well aware of the fragility of existence. He breathes the very breath of God. The fiat of creation concerns him at every instant. Man and soil subsist only by a daily act of renewal. Life lives at the edge of death and should not be taken for granted. "Life," said Montaigne, "is a tender thing, and easy to be distempered." Life, wrote the psalmist, is the property of God and is never independent of the creator.

The eighth strophe (vss. 31-35) concludes the hymn with a lyrical burst of delight: "Let Yahweh rejoice in his works!" (Vs. 31*b*.) The poet thereupon wishes to sustain his response to the divine joy: "Let me sing a psalm to my God as long as I have my being!" (Vs. 33*b*.) Two thoughts of a dark portent, however, come to haunt and to disturb his mind. What about the earthquakes and the volcanoes? (Vs. 32.) And more perplexing still, what about the presence of human wickedness in the midst of a generally good universe? The poet may not have been so completely deaf, after all, to the discordant notes which jar the universal harmonies. He was unable to ignore them altogether. Nevertheless, he could not be prevented from concluding, "I, for one, shall rejoice in Yahweh." He was confident that someday evil would be eradicated from the world and that Yahweh would reign benevolently over all.

Ps. 104 has received greater attention than many other poems of the Psalter, for it presents a number of striking parallels with the hymn composed in the fourteenth century B.C. by Pharaoh Amenhotep IV (Akhenaten).[2] This poem, which was addressed to the sun-god, contains a number of passages quite similar to various developments of the Hebrew psalm:

(a) When thou settest in the western horizon,
    The land is in darkness, in the manner of death. . . .
    Every lion is come forth from his den;
    All creeping things, they sting. (Cf. Ps. 104:20 ff.)

(b) At daybreak, when thou arisest on the horizon . . .
    All the world, they do their work. (Cf. Ps. 104:22-23.)

(c) All beasts are content with their pasturage;
    Trees and plants are flourishing.
    The birds which fly from their nests . . . (Cf. Ps. 104:11-14.)

(d) The ships are sailing north and south as well,
    For every way is open at thy appearance.
    The fish in the river dart before thy face;
    Thy rays are in the midst of the great green sea. (Cf. Ps. 104:25-26.)

(e) How manifold it is, what thou hast made!
    They are hidden from the face (of man).
    O sole god, like whom there is no other!
    Thou didst create the world according to thy desire,
    Whilst thou wert alone. . . . (Cf. Ps. 104:24.)

(f) The world came into being by thy hand,
    According as thou hast made them.
    When thou hast risen they live,
    When thou settest they die. (Cf. Ps. 104:27 ff.)

It is difficult to deny the similarity of theme and, in some cases, of style which exists between the passages quoted and the corresponding lines of the Biblical hymn. One may therefore admit the hypothesis according to which the Hebrew poet was acquainted in some way with the ancient Egyptian piece. Yet there are also wide differences between the two poems. The Egyptian hymn contains a number of details which would have appealed greatly to the He-

---

[2] See English translation by John A. Wilson in James B. Pritchard, ed., *Ancient Near Eastern Texts . . .*, pp. 369 ff. Quoted by permission of the publisher, Princeton University Press.

brew psalmist, had he been aware of them. For instance, Akhenaten described the mystery of human and animal birth:

> Creator of seed in women,
> Thou who makest fluid into man,
> Who maintainest the son in the womb of his mother . . .
> Thou suppliest his necessities.
> When the chick in the egg speaks within the shell,
> Thou givest him breath within it to maintain him.

Now the miracle of embryology fascinated the Hebrews (cf. Job 10:8-11; Ps. 139:13-16). Yet the author of Ps. 104, praising Yahweh, the giver of life, is utterly silent about human and animal fertility.

Likewise, the Egyptian poet expressed the daring thought that the creator was embracing in his gracious care men of all lands and races:

> The countries of Syria and Nubia, the *land* of Egypt,
> Thou settest every man in his place,
> Thou suppliest their necessities:
> Everyone has his food, and his time of life is reckoned.
> Their tongues are separate in speech,
> And their natures as well;
> Their skins are distinguished,
> As thou distinguishest the foreign peoples. . . .
> All distant foreign countries, thou makest their life (also).

The idea of a providence watching over all men regardless of particularities of land, tongue, or skin, is rather daring in ancient and even in modern civilization. One might imagine that the Hebrew psalmist, whose horizon was exceptionally wide, would have welcomed this concern for world-wide humanity. But there is no trace of it in his hymn.

Even if one admits the conjecture of a literary relationship, one should also recognize that the Hebrew poet has submitted his Egyptian model to a remarkable process of adaptation—indeed, of re-creation—and has succeeded in producing a thoroughly original masterpiece. In the hymn of Akhenaten the godhead is totally contained in the sun and constitutes the unifying motif of the whole. In the Hebrew psalm, on the contrary, far from being the force behind the life of the world, the sun is dismissed in two lines (vss. 19*b* and 22*a*), as the obedient slave who knows his position and fulfills his duty with meticulous care. "The sun knoweth its going down" (vs. 19*b*). The unifying motif of the psalm is not the sun, but Yahweh, the creator and upholder of nature. The Egyptian god is part of nature. Yahweh is free as well as self-sufficient. His purpose is the joy of his world and the prosperity of man and beast.

More profound and more lucid thinkers came after him. For example, Paul knew "that the whole creation groaneth and travaileth in pain together until now" (Rom. 8:22). While the psalmist shouted quite abruptly, "Let sinners be consumed out of the earth!" (vs. 35), the Christian apostle affirmed that "the earnest expectation of the creature waiteth for the manifestation of the sons of God" (Rom. 8:19).

V

The psalmists had a profound appreciation of the beauty of the world, but they did not commune with nature as such. They were not "out of tune" with

> "This sea that bares her bosom to the moon;
> The winds that will be howling at all hours,
> And are up-gathered now like sleeping flowers."

Moreover, they did not lose themselves in some mystical marriage with those mysterious forces of life which they sensed all around them, because they were not suffering from spiritual loneliness. A romantic poet like Wordsworth condemns himself and lays bare his secret illusion when he writes,

> "Great God! I'd rather be
> A Pagan suckled in a creed outworn;
> So might I, standing on this pleasant lea,
> Have glimpses that would make me less forlorn . . ."

The psalmists did not go out at night or at sunrise in order to escape from their isolation and to find in nature a confidant and a solace. They were "out in the fields with God," but it was not in the brooks or in the stars that they found the company of the divine. It was because they were already in intimate communion with God that they discerned the trace of his hand in the loftiness of the heavens and in the stability of the earth. They did not believe in him because they looked at creation. They affirmed creation because they believed in him. The pagans or the romantic poets made a deity out of every mystery of the world, but the psalmists read into the spectacle of nature the faith which they had received as members of the covenanted people. For this reason the motif of nature in their hymns is always subordinated to the motif of God's activity and purpose. The world has been created and is being maintained, not for its own sake, but in order to provide an adequate setting for the drama which takes place within the history of mankind. Even a hymn like Ps. 148, in which the personified elements of nature are called on to join as participants on the cosmic stage with men and women of all conditions and ages in a chorus of praise for the sovereign of creation, finds its climax in the final strophe, wherein God is worshiped no longer for his rule over nature but for his love of Israel, "a people near unto him" (Ps. 148:14).

The psalmists hailed a creative God who was free from his creation and at the same time was constantly providing for its perpetuation, and thus they were not themselves imprisoned by the forces of a blind and impersonal nature, nor were they left abandoned on a ship without a skipper. Their faith in the creator delivered them from fatalism in all its forms, and it enabled them to find a sense in the history of mankind. They worshiped God, not only as the creator and the sustainer of the universe, but also and primarily as the ruler, judge, and redeemer of man within history.

2 | WORSHIP OF THE LORD OF HISTORY

BIBLICAL faith is different from any other because it does not proffer a technique whereby man compels the deity to act according to his own desires. Biblical faith attempts to place man at the disposal of God rather than God at the disposal of man. "Thy will be done!" Such is the prayer of the Bible. This is the reason for which the ancient Hebrews discerned a meaningful pattern in history. They believed that one God intervenes in the life of nations as well as in the destiny of individuals in order to pursue across the centuries and from generation to generation a just and moral purpose.

Some religions ignore history altogether, for they assume with unrelieved pessimism that the world is the prey of an impersonal force—which they call chance, fate, necessity, or scientific determinism—and they consequently teach their initiates how to escape from the evil realities of this earth and to achieve as individuals a mystical salvation.

Other religions hold a fragmentary view of history, for they are centered around the success of one tribe, one dynasty, one city-state, one fatherland, one empire, to the exclusion of all others. The deities they worship are nothing more than the projection of the life of a particular group. They identify the will of their gods with the needs and ambitions of a closed society. Thus they do not survive its fall. The god Ashur dies with the city of Nineveh and the god Marduk with the city of Babylon. There lies the hidden falsehood of the slogan which characterizes all religious nationalisms, "My country, right or wrong!"

Biblical religion alone is concerned with the whole of history. "All the earth is mine," declared from the beginning the God of the covenant (Exod. 19:5). The Hebrews remembered that they had come into national birth in order to fulfill a mission of blessing for mankind (Gen. 12:2-3). They knew that their ancestors had been delivered from Egyptian slavery in order to become the holy people of God (Exod. 19:4-6), but they never claimed that they had been chosen for this unique task on account of any special genius or achievements of their own. They acknowledged that they were "a stiff-necked people" (Deut. 9:6). As they could not explain their election on the basis of their own merits, they merely hailed in wonder the incomprehensible love of the God who had elected them (Deut. 7:7-8). The prophets of the eighth and seventh centuries reminded them of the obligations placed upon them by the ancient covenant: "You alone have I known of all the families of the earth. Therefore I will punish you for all your iniquities" (Amos 3:2). When "the Assyrian came down like the wolf on the fold," the prophets recognized in the impending catastrophe the righteous judgment of the master of all history. "Ho! Assyrian, the rod of mine anger!" (Is. 10:5.) The northern kingdom of Israel was annihilated (722 B.C.). The southern kingdom of Judah was spared for a while, but it succumbed in its turn under the blows of Babylon and its population was carried away into exile (597-586 B.C.). The Judeans bowed their heads in humiliation and accepted their national death as the retribution of their national failure. Yet they survived the loss of their king, land, and temple. Their descendants became the Jews—a spiritual congregation. Therein lies the miracle of their history. They were the people which would not die. Chiefly on account of the ministry of Jeremiah, Habakkuk, Ezekiel, and Second Isaiah (the anonymous seer whose poems are now preserved in Is. 40-55), the sons of the ancient covenant, without king, land, or temple, maintained themselves as a closely knit community.

When the Persian empire conquered Babylon and became the new power of the ancient world, the Jewish exiles were allowed to return from Babylonia to Jerusalem (538 B.C.) and to rebuild their sanctuary on the ruins of the old (516 B.C.). National life was restored after a fashion, but internal factions and constant struggles against greedy neighbors deprived them of political and economic security. Then a handful of worshipers, in the shadow of their shabby Temple, reflected on their national past, meditated on their present trials, and turned their gaze toward the future. They hoped for the advent of a realm of justice for all. They prayed for the coming of a true kingdom of peace. They saluted the city of God.

Many hymns of the Psalter were composed for the worship of the lord of history. Some of them, like Ps. 114, recalled the past and made it live into a cultic present, especially the Exodus from Egypt. Others, like Ps. 46, faced without fear the perils of the moment. Still others, like Ps. 47, acclaimed the universal judge. Lastly, some hymns called "Royal Psalms," like Ps. 110, hailed the advent of the messianic king.

I

The Lord of the Passover
(Psalm 114)

I

1. When Israel went out of Egypt,
    The house of Jacob, from a stammering people,
2. Judah became [God's] sanctuary,
    Israel, his dominion.

II

3. The sea looked and it fled,
    The Jordan turned back,
4. The mountains skipped like rams,
    The little hills like lambs!

III

5. What aileth thee, O thou sea, that thou fleest,
    Thou Jordan, that thou turnest back?
6. Ye mountains, that ye skip like rams,
    And ye little hills, like lambs?

IV

7.   At the presence of the sovereign, tremble, O thou earth!
         At the presence of the God of Jacob,
8.   Who turneth the rock into a pool of waters,
         The flint into a fountain of waters!

This exquisite poem belongs to the section formed by Pss. 113-118, which is called "Egyptian Hallel" or "Egyptian Praise" in the Jewish liturgy (Ps. 136 is known as the "Great Hallel"). These hymns were and are still sung at the festival of the new moon, every fourth Sabbath, and also at the celebration of the Passover and other feasts. The Gospels probably referred to these psalms when they described Jesus and his disciples as "having sung the hymns" (Mk. 14:26, Mt. 26:30) after the last supper.

Ps. 114 is a masterpiece of poetic conciseness, filled at once with hyperbole and understatement. It reveals the unity of the theme of nature with that of history. When God intervenes in the realm of man, the natural elements retreat in awe. Let man take heed and respond!

In the first strophe (vss. 1-2) the birth of the nation is swiftly and precisely stated. Egypt, "the house of bondage," is the country of a people of strange language, or, more literally translated, "a stammering people," i.e., speaking an obscure and ambiguous tongue comparable to stammering. In other words, the psalmist meant more than "foreign." He suggested probably "different and shady, strange and heathen," not only in speech but also in behavior and mentality. The temptations of the Egyptian culture, materially and intellectually far superior to that of the Hebrews, remained very pressing throughout the centuries of Biblical history. Indeed, in the times of Hosea and Isaiah (eighth century B.C.), Israel and Judah tried to renew the Egyptian alliance inaugurated by Solomon in a vain effort to resist the Assyrian onslaught. Still later, after the Babylonian emperor had subdued the city of Jerusalem, a number of Judeans in order to save themselves from exile in Babylonia escaped into Egypt and settled in the valley of the Nile. In fact, they lost their faith there, for the aged prophet Jeremiah, who had apparently been forced to follow them into that land of the dead, witnessed with impotent sorrow his compatriots burning incense "to the queen of heavens," namely, Isis, the Egyptian goddess (Jer. 43-44).

The Passover is the memorial celebration of the Exodus from Egypt, when the redemption from slavery is liturgically lived anew, and the destiny of Israel is solemnly reaffirmed. "Judah became his sanctuary." The name of God is not even explicitly mentioned, as if the poet kept it in reserve for the climactic admonition of the fourth strophe (vss. 7-8). The Hebrew word which is translated here by "sanctuary" should be taken in its original meaning of "peculiar and exclusive property," set apart and reserved for a holy use. An oracle from the prophet Jeremiah throws some light upon this idea; it contains the same word, rendered by "holiness."

> "Thus saith Yahweh:
> I remember thee, the kindness of thy youth,
> The love of thine espousals,
> When thou wentest after me in the wilderness,
> In a land that was not sown.
> Israel was *holiness* unto Yahweh,
> The first fruit of his increase" (Jer. 2:2-3).

In other words, the Hebrews were delivered from slavery in order to become the special people of God. Israel has a unique mission among the nations of the earth. It belongs entirely to its Lord. The psalmist echoes in poetic style the tradition of the covenant in which Yahweh declares that he brought the Hebrews unto himself in order to make them his "peculiar treasure above all people . . . a kingdom of priests, and a holy nation" (Exod. 19:4-6). Redemption from bondage meant more than political freedom. Or rather, political freedom was not the purpose of the redemptive act. Bought from slavery, Israel must live up to its purpose. It must incarnate a way of life. It must shine in the world like the shrine of the holy God. The Passover is the sacramental reminder of Israel's high calling. *Noblesse oblige.*

In the second, third, and fourth strophes (vss. 3-4, 5-6, 7-8), the psalmist selected from the stories of the Exodus, the wandering in the wilderness, and the entry into the promised land, a few suggestive details. The divine maker of history is also the ruler of nature, and he summons the elements as the witnesses and instruments of the people's destiny. The sea divides itself and transforms imminent death into life. The Jordan turns back and opens the gate to the promised country. The mountains shake and leap like the animals of the spring flock, as God seals with his people the covenant which binds them to his design. The whole earth is commanded to tremble before the face of Yahweh. It will be noted that the verbs which recall the old traditions are used in the present tense, for history is no longer past. The festival derives an everlasting meaning from the event of Israel's birth. The God who ruled then is ruler still. He is the sovereign eternal.

Why did the poet allude, in the last strophe, to the ancient story of the water which gushed out of the rock at the stroke of Moses (Exod. 17:1-7; Num. 20:2-13)? Is it not because he found there a symbol of God's providence in all the wanderings of the people across the wilderness of the world? Passover is the festival of spring as well as the commemoration of redemption. The rams and the lambs, used as poetic metaphors in the second and third strophes, bring precisely to mind the meat of the Passover feast. Together with the water of life, which springs out of barren places, they point to the goodness of the divine purpose. Let all the earth recognize his presence when he brings his people unto himself; let all the earth adore him as its true *Adhôn* (sovereign). The pagan deity of the vernal fertility (whom the Greeks later called "Adonis") is a fiction of man's imagination, but Yahweh is the master of life and of all history.

Christians have been moved by a sure instinct to draw the lines from the Passover of the Old Testament to the Easter of the New Testament. In Christ, "our passover," we receive a redemption from the bondage of sin and the prison of death. In Dante's vision the travelers read in this psalm the meaning of their spiritual pilgrimage:

"In exitu Israel de Ægypto!"
Sang they all together in one voice,
With whatso in that Psalm is after written.
Then made he sign of holy rood upon them,
Whereat all cast themselves upon the shore . . ."

Biblical faith affirms that every generation must make its "Exodus from Egypt" and needs to be redeemed from spiritual slavery before receiving life and the power to fulfill its mission.

II

"The Lord of Hosts Is with Us"
(Psalm 46)

I

1. God is for us refuge and strength,
    A very present help in trouble.
2. Therefore will we not fear, though the earth be moved,
    And the mountains stumble into the midst of the seas.
3. [The ocean] may roar and its waters may foam,
    The mountains may tremble with the swelling thereof:
    [Yahweh of hosts is with us;
    A fortress unto us is the God of Jacob!]

II

4. [There is] a river, the streams thereof gladden the city of God,
    The holy place of the tabernacles of the Most High.
5. God is in the midst of her: she shall not be moved;
    God shall help her, and that right early.
6. Nations are in tumult, kingdoms are moved;
    He uttereth his voice: the earth melteth.
7. Yahweh of hosts is with us;
    A fortress unto us is the God of Jacob!

III

8. Come, behold the works of Yahweh,
    What desolations he maketh in the earth!

9. He causeth wars to cease unto the ends of the earth;
       The bow he breaketh and he splitteth the spear,
       The chariots he burneth with fire.
10. "Be still, and know that I am God.
       I shall be exalted among the nations, exalted in the earth!"
11.   Yahweh of hosts is with us;
       A fortress unto us is the God of Jacob!

This psalm inspired Martin Luther to compose his greatest hymn, *"Ein feste Burg ist unser Gott."* It has been rightly called "the Song of Songs of Faith" (Kittel). With absolute trust in Yahweh, "the God of Jacob" and the master of the universe, the holy people shall not fear. The experience of divine presence is so overwhelming that, whatever may happen, human anguish is overcome. Surely, true faith is the only basis of true staith (Is. 7:9). It gives a sense of security that no fortress made of stone can provide.

The poet developed his theme in three strophes. Each of them was probably followed by a refrain[1] intended for choral response. Three aspects of the activity of God are in turn contemplated: (1) Yahweh is the lord of creation; (2) Yahweh is the lord of history; (3) Yahweh is the lord of eternal peace.

In the first strophe (vss. 1-3) the theme is unfolded against a background of cosmic conflagrations. The poet was perhaps living at a time of imminent war. His fellow men were the prey of panic and they were frantically engaged in rushing defensive preparations before the enemy attacked. Walls and towers were repaired and strongholds were reinforced. Boldly and deliberately the psalmist faced a much more frightening prospect than the threat of an invading army. He looked back at the primeval chaos, he looked ahead to the end of the world. Let it be supposed, he said in effect, that the earth itself would be moved from its foundation; even if the natural elements were upset and the original ocean overflowed

---

[1] Most scholars agree in restoring at the end of vs. 3 the refrain which appears identically in vss. 7 and 11. It will be noted that the marginal sign "Selah" (the meaning of which is not known) is found not only at the end of vss. 7 and 11 but also at the end of vs. 3. In addition, the present text offers a lack of transition between vss. 3 and 4, and the abruptness is removed if the refrain is inserted there. Lastly, the division in three strophes provides a structural support for the threefold development of the ideas.

its bounds, what of it? Yahweh of hosts is our God. He is the lord of creation. His omnipotent will shall prevail. Thus, with utter serenity and calm, the psalmist bade the people stand up and sing, "God is our refuge and strength; a very present help in anguish." Such an unshakable trust may not alter the material situation, but it actually makes man triumph over any physical defeat and therefore causes him to transform the woes of the present into a spiritual victory. "Immanuel! God is with us!" (Is. 7:14; 8:8.) This is not an affirmation of arrogant militarism. Although the psalm has been used by marching soldiers and conquerors who thought to enlist God on their side, it represents the attitude of the prophets like Hosea, Isaiah, Jeremiah, and Habakkuk, who claimed that "the righteous shall live by his faith" (Hab. 2:4).

The vision of outward destruction which dominates the first strophe is suddenly over and makes room with unexpected contrast for the image of "the city of God" in the second strophe (vss. 4-7). Many commentators find here an allusion to the earthly Jerusalem and for this reason classify the psalm with the "Hymns of Zion." The text, however, does not support such an interpretation. Jerusalem has no river worth mentioning. The torrent of Kidron flows only for a few weeks after the winter rains, and the spring of Gihon is barely sufficient to feed the pool of Siloam through Hezekiah's tunnel (II Kings 20:20). The "river" of which the poet sang in quiet rapture does not make glad a city of the earth but the "sanctuary of the tabernacles of the most High." The "city of God" is the new Jerusalem which, at the end of history, will shelter the assembly of the saved.

"Thine eyes shall see Jerusalem,
A serene dwelling place, an immovable tabernacle. . . .
Yahweh shall be for us a place of broad rivers and streams,
Wherein shall go no galley with oars,
Neither shall gallant ship pass thereby . . ." (Is. 33:20-21).

While "the earth melteth," such a city "shall not be moved." In the darkness which will precede the great tribulation, God shall succor his own, "and that right early" (vs. 5*b*). This expression literally means "at the turn of the morning," and commentators have thought that it alludes to the unexpected lifting of the siege which Sennacherib, the Assyrian emperor, laid around the city of Jerusalem in 701 B.C. "And it came to pass that night, that the angel of Yahweh went out and smote in the camp of the Assyrians an hundred fourscore and five thousand: and when [the people of the city] arose *early in the morning,* behold, they were all dead corpses. So Sennacherib king of Assyria departed" (II Kings 19: 35-36). This historical event played an important part in the formation of the prophetic picture of the "immovable city." But neither the great prophets nor the psalmist believed in the inviolability of Zion. The context of the psalm shows that the poet was thinking in eschatological terms. He was depicting the "end" (in Greek, *eschaton*) of history. He was not referring to a limited happening of the recent past. He was looking for the eternal city, watered by the streams of grace, the "blest river of salvation." This interpretation is confirmed by the last part of the hymn.

The third and concluding strophe (vss. 8-11) calls every member of the holy community "to consider," to contemplate, to examine in the gaze of prophetic vision (vs. 8*a*), the "deeds" of the lord of the nations. The era of eternal peace has begun.

"And it shall come to pass in the last days,
  That the mountain of the house of Yahweh
  Shall be established in the top of the mountains . . .
  And he shall judge among the nations,
  And he shall rebuke many peoples,
  And they shall beat their swords into plowshares,
  And their spears into pruning hooks:
  Nation shall not lift up sword against nation,
  Neither shall they learn war any more." (Is. 2:2-4; cf., Mic.
    4:1-3.)

The psalmist has become a prophet. The words of God are introduced in the first person as in the prophetic oracles: "Be still!" (Vs. 10.) Literally they read, "Let your hands drop! Desist! Ground your weapons!" It is useless to resist the power of the almighty ruler. This negative command is then followed by a positive appeal: "Know that I am God! I shall be exalted among the nations, exalted in the earth." Again the psalmist echoes the prophet, "Yahweh alone shall be exalted in that day!" (Is. 2:11, 17.)

This psalm has often been compared to the famous lines of Horace in which the virtuous man remains undaunted in the midst of the most adverse calamities:

> *"Dux inquieti Adriae,*
> *Nec fulminantis magna Jovis manus,*
> *Si fractus illabitur orbis,*
> *Impavidum ferient ruinae."*

> "Let the wild winds that rule the seas,
> Tempestuous, all their horrors raise;
> Let Jove's dread arm with thunders rend the spheres;
> Beneath the crush of worlds undaunted he appears."

Calvin aptly remarks, with his accustomed brusqueness and irony, "As no such person as [Horace] imagines could ever be found, he only trifles in speaking as he does." Indeed, the contrast between the stoic hero and the holy people of God is obvious. There, one man stands courageous but defiant. Here, a community finds fortitude in its reliance on a God who will not fail his own, though the heavens fall, and the earth be moved out of its place.

Christians have inherited the faith and the hope of the prophets and they have therefore also found in such a hymn as this a poetic impetus to formulate their specifically Christian expectations. Thus it is of the church that the poet now sings,

> "In vain the surge's angry shock
> In vain the drifting sands:
> Unharmed upon the eternal rock
> The eternal City stands."

The Christian church, however, should take care not to identify herself too glibly with that eternal city. Perhaps a lesson is in store

for her if this psalm is interpreted as an "Eschatological Hymn."
The community of God lives, suffers, and fights on earth, to be sure,
but the eternal city is not to be confused with any stronghold of
this world, be it Rome, Geneva, or Canterbury. The church militant should not play with the illusion of having "God in the midst
of her." *Immanuel* is a motto of condemnation as well as of confidence. The psalmist waited for the day of the Lord. So also shall
the Christian wait.

III

The King of All the Earth
(Psalm 47)

I

1.   All ye peoples, clap your hands!
        Shout unto God with the cry of jubilation!
2.   For Yahweh Most-High is to be feared,
        A great king over the whole of the earth.

3.   He is subduing peoples under us,
        And nations under our feet.
4.   He is choosing our inheritance for us,
        The excellence of Jacob, whom he hath loved.

5.   God is gone up with a shout,
        Yahweh, with the blast of the trumpet.

II

6.   Sing praises to God, sing praises!
        Sing praises to our king, sing praises!
7.   For God is king of the whole of the earth;
        Sing praises with a contemplative psalm!

8.   God hath become king over the nations,
        God sitteth upon his holy throne.
9.   The princes of the peoples are gathered,
        The people of the God of Abraham.

10.   For unto God belong the shields of the earth.
        He is greatly exalted.

This psalm is generally designated as a "Hymn of the Enthronement of Yahweh," but the expression should not be taken in a concrete or literal way. It refers to a dramatic ceremony which may have taken place at the celebration of the New Year festival, during which the worshipers acclaimed the kingship of their heavenly Lord over the universe and all the nations of the earth. Possibly they used a ritual derived from the anointing of earthly monarchs. According to the books of Kings, after "Zadok the priest . . . anointed Solomon, . . . they blew the trumpet, and all the people said, Long live the king . . . ! And all the people came up after him, and the people piped with pipes, and rejoiced with great joy, so that the earth rent with the sound of them" (I Kings 1:39-40). Some scholars suggest that a similar ceremony was held every New Year in honor of Yahweh and that the ritual included a procession of the ark, which was afterward replaced with great solemnity in the Temple as if Yahweh himself had ascended his royal throne. Although such an "enthronement" was practiced in honor of Marduk in Babylon, there is no allusion to a similar rite in honor of king Yahweh in the Old Testament. However, the Hebrews certainly conceived their God in imagination as a monarch. During the vision of his call the prophet Isaiah "saw the Lord sitting upon a throne, high and lifted up, and his train filled the temple" (Is. 6:1), and he declared, "Mine eyes have seen the king, Yahweh of hosts!" (Is. 6:5.) It seems likely that Ps. 47 was composed in order to celebrate the kingship of God at the occasion of the New Year festival, but the term "enthronement" is probably not fitting unless it is used metaphorically.

The poem divides itself equally into two strophes, which are separated at the climactic moment of the ceremony by the blast of the trumpet. Each strophe presents itself in three parts, which in English might correspond to two quatrains and a distich.

The first strophe (vss. 1-5) begins with a call to worship which is issued to "all peoples" (vs. 1), not only to the members of the Hebrew congregation, but to all foreign nations, because Yahweh is not merely the God of Israel, but "a great king over the whole of the earth" (vs. 2). It will be observed that the experience of fear is not incompatible with the manifestations and even the authentic feeling of joy and exultation. Modern man, especially when he belongs to an established and respectable church, is practically unable to understand the mixture of awe and frenzied gaiety which seized the ancient Hebrews as they were engulfed in the act of corporate worship. The reason for this marriage of fear and joy is given in the second part of the first strophe (vss. 3-4). It appears that the celebration of the New Year carries the corporate mind of the worshipers into a kind of future which is made liturgically present. They live cultically at the end of history when God's kingdom shall truly be world-wide. The principalities and empires which for centuries have been treading Israel underfoot shall at last be overcome by the king of the earth. "He is subduing peoples under us, and nations under our feet" (vs. 3).

Some critics are uneasy about this outburst of political imperialism and, by omitting a single letter at the end of vs. 3*a* and of vs. 3*b*, they obtain the following reading, "He is subduing peoples under *him*, and nations under *his* feet." It is possible that such was the original text of this verse, for we know that the passion of nationalism increased during the postexilic period of Judaism, while the Biblical manuscripts were still in a relatively fluid and unfixed form. Nevertheless, there is no scientific evidence to support such a correction here. It is preferable to accept the traditional text as it stands and to admit that, in this psalm as well as in some others and in many poems of the exilic and postexilic prophets, an inclusive universalism in religion is found side by side with nationalistic egocentricity. In the course of their long history the Hebrews experienced more buffeting from foreign potentates than any other nation. They should not be justified when they display a spirit of vindication against their enemies. Nevertheless, one should perhaps try to understand the growth of bitterness and even hatred in the background of humiliation and bloodshed. The strophe ends with the climactic lines which mark the central moment of the cultic act. The trumpet *(shôphar)* is still blown today in the synagogues to welcome the New Year. The sound of the horn breaking through the absolute silence of the congregation creates an eerie atmosphere and a sense of tension which is hardly equaled in other religious celebrations.

The second strophe (vss. 6-9) explodes with emotional release. In the first part (vss. 6-7) the rhythm of the original Hebrew produces an effect of syncopation which befits the psychological mood expressed by the words:

> 6. *Zammerû Elohîm zammerû*
>   *Zammerû lemalkenû zammerû*
> 7. *Kî melek kol haaretz*
>   *Elohîm zammerû maskîl*

The invitation to "sing praises" which is repeated five times summons the whole orchestra and chorus to join in the singing of the "maskil," probably an elaborate piece of contemplative music using all the resources of instrumental and vocal art. Those people knew how to enjoy their religion. As the trumpet had signified that Yahweh had symbolically ascended his heavenly throne at the end of time, the congregation reached a pitch of excitement and of religious fervor which can hardly be imagined today. A thrilling thought it was, indeed, that Yahweh, who loveth Jacob, is the king of the whole world. No earthly allegiance is possible. At the same time no power which now dominates the earth or part thereof shall endure before the true ruler of the universe.

Such a thought is too stupendous and too intoxicating to be allowed to lapse without repetition. "God hath become king over the nations" (vs. 8). It is quite remarkable, then, that in the second part of the second strophe, the psalmist corrects the nationalistic hope expressed in the first strophe by entertaining a truly universalistic expectation, nay, a vision which is already realized liturgically: transported in spirit at the end of history, the community sings that the invitation made to the nations at the beginning of the hymn has now been answered. "The princes of the peoples are gathered as the people of the God of Abraham" (vs. 9). The promise made of old is fulfilled, "In thee shall all the families of the earth find blessing" (Gen. 12:3). There is no longer any distinction between the people of God and the foreign nations, for "the shields of the earth belong to God. He is greatly exalted" (vs. 10).

It is understandable that Christians have used this hymn in the liturgy of the Ascension. They believe that the hope of a united humanity will remain an empty dream until it is grounded on the acknowledgment of the royalty of Christ, in whom alone there is "neither Jew nor Greek."

IV

The Messianic King
(Psalm 110)

I

1. Oracle of Yahweh to my sovereign: "Sit at my right hand
   Until I make thine enemies thy footstool!"
2. The scepter of thy strength shall Yahweh send from Zion.
   Rule thou in the midst of thine enemies!

II

3. Thy people shall offer themselves freely in the day of thy might,
   In the beauties of holiness, from the womb of dawn,
   To thee shall be the dew of thy youth.

III

4. Yahweh hath sworn it and he shall not repent:
   Thou art priest forever
   According to the order of Melchizedek.

IV

5. The Lord shall be at thy right hand,
   He shall smite the kings in the day of his wrath,
6. He shall judge among the nations, filling [the valleys] with corpses,
   He shall crush their head over the wide earth.

V

7. He shall drink of the brook on the way;
   Therefore shall he lift up his head.

This hymn has received a great many different interpretations. Some commentators think that it was composed at an early date in honor of David (ninth century B.C.). Others, on the contrary, believe that it celebrates some king-priest of the Maccabean period (second century B.C.). Still others are compelled to conclude that, although the psalmist may have been inspired by a historical monarch, he was probably thinking of the messianic king, the agent of God who would come on the last day of history to deliver Israel from the yoke of the foreign nations and establish the kingdom of justice.

The text bristles with difficulties and seems to have been corrupted in the transmission of the manuscripts. At several points, the ancient versions differ widely from the Hebrew text we now possess. In addition, the language is frequently obscure and the poetic structure uncertain. Thus the translation and strophic arrangement which have been offered above represent only a provisional attempt to introduce the study of the psalm.

The first strophe (vss. 1-2) opens with the most unusual formula, "Oracle of Yahweh." This expression, which occurs frequently in the prophetic books but exceptionally in the Psalter (cf. Ps. 28:2), denotes a poem in which God himself speaks in the first person through a human mouthpiece. It seems therefore that the psalmist compares himself to a prophet and that he considers this hymn as a revelation of God.

The oracle is addressed to "my sovereign" *(Adhôn)*, a designation of majesty and lordship which may be applied not only to human kings and governors but also to God himself. The Gospels have preserved what might be called the earliest interpretation of the first strophe when they recorded the following exchange between Jesus and the Pharisees: "Jesus asked them, saying, What think ye of Christ? whose son is he? They say unto him, The son of David. He saith unto them, How then doth David in spirit call him Lord, saying, The LORD said unto my Lord, Sit thou at my right hand, till I make thine enemies thy footstool? If David then call him Lord, how is he his son? And no man was able to answer him a word." This discussion (Mk. 12:35-37; Mt. 22:41-46; Lk.

20:41-44) reveals the perplexity that such a poem arouses in the minds of its readers, ancient and modern.

Were the hero a historical monarch, it would be surprising that he be invited to sit at the right hand of God until victory is won by God himself. Should he not take actual command of the battle which is being waged against his enemies? Moreover, one can hardly suppose that this king, like David (II Sam. 10:6-14), stays in Jerusalem while his war is being fought for him, since the psalmist declares, "Yahweh shall send the rod of thy strength out of Zion" (vs. 2*a*). More baffling still is the command, "Rule thou in the midst of thine enemies" (vs. 2*b*). Does this unusual construction, "Rule in the midst of . . . ," indicate the special nature of this hero's sovereignty? Does it suggest that this ruler will not administer his realm from afar but that he will live close to his submitted foes and that the antagonism and bitterness which their crushing has necessarily engendered among them will be transformed into a willful obedience? Does it mean that the opponents of this ruler will not only be subdued but also converted into peaceful subjects? It is not possible to answer these questions with any degree of certainty. Poetry, however, has the virtue of suggesting more profound ideas and sentiments than mere words signify literally. Is it legitimate to bring this line alongside with the saying, "Behold, the kingdom of God is in the midst of you" (Lk. 17:21)?

The second strophe (vs. 3) is even more difficult than the first. According to the Hebrew text the people shall become "free-will offerings" in the day of their sovereign's might. A free-will offering was a sacrifice not required by law. The poet may therefore indicate that the people will offer themselves freely, will co-operate willingly, will serve beyond the call of duty or above the requirements of a code. They will be animated by loyalty and sacrificial love. They will be like priests "in the beauties of holiness," clad in the sacerdotal attire which befits the offering of free-will sacrifices. "From the womb of dawn, thou hast the dew of thy youth." The imagery is daring, even for Oriental poetry. Does the sentence mean that "thy young men will serve thee eagerly"? Ancient translators, however, seem to have read a slightly different

text with a widely different meaning. From a careful comparison
between the Hebrew and the Greek and other versions, it is possible to render the whole verse as follows:

> 3. With thee is nobility from the day of thy birth;
>   In the splendor of holiness, from the womb of dawn,
>   I have brought thee forth as the dew.

If this is the correct meaning of the original, the psalmist is describing the divine origin of the hero. A similar idea is found in
another royal psalm:

> "Yahweh said unto me, Thou art my son;
>   This day have I begotten thee" (Ps. 2:7).

God's vice-regent on earth is not an ordinary man. In some way
which can be expressed only in poetic style, his origin is divine.

The third strophe (vs. 4) adds a new and startling qualification
of the mysterious king. In the ancient Near East as well as in
Israel human monarchs were endowed with sacerdotal functions
(II Sam. 6:18; I Kings 8:14). But the priesthood of this prince
is of a different order. The figure of Melchizedek belonged to the
distant past (Gen. 14:18-20). The name itself suggested the idea
of righteous kingship, and inasmuch as this man was described in
the traditions of the fathers both as "king of Salem . . . and priest
of God Most-High," the psalmist could easily appeal to that hallowed memory in order to picture the unique combination of kingship and priesthood which would be found in the messianic ruler.
A king defends his own subjects, and a priest represents the people
before God. The messianic king shall be priest forever.

The fourth strophe (vss. 5-6) reverts to the theme of the last
battle of history. It will be the Lord's fight, and the battlefield
will be strewn with the bodies of the slain (cf. Ezek. 39:12). Several poems of the exilic and postexilic prophets similarly paint in
horrible colors the last day of history.

"I shall tread the wine press alone,
  And of the nations there shall be none with me,
  And I shall tread them in my wrath,
  And I shall trample them in my fury,
  And their blood shall be sprinkled upon my garments
  And shall stain all my raiment" (Is. 63:3).

Apocalyptic visions as wild as these may have seemed antiquated and barbarian during the nineteenth century, although they inspired such startling lines as:

"Mine eyes have seen the glory of the coming of the Lord;
  He is trampling out the vintage where the grapes of wrath
    are stored . . ."

In the middle of the twentieth century the bizarre and bloody imagery of the psalm loses a great deal of its fantastic character and does not appear to be far removed from the realities of history. Certainly the modern reader may agree that the fulfillment of divine justice entails the annihilation of evil forces, and the psalmist, at least, was not unaware of their magnitude. But he now turns swiftly to another theme in order to conclude his poem with an entirely different note.

Most interpreters agree that the last distich (vs. 7), through an abrupt change of subject, returns to the description of the royal hero. A single, concrete touch, apparently trivial, suggests an inward attitude and perhaps evokes the central act of his mission. A humble man, in spite of the wonders of his birth and of his ordination, he will stoop down as a simple nomad tormented by thirst. "He shall drink of the brook on the way"—and his final exaltation will be preceded and perhaps explained by his humiliation. Again, the Christian interpreter must be cautiously aware of easy and illegitimate rapprochements, but he will, at the same time, brood over these enigmatic lines in the light of his devotion to the "king of sorrow" who, "being in the form of God . . . was made in the likeness of men . . . and became obedient unto death, even the death of the cross. Wherefore God also hath highly exalted him"

(Phil. 2:6-9). While messianic hope in New Testament times was colored by military dreams of revenge against the Roman oppressors, a simple man, a poor man among the poor, who drank "of the brook on the way," fired the faith and the loyalty of men and women who were destitute like him and who hailed him as the new "king of Salem, which is, king of peace" (Heb. 7:2). They did not recognize him as a sovereign after the manner of men. They discovered in his kingship a priestly significance. For, as Milton wrote in *Paradise Regained,* his

> "crown,
> Golden in show, is but a wreath of thorns,
> Brings dangers, troubles, cares, and sleepless nights . . .
> When on his shoulders each man's burden lies . . . ."

V

The poets who composed these hymns of praise did not distinguish clearly between the theme of nature and that of history, for they moved from one plane to the other (as in Ps. 114) without any sense of confusing two separate realms of God's activity. They discerned behind both of them the single hand of the creator of the universe and of the ruler of the nations.

Pagan thinkers could ask, and may still ask today, in a state of perennial doubt whether men and gods are not the prey of accidental forces or of a monstrous, impersonal "necessity." Greek poets and modern philosophers have found no meaning in a universe whose destiny is determined either by chance or by immutable laws. With them, some of us are tempted to repeat:

> ". . . We are all, like swimmers in the sea,
> Pois'd on the top of a huge wave of fate,
> Which hangs, uncertain to which side to fall.
> And whether it will heave us up to land,
> Or whether it will roll us out to sea . . .
> We know not. . . ."[2]

---

[2] Matthew Arnold, "Sohrab and Rustum."

The psalmists, on the contrary, never doubted in their "Hymns of History" the goodness of the creator's purpose nor his power to fulfill it. The same Yahweh who made heaven and earth and keeps the stars in their course also controls the affairs of men and the rise and fall of nations. In his own time he will establish a peaceful kingdom and complete the work of his creation.

The Hebrew poets did not derive their faith in a victorious creator from their observation of "universal harmonies," but they readily recognized in nature the "Vicayre of the Almighty Lord," and they acknowledged with awesome gratitude that "the world is charged with the grandeur of God." Likewise, it was not through their interpretation of historical events that they reached their certitude in the righteousness of God's judgments and the ultimate fulfillment of his creation, but they used their conviction as a key to open the riddle of the past and the mystery of the future. "It is not what happens that matters, but why it happens," wrote a Greek historian. The psalmists would have preferred to say, "What happens always matters, for it displays the intention and the will of the lord of history."

i

In the first place, the Hebrews celebrated in their hymns the distinctive qualities of the God of the covenant, his faithfulness and his grace.

> "Remember his marvelous works that he hath done,
>   His wonders, and the judgments of his mouth;
> O ye seed of Abraham his servant,
>   O ye sons of Jacob his chosen one. . . .
> He remembereth his covenant forever,
>   The word which he declared for a thousand generations"
>   (Ps. 105:5-6, 8).

However, even in their hymns of praise, the psalmists brought back to their fellow worshipers the unhappy memories of their national tradition—trials in the wilderness, military defeats and oppression, famines and plagues—as a solemn sign of divine retribution for man's stubbornness and revolt. They recalled in worship

"old, unhappy far-off things,
And battles long ago,"[3]

not because they were interested in the past for its own sake or
yielded to the deleterious tides of nostalgia, but because they discovered in the story of ancient ages "the righteous deeds of Yahweh" (cf., e.g., Ps. 78:3-8).

The continuity of God's holy people is at stake. The past moves
into the present which sows the seeds of the future. Each generation must pay heed to the lessons set forth by the misdeeds and
misfortunes of its ancestors in order to warn and educate its descendants. The psalmists worshiped within the perspective of time;
thus in their hymns praise was intimately mingled with their acknowledgment of solidarity with the fathers—even praise to God
for his chastenings as well as for his protection. Pride in the election of one's race or church is legitimate only when it is sobered by
the shame of failure (cf., e.g., Ps. 66:8-12).

God's favor is extolled side by side with his judgments of condemnation, and his sternness itself is a sign of his love. He pun-
ished, but he did not destroy. He chastened, but in a measure,
slowly educating the covenanted people within the frame of his
"Grand Design."

ii

In the second place, the Hebrews hailed in their hymns of history Yahweh's control over human affairs not only as a memory
of the distant past but also as a contemporaneous reality. The
same God who created the world now rules and overrules the nations of men.

"By the word of Yahweh were the heavens made . . .
For he spake, and it was done;
He commanded, and it stood fast.
Yahweh bringeth the counsel of the nations to nought;
He maketh the scheming thoughts of the peoples of none effect"
(Ps. 33:6, 9-10).

---

[3] William Wordsworth, "The Solitary Reaper."

To be sure, there were moments when the burden of national humiliation weighed so heavily on the mind of Israel as to arouse anxious questioning of a theological nature: one prophet even asked, "Art thou not from everlasting, O Yahweh, my God, my Holy One? Thou canst not die!" (Hab. 1:12.) The thought of Yahweh's death appeared so blasphemous to some scribes that the text was corrected to read, "We shall not die." But the psalmists in their hymns never indulged in such skepticism. They continued to praise the great controller of history, and only occasionally did they introduce in those hymns a brief and humble prayer for him to intervene.

"Not unto us, O Yahweh, not unto us,
    But unto thy name give glory,
    For thy mercy, and for thy truth's sake!" (Ps. 115:1.)

Since Yahweh is always the master of history, the efforts of the nations to overthrow Israel will be futile.

"Why do the nations rage,
    And the peoples imagine a vain thing?
The kings of the earth set themselves,
    And the rulers take counsel together
Against Yahweh and against his anointed . . .
He that sitteth in the heavens shall laugh:
    The Lord shall have them in derision!" (Ps. 2:1-2, 4.)

A faith of this metal, quite similar to that displayed in Ps. 46, could withstand the blows of foreign imperialism and the even more insidious threats of pagan seduction. Borrowing the eternal look of God, the psalmists could overcome in worship the baffling spectacle of the present, for their faith enabled them to live ahead of their time, at the day when God would intervene in the fullness of his power.

iii

In the third place, therefore, the psalmists contemplated the future with the eyes of faith. Not only in Ps. 47, but in many other "Eschatological Hymns," the congregation gathered in worship at the Temple for the celebration of the great festivals acclaimed and welcomed Yahweh as the judge and king of the earth, already taking his seat as if it were the end of history.

"For God is the judge,
    He putteth down one and lifteth up another.
  For in the hand of Yahweh there is a cup,
    And the wine foameth, charged with spices,
  And he poureth it out: even to the dregs thereof
    Will all the wicked of the earth [. . .] drink it" (Ps. 75:7-8).

". . . For he cometh,
    For he cometh to judge the earth,
  He shall judge the world with righteousness,
    And the peoples with his truth" (Ps. 96:13).

No fear is entertained for the remnant of Israel, and the invitation is issued to sing in humble confidence and joy.

"O come, let us worship and bow down;
    Let us kneel before Yahweh our maker.
  For he is our God,
    And we are the people of his pasture,
      And the sheep of his hand" (Ps. 95:6-7).

Yet the people of God's pasture, even as the foreign peoples, was prone to perpetrate evil, and although the poets who composed the eschatological hymns did not confess or condemn the sinfulness of their own "church" with the lucidity and courage of the great prophets (the genre which was appropriate to this task was not the hymn of praise but the "National Lament" and the "Public Confession"), nevertheless they coupled their invitation to worship the creator of nature (as in Ps. 95:1-5) and to trust the love of the "Shepherd-God" (as in Ps. 95:7*ab*) with—immediately following—a stern and sharp warning of truly prophetic inspiration:

"Today, O that ye would hear his voice!
'Harden not your heart, as at Meribah,
    As in the day of Massah in the wilderness:
When your fathers tempted me,
    Proved me, and saw my work.

Forty years long was I grieved with that generation,
  And said, It is a people that do err in their heart,
  And they have not known my ways:
Wherefore I swore in my wrath,
  That they should not enter into my rest' " (Ps. 95:7c-11).

Here is an abrupt end for a hymn of praise, but such a concluding note reveals how uneasy some of those poets must have felt when confronted by the discrepancy which opposed the promises of faith to man's obstinacy.

iv

Lastly, the hymns of history included a number of "Royal Psalms," like Ps. 110, which were sung at festivals when the worshipers celebrated in the Temple the imminent renewal of creation through the advent of Yahweh's viceroy, his "anointed," or "messiah."

The institution of a human monarchy was not congenial to the spirit of Hebrew religion. From Jotham's fable on "King Bramble" (Judg. 9:7-15) to the prophets' denunciation (*i.e.,* Hos. 8:4; cf. I Sam. 8:11-18), one detects a long line of antagonism to an alien institution which carried within it the dangers of polytheistic corruption, and this deep current of opposition appears to be largely justified by the record of most Hebrew kings. The "sad story" tells, as in *Richard II,*

"How some have been depos'd; some slain in war;
  Some haunted by the ghosts they have deposed."

When the kingdoms of Israel and Judah were finally wiped out by Mesopotamian imperialism, one might have thought that

"God said, I am tired of kings,
  I suffer them no more;
  Up to my ear the morning brings
  The outrage of the poor."[4]

---

[4] Ralph Waldo Emerson, "Boston Hymn."

It is probably on account of sorry memories that the eschatological hope, by and large, looked for the coming of Yahweh himself as the king of the new world. Yet the idea of a righteous and humble ruler who would truly serve God and reign in the midst of his people continued to shape the expectations of many, perhaps in accordance with the obscure human need for a concrete representation of the divine, for a mediator between God and man, for an intermediary who would unite heaven and earth. The great prophets had, time and again, spoken in various ways of a prince of the Davidic house, who would at the end of days rule the people of God with equity. Similarly the psalmists, in some of their hymns, looked for the advent of the Lord's anointed.

Several of the royal psalms were probably written—at least in part—in the honor of a human king at the occasion of his accession to the throne, but they probably received their finally edited form and certainly obtained their liturgical use in the context of the "messianic hope." They describe the expected king as the "son" of the Almighty (Ps. 2:7; cf. Ps. 110-3; Is. 9:6). His rule shall redress the injustices of society (Ps. 72:4, 12) and bring life and prosperity to earth (Ps. 72:6). His kingdom shall be universal as well as eternal.

> "Yea, let all kings fall down before him;
>   Let all nations serve him. . . .
> May his name endure forever:
>   May his name be continued as long as the sun!
> Let men bless one another and be blessed in him,
>   And let all nations bless him and call him happy!"
>   (Ps. 72:11, 17.)

The original poets of the royal psalms may not have thought of the messiah to come, but as the messianic hope took root and grew through centuries of foreign oppression and of domestic misrule, such songs became charged with a potency which, in the days of the Roman empire, inflamed the minds of two extremely divergent groups: on the one hand, the Zealots, who repeatedly took arms against the foreign yoke and led Jerusalem to its bloody end (A.D.

70); on the other hand, the disciples of an obscure prophet whom the Roman procurator mistook for a fanatic "messiah" and had crucified as "king of the Jews." These disciples reinterpreted in the light of that event the royal psalms of their hymnal, and they saluted their master as "the one who was to come," Immanuel, God-Is-with-Us.

The psalmists who sang praises to the lord of history reflected in their poems the ambiguity of the Old Testament faith in general; although they were given the vision of a united humanity, some of them could not unshackle their hope of a universal realm from the narrow straps of nationalistic pride, and these needed to pray, "Save us from our tribal gods!" Nevertheless they grasped a remarkably bold truth when they perceived that God is not the projection on an infinite screen of a nation's ambition or power, and that evil is a human reality to which not even—or especially— a people with a unique mission is abjectly submitted and from which it cannot escape. It is the presence of that evil within the human heart which estranges man on earth from his maker. Thus, if God himself comes to his "church" in the drama of worship, some mode of religious survival is possible, and the present can be lived day by day. The psalmists believed that God made himself revealed and "available" to his holy congregation gathered in the Temple. They celebrated him, therefore, in their hymns, not only as the sovereign of nature and as the ruler of history, but also, and always, as the lord of Zion.

3 | WORSHIP OF THE LORD OF ZION

INASMUCH as the Psalter was originally the hymnal of the Second Temple (about 516 B.C.-A.D. 70), all the hymns and prayers which it contains were used for worship at the sanctuary of Jerusalem. Nevertheless a few psalms were more explicitly concerned with the significance of ceremonial adoration and they may therefore be grouped together as "Hymns of Zion."

It would be a grave error—sometimes committed by Christian interpreters, especially of a nonliturgical Protestant tradition—to consider the Temple esplanade merely as a place for the slaughter of rams and bullocks, or to view the Temple services as little more than theatrical performances. Such an attitude betrays a misapprehension of the true spirit of drama as well as a lack of understanding of the relation between faith and ritual.

The love of the psalmists for Zion reveals something more than a sentimental attachment to religious pageantry. Behind the symbolism of sacerdotal garb and ornament, above the solemnity of procession, posture, and act, beyond the aesthetic impressiveness of orchestral and choral music, the people perceived and received the sacrament of the real presence of God.

Assembled in the Temple for worship, priests, musicians, and congregation realized an experience of covenantal oneness in two dimensions: they were knit together as a sociological whole, and they felt the awesome nearness of the maker of heaven and earth who, in his gracious condescension, consented to tabernacle in the holy of holies.

The ancient Hebrews sensed the truth which has been recently

93

rediscovered by modern psychologists: there is an intimate connection between body and soul. Thus the most spiritual worship may not be separated from outward form and dramatic expression. That the Temple services, at their best, impressed the men of the old covenant at the very core of their religious life can be seen from several descriptions preserved in their literature. The Chronicler, for instance, pictured in terms of what he witnessed in his time (fourth century B.C.) the initial ceremony of the Temple dedication:

"The Levites which were the singers, all of them of Asaph, of Heman, of Jeduthun, with their sons and brethren, being arrayed in white linen, having cymbals and psalteries and harps, stood at the east end of the altar, and with them an hundred and twenty priests sounding with trumpets. And it came to pass, as the trumpeters and singers were as one, to make one sound to be heard in praising and thanking Yahweh; and when they lifted up their voice with the trumpets and cymbals and instruments of music, and praised Yahweh [singing antiphonally],

> For he is good,
> For his mercy endureth forever!

that then the house was filled with a cloud, even the house of Yahweh; so that the priests could not stand to minister by reason of the cloud, for the glory of Yahweh had filled the house of God" (II Chron. 5:12-14).

Here is an attempt to express by intelligible words some ineffable certainty that the very God of the universe came and dwelt in his sanctuary.

Another description, written by Jesus ben Sirach (Ecclesiasticus, at the beginning of the second century B.C.), conveys in the style of Oriental imagery the profundity of worshipful emotion which captured the participants of a Temple ceremony:

"How glorious he [the high priest] was, surrounded by the people,
As he came out of the sanctuary!
Like the morning star among the clouds,
Like the moon when it is full;

Like the sun shining forth upon the sanctuary of the Most
   High; . . .
And when he finished the service at the altars,
To adorn the offering of the Most High, the Almighty,
He stretched out his hand to the cup,
And poured out some of the blood of the grape;
He poured it out at the foot of the altar,
A fragrant odor unto the Most High, the King of All.
   Then the descendants of Aaron shouted;
They sounded the trumpets of beaten work;
They made a great sound heard,
For a reminder, before the Most High.
   Then all the people made haste together,
And fell upon their faces on the ground,
To worship their Lord,
The Almighty, the Most High.
The singers too praised him with their voices; . . .
And the people intreated the Lord Most High,
With prayer before him who is merciful,
Until the worship of the Lord should be finished,
And they completed his service.
   Then he came down and lifted his hands
Over the whole assembly of the descendants of Israel,
To pronounce the blessing of the Lord with his lips,
And to exult in his name" (Ecclus. 50:5-7*a*, 14-18*a*, 19-20).[1]

Even when proper allowance is made for the obvious dangers of
such a ceremonial, one may easily admit that some inward and
spiritual event of magnitude took place then and there. Men were
lifted out of the routine and mediocrity of their daily life and
brought into communion with God. Theirs was a genuine experience of corporate encounter with a majestic deity, lord of nature,
and controller of history, who assented to sojourn in the "thick-
darkness" of a Temple made by human hands.

The hymns of Zion confer an articulate meaning on the depth
of passion which possessed the worshipers. They introduce an intellectual content into religious emotions which would otherwise
vanish into sterile sentimentalism. They interpret the act of ad-

---

[1] Tr. Edgar J. Goodspeed, in *The Complete Bible, An American Translation* (Chicago: The University of Chicago Press, 1939). Quoted by permission of the publisher.

oration, but they do so in poetry, and thus propose—in Milton's words—

> "thoughts that voluntary move
> Harmonious numbers."

Through most centuries of the Dispersion, Jews came back to Jerusalem as eager pilgrims to participate in the celebration of the festivals; although they prayed wherever they lived, they looked at Zion as the concrete symbol of divine inhabitation on the earth. There, in some unique way, the creator dwelt. There the church of dispersed Israel was visible as a united body. There the past and the future of history were liturgically overcome. There confession was uttered, forgiveness was received, vows were paid, resolutions were taken, and life received meaning.

Some of the hymns of Zion, like Ps. 122, were sung by pilgrims on their way to the holy city. Others, like Ps. 15, were liturgical songs of entrance to the sanctuary. Still others, like Ps. 24, gave lyrical expression to the supreme mystery of the cult: the presence of God in his Temple. Lastly, some hymns, like Ps. 84, revealed the longing and faith of those exiled in a foreign land far from Zion.

I

On the Way to Zion
(Psalm 122)

I

1.   I was glad when they said unto me,
           Let us go into the house of Yahweh!
2.   Our feet are [already] standing
           Within thy gates, O Jerusalem!

II

3.   Jerusalem! Thou art builded as a city
           That is compact together:

4.   Whither the tribes go up,
           The tribes of Yahweh;
       As a testimony to Israel
           To give thanks to the name of Yahweh.

5.   For there are the thrones of judgment,
           The thrones of the house of David.

III

6.   Pray for the peace of Jerusalem!
           May they be secure that love thee!
7.   Peace be within thy walls,
           And security within thy towers!

8.   For my brethren and companions' sakes,
           I will now say, Peace be within thee!
9.   For the sake of the house of Yahweh our God,
           I will earnestly seek thy good.

In the present Psalter, fifteen poems (Pss. 120-134) are grouped together under the title of "Songs of Degrees" or "Songs of Ascents," for they were used by pilgrims on their way to the sanctuary. Ps. 122 offers perhaps the best example of "Pilgrim Songs," for it expresses some of the emotions, sentiments, and thoughts which were entertained by a man plodding along to Zion.

The first strophe (vss. 1-2) recalls the moment of rapturous joy which seized the psalmist when he decided, in company with other members of his distant community, to make the pilgrimage in order "to give thanks to the name of Yahweh" (vs. 4*d*). Although the verb used in vs. 2 appears in the perfect tense, he is probably still far from the holy city, but he anticipates vividly the thrill of arrival, as if his "feet were [already] standing within [the] gates."

In the second strophe (vss. 3-5), the city appears suddenly from the top of the road, as it still does to the traveler who approaches Jerusalem from almost any direction. The compactness of its houses rises within its ramparts and towers above the narrow valleys which surround it on three sides. It is like a block of light-beige stones, sparkling under the deep blue sky, with its multitude of flat roofs and small domes crowding within the city walls. After days and perhaps weeks of hard trekking on rocky paths, the wayfarer is at last in sight of the goal. A shout rises from his throat: "Jerusalem!" (Vs. 3a.) But the poet means more than the concrete observation of a fact, or a feeling of artistic admiration. Indeed the expressions used in vs. 3b suggest a double sense: not only the closeness and intricacy of stones, but also the harmony of the worshipers who assemble there for the single purpose of giving thanks in the house of Yahweh. The poet not only sang of a city "that is compact together," but also thought of a spiritual reality. He hailed the place "where people gather together in unity." The secret of true poetry lies in its ability to cast a spell on its hearers and to bring to their minds some inward truth barely delineated by its words. These lines are charged with centuries of a faith which has held the earthly Jerusalem in hallowed imagination and seen in it the symbol of a "city which hath foundations, whose builder and maker is God" (Heb. 11:10). The psalmist was thinking, not only of the cementing of stones, but also of the solidarity and reciprocal companionship of a human society. His singing is echoed by the strains of a Christian poet:

> "City of God, how broad and far
> Outspread thy walls sublime!
> The true thy chartered freemen are,
> Of every age and clime. . . .
> How gleam thy watch-fires through the night
> With never-fainting ray!
> How rise thy towers, serene and bright,
> To meet the dawning day!"

The thought of Zion as the rallying center of the tribes that are scattered in the land and even in the world is developed in vs. 4. They "go up" to the Temple "as a testimony for Israel." There individuals and families regain a concrete consciousness of themselves as belonging to the elected people of God, as forming a part of the incarnate body of his will for man on earth, as the "church" of the covenant. There also are memories of a great past, "the thrones of the house of David," when justice—so the psalmist liked to believe—was administered with equity. A certain mood of melancholy seems to be lingering here as if he were "thinking of days that are no more." No specific statement is made, but the rapturous joy of the opening lines is sobered by the haunting presence of historical reality. And thus, without the need of a transition, the mood subsides with the third strophe (vss. 6-9) into a call for prayer.

"Pray for the peace of Jerusalem!" (Vs. 6*a.*) The phrase is filled with assonances: *"Shaalû shelôm Yerûshalayîm!"* Ask not only for peace but also for the health, the prosperity, the fullness, the total welfare, the wholeness, the oneness, the fulfillment of Jerusalem! A common love should make men brothers. A social sense springs from religious allegiance.

The psalm closes as it began (cf. vs. 1 with vs. 9). Loyalty to the city or to the Hebrew brotherhood is motivated by devotion to the "house of Yahweh *our* God." It is for the sake of the people of God and of the earthly home of God that the poet finally pledges to Jerusalem, "I shall earnestly seek thy good" (vs. 9). Care for the welfare of individuals is rooted in a filial fealty for the church of God. The external institution is the necessary shell of an inward core. The church is the "kirk," that is to say, the society of those who acknowledge the "lordship" of God (from the Greek *kyriakos,* "pertaining to the Lord"—hence "kirk" and "church").

According to a traditional and possible etymology the name "Jerusalem" means "city of peace." The psalmist was probably thinking of this when he invited the pilgrims to "pray for the peace of Jerusalem." He knew the internal divisions which seethed behind the unity of its walls. He did not speak of the mystery of iniquity which insidiously worms its way into the best of man's endeavors or corrupts God's work in the human realm, but he asked for the appropriate intercession. No prayer, indeed, is more fitting than a request for the perfecting, at last, of what was meant to be.

Another pilgrim made his way to Zion, "and when he was come near, he beheld the city, and wept over it, saying, If thou hadst known, even thou, at least in this thy day, the things which belong unto thy peace!" (Lk. 19:41-42.) If the Christian church claims the right of inheritance to Zion, it must also undergo the same kind of judgment. "O Jerusalem, Jerusalem, . . . how often would I have gathered thy children together, even as a hen gathereth her chickens under her wings, and ye would not! Behold, your house is left unto you desolate" (Mt. 23:37-38). The psalmist is calling still, to Jewry and Christendom alike, "Pray for the peace and the unity of Jerusalem!"

II

At the Gates of Zion
(Psalm 15)

I

1.   O Yahweh, who shall sojourn in thy tent?
        Who shall dwell in thy holy hill?

II

2.   He that walketh uprightly, and worketh righteousness,
        And speaketh the truth in his heart;
3.   He that backbiteth not with his tongue,
        Nor doeth evil to his neighbor,
        Nor bringeth a reproach to his friend.

III

4.   In his eyes a vile person is contemned,
        But he honoreth them that fear Yahweh;
        He sweareth to his own hurt, and changeth not.
5.   He putteth not out his money to usury,
        Nor taketh a bribe against the innocent.

IV

He that doeth these things
Shall never be moved.

This psalm does not belong among hymns of praise, but it may be studied at this place, for it was used by worshipers who had come from near and far to present themselves before the lord of Zion and who sought admittance to the courts of the Temple.

The first two lines (vs. 1) ask a question to which the body of the psalm provides the answer (vss. 2-3, 4-5). In order to be "a guest" of Yahweh and to "sojourn" in his tent, the pilgrim must behave "with integrity" all the days of his life. His religion may not be divorced from his ethics. He must practice at home and in his profession or business the ideal of existence to which he subscribes in the sanctuary. He must have a singleness of purpose and carry it out in all situations. He must do his duty and accomplish what is right. More than this, he must think inwardly what he utters outwardly. There must be complete agreement between his deeds and his speech, and between his speech and his secret intent. This is the basic principle which must inspire his whole conduct (vs. 2).

The true worshiper of Yahweh will therefore have a sense of responsibility toward the community to which he belongs. He will resist those temptations which, in all ages, seem to beset particularly the pious and the devout—slandering, or calumny, or mere gossiping—which bring hatred and bitterness, destroy friendship, and divide the "church." Communion with God means peace and fellowship with men (vs. 3).

However, the guest of God will not practice the virtues of social gentleness at the price of his religious loyalty. "Gracious living" does not mean compromise with evil. Tolerance is sometimes a word which covers up a lack of solid conviction. The true worshiper of Yahweh will have no dealings with "a vile person," even one of influence and high estate, but he will honor the God-fearing man, however poor and socially inconsequential (vs. 4*ab*). He will be a man of his word and he will respect his oath, even "to his own hurt" (vs. 4*c*). He will not take advantage of his fellow men in distress who need a loan in order to survive (the practice of usury was a constant concern of Hebrew law: see Exod. 22:25 [pre-Davidic]; Deut. 23:19 [pre-exilic]; Lev. 25:36 [postexilic]), nor will he consent to testify falsely—and for a reward—against the innocent (vs. 5).

The conclusion rings with a note of calm certainty: "He that doeth these things shall never be moved" (vs. 5*c*). Indeed the final answer goes much farther than the initial question anticipated. Such a man will not only "sojourn" for a while "in the house of Yahweh"; he will obtain in his existence a stability and a solidity which cannot be shaken. His life will be built on a rock. He can neither stumble nor fall.

> ". . . There are wanderers o'er Eternity
> Whose bark drives on and on, and anchor'd ne'er shall be,"

like Byron's Childe Harold, but there are also those who discover what a true home can be. Not only will they lodge for a night in the tent of God, but they will "dwell upon his holy hill" even after they have returned to the meandering tracks of the world's sandy wastes.

It is quite possible that the question was asked by pilgrims while they were waiting outside the Temple courts, and that the answer was intoned by the keepers of the gates whose function was precisely to weed out undesirable individuals. Or else, vice versa, the doorkeepers may have put the question first, and the would-be worshipers, like the catechumens of the early church, answered by reciting the list of requirements for admittance; thereupon the threshold attendants replied antiphonally with the concluding sentence (vs. 5c), and opened the doors. In like fashion the famous shrines of Mesopotamian, Egyptian, and Graeco-Roman religions were accessible only to those who gave evidence of their ritual purity and general fitness.

This psalm, however, is truly remarkable in one respect. Its list of requirements for admittance before the lord of Zion does not include any prescription of a ritual nature, nor does it concern itself with any legal abstinence or cleansing. It deals exclusively with inward attitude, purity of heart, honesty of will, and deeds of ethical decency. This is characteristic of the psalmists in general, who, like the great prophets, believed in the religious necessity of wholesomeness in morality. They could not admit the coexistence of Temple piety with market-place duplicity. To be sure, this poet is not moved by the hard-tempered sharpness of an

Amos, an Isaiah, a Micah. He does not even feel the need of pole-
mizing against the hypocrisy of double-minded worship. He does
not attack the validity of sacrificial offering and of Temple ceremonial. He does not ask with awesome anxiety,

> "Wherewith shall I come before Yahweh,
>   And bow myself before the high God?
> Shall I come before him with burnt offerings,
>   With calves of a year old?
> Will Yahweh be pleased with thousands of rams,
>   Or with ten thousands of rivers of oil?
> Shall I give my first-born for my transgression,
>   The fruit of my body for the sin of my soul?" (Mic. 6:6-7.)

Nor does he provide the profound and all-inclusive answer,

> "He hath shewed thee, O man, what is good;
>   And what doth Yahweh require of thee,
> But to do justly, and to love mercy,
>   And to walk humbly with thy God!" (Mic. 6:8.)

Nevertheless some of the criticism directed against this psalm
does not appear to stand a serious examination.

It has been said, for instance, that the picture of the guest of
Yahweh is inadequate because it omits all mention of man's duty
to God, and thus reduces religion to the practice of morality. But
this is a strange charge, indeed, to be made against a "song of entrance" before the lord of Zion. Jesus stressed also the need of
social decency in daily life, and the parable of the sheep and the
goats (Mt. 25:31-46), detached from the context of the whole
gospel, lies open to a similar condemnation. The psalmist concen-
trated his admonitions on ethical conduct, precisely because men,
in all times, have too easily paid lip service to their faith without
carrying out its demands in the realm of secular living. "Why call
ye me, Lord, Lord, and do not the things which I say?" (Lk. 6:46.)
Some may even consent to make heavy sacrifices in time, work,
and money for the cause of God, as if they were thereby purchasing
the right to behave far less nobly than a pagan. "Men will wrangle

for religion; write for it; fight for it; die for it; anything but—
live for it," wrote Caleb Colton. The psalmist bids us simply to
live our faith.

Again, it has been said that the picture of the guest of Yahweh
is on the whole unsatisfactory because the ethics it proposes con-
sist mostly of outward prohibitions. But let any man try to observe them, and let him discover for himself that they may require
an uncommon nobility of character. A man who "walketh with integrity" is endowed with psychological health; he enjoys an integrated personality; he has reached emotional maturity; he is well
adapted to his environment and yet he dominates it through his
influence. He may not be a saint or a hero, but he is a man in the
full sense of the term. As a matter of fact, the psalmist's program
is far from being confined to negative externals. Its fulfillment pre-
supposes an inner life of deep consecration to God and genuine love
for fellow men. One has the right, however, to ask, "Who is he that
walketh with integrity, and whose very faithfulness is not perverted
by a sense of pride in his own achievement?" The question is raised
in another liturgy of entrance which has been preserved in Ps. 24.

III

Before the King of Zion
(Psalm 24)

I

1.   The earth is Yahweh's, and the fullness thereof;
         The world, and they that dwell therein.
2.   For it is he that hath founded it upon the seas,
         And established it upon the streams [of the deep].

II

3.   *Who shall ascend into the hill of Yahweh?*
         Or who shall stand in his holy place?
4.   He that hath clean hands, and a pure heart,
         Who hath not lifted up his soul unto vanity,
         Nor sworn deceitfully.

5.   He shall receive the blessing from Yahweh,
      And righteousness from the God of his salvation.
6.   This is the generation of them that seek him,
      That seek thy face, O God of Jacob!

III

7.   Lift up your heads, O ye gates;
      And be ye lifted up, ye everlasting doors!
      And the king of glory shall come in.
8.   *Who is this king of glory?*
      Yahweh, strong and mighty!
      Yahweh, mighty in battle!

9.   Lift up your heads, O ye gates;
      Even lift them up, ye everlasting doors!
      And the king of glory shall come in.
10.   *Who is he, then, this king of glory?*
      Yahweh of hosts!
      He is the king of glory!

Ps. 24 is perhaps the most challenging and thought-provoking among the hymns of Zion, for it celebrates the entrance, not only of man, but also of God himself, into the holy place. There is little doubt that the present poem is composite, but it must be added that its three component parts now form an artistic, liturgical, and theological unity.

i

Those who are tempted to liken the lord of Zion to the other deities that dwell in man-made shrines must, from the start, be shaken out of their illusion (vss. 1-2). Earth and mankind belong to the God of Israel. "All the earth is mine!" This is the claim of the God who chooses for himself "a peculiar people" (Exod. 19:5-6). And not only the earth, and all that it contains, but also "the world" in its immensity, for Yahweh is creator of the universal nature.

In a similar vein, at the dedication of the first Temple (which had been erected by pagan architects trained in the aberrations of sun worship), Solomon's prayer aimed at dispelling popular confusions and began with the word which was in everybody's mind: "The sun! Yahweh hath set it in the heavens!" (I Kings 8:12, according to the Greek text of the Septuagint.)

No doubt about it: the master of heaven, earth, and abyss is not confined within the walls of an abode made of stone and wood. Still, he is fully present in his Temple as a guide and protector of his people. Thus, as the supreme moment of ceremonial encounter with God himself approaches, the worshipers remind one another in music and song of the *divinity* of God. The creator of the universe, who gave to man a habitation by establishing the earth on the deep, is here.

ii

The opening hymn has been sung, and the question is therefore inevitable: "Who is able to stand before Yahweh, this holy God?" (I Sam. 6:20.) In the second part the psalmist presents a "catechism" of admission (vss. 3-4, 5-6) which is much more comprehensive than the entrance liturgy of Ps. 24.

The guest of Yahweh must be endowed with four qualifications which are arranged to proceed from purity of deeds ("He that hath clean hands") to purity of speech ("Nor sworn deceitfully") by passing through inward truthfulness ("a pure heart") and unadulterated faith ("Who hath not lifted up his soul unto vanity," *i.e.,* idols). No one will be admitted into the presence of God if his hands are stained with the blood of crimes or the mud of shady dealings. Moral acts stem from cleanness of thought and will, or else they are but short-lived pretense. Furthermore, no man possesses an immaculate mind and an unsullied power of resolve unless he is free from idolatrous pursuits. He cannot harbor in secret a worship of false deities, those gods created by the dozen in the image of man's selfish desires. Idolatry always translates itself into moral compromises. Monotheism, in the days of the psalmist as in our time, represents more than a belief of the intellect. It means a complete dedication of the will and an absolute refusal to worship those projections of the self whose names may vary and die (Moloch, Ashtoreth, Baal, or Mars, Venus, Mercury), but whose realities survive.

The psalmist, however, is not satisfied with providing the pilgrims merely with a catalogue of moral and religious virtues. He seems to have discerned how short man falls of perfection and he whispers in effect, centuries before the apostle Paul, "Who is sufficient for these things?" (II Cor. 2:16.) Man's strength to be faithful comes not from himself. His righteousness is of God (vs. 5). It cannot be achieved by his own efforts; it is received from the "God of his salvation." He must strive after the inward purity which produces righteous living, but ultimately it is God who purifies.

> "Like the stain'd web that whitens in the sun,
>   Grow pure by being purely shone upon."[2]

With vs. 6, this strain of meditation is pursued still farther. The righteous man seeks the righteousness of God by seeking God's own presence, in the midst of the worshiping community. "This is the generation of them that seek him" (vs. 6*a*). Better than Jacob at Peniel (Gen. 32:24-31) who, left alone in a dark canyon, fought all night long and saw the face of God, thereby to become a new man, the pilgrims are seeking in worship the face of God and thus obtain the blessing of righteousness. Indeed the psalmist's emotion transforms his meditation into a prayer, and he repeats, "That seek *thy* face, O God of Jacob!" (Vs. 6*b*.)

iii

As the worshipers enter the sacred courts there is no longer any concern for man. A triumphal song (vss. 7-10) celebrates the advent of God himself in his holy place. In all probability the psalmist has incorporated in his hymn an ancient liturgy composed in the tenth century B.C. when the ark was for the first time carried into the city of Jerusalem (II Sam. 6:12-19).

---

[2] Thomas Moore, "The Veiled Prophet of Kohrassan."

As the procession advances toward the gates the choir without addresses antiphonally the choir within in a sublime dialogue which reveals the profundity of Hebrew theological thinking on the double mystery of God's transcendence and cultic immanence: God is coming in! But what doors are large and high enough to admit the creator of the universe? Is not such an entrance incongruous?

Old Testament thinkers, in other centuries, were aware of this awesome contradiction (cf. Jer. 23-24; Is. 66:1; Ps. 113:4; II Chron. 2:6), and the question was asked,

"But will God indeed dwell on earth?
  Behold, the heaven and heaven of heavens cannot contain thee;
  How much less this house . . ." (I Kings 8:27).

God is not conceived, even in ancient times, merely in dimensional terms. He does not really dwell in a temple. He does not even dwell *in* heaven. That is the reason for which the hymnic invitation of this psalm could be used for the welcome of the king of creation by the choirs of the heavenly Sabbath, as Milton used it in *Paradise Lost:*

> " 'Open, ye everlasting gates!' they sung;
>   'Open, ye Heavens, your living doors! let in
>   The great Creator, from his work returned
>   Magnificent, his six days' work, a World!' "

At the gates of the city of David the call is renewed, more urgent, more imperative, and the inquiry is thrown back:

> "Who is *he*, then, this king of glory?"

This time, the final response gives the full name of the God of Israel:

> "Yahweh of hosts!
>   He is the king of glory!"

With him, the universe enters into Zion.

Thus, by means of poetic language and dramatic ceremonial, the ancient Hebrews were able to convey the startling mode of God's coming toward his "church." The paradox of a transcending deity who desires to be near the children of men remains entirely unexplainable in logical terms—no more and no less than the Christian "scandal" of the Incarnation. But the reality of God's presence is not to be denied, and sinful man, by the miracle of grace, may seek, and see, his very face.

In bringing together a hymn of creation (vss. 1-2), a pilgrims' liturgy of entrance (vss. 3-6), and what probably was at first the hymn of reception for the ark in the city of David (vss. 7-10), the psalmist defined with great beauty and power the prerequisites and the nature of the supreme act of religion: that instant when heaven and earth fade away and the eternal God, in loving grace, meets his mortal creature.

From cultic immanence to psychological communion the transition was but a step, and it was made by other psalmists. But the imagery of the Temple persisted. Fellowship with God should not degenerate into an easy, flippant, sometimes downright irreverent, comradeship. When the apostle wrote to the "moldy saints" of Corinth, "Know ye not that ye are the temple of God?" (I Cor. 3:16) he hastened to add, "If any man defile the temple of God, him shall God destroy" (I Cor. 3:17).

Communion with God means man's transformation. The pilgrims who seek admittance to Zion must receive a righteousness which was not hitherto their own. The gates must raise their lintels.

> "Then may the senses fall
> Vanquished indeed, nor dread
> That this their dear defeat he counted sin:
>   For every door of flesh shall lift its head,
> Because the King of Life is entered in."[3]

Here lies the artistic, liturgical, and theological unity of the psalm.

---

[3] Evelyn Underhill, "Supersensual."

IV

Far from Zion
(Psalm 84)

I

1. How amiable are thy tabernacles,
    O Yahweh of hosts!
2. My soul longeth, yea, even fainteth
    For the courts of Yahweh:
My heart and my flesh cry out
    For the living God.

3. Yea, the sparrow hath found an house,
    And the swallow a nest for herself,
    Where she may lay her young.
    ... Thine altars! O Yahweh of hosts,
    My king, and my God!

4. Blessed are they that dwell in thy house:
    They will be still praising thee.

II

5. Blessed is the man whose strength is in thee;
    In whose heart are the highways [to Zion].

6. Passing through the valley of weeping,
    They make it a place of fountains;
    Yea, the early rain covereth it with blessings.
7. They go from strength to strength,
    To appear before God in Zion.

8. Yahweh, God of hosts, hear my prayer,
    Give ear, O God of Jacob:
9. Behold our shield, O God,
    And look upon the face of thine anointed!

III

10. Because a day in thy courts is better
    Than a thousand [elsewhere],
I had rather be a doorkeeper in the house of my God,
    Than to dwell in the tents of wickedness.

11.   For Yahweh is a sun and shield:
       He will give grace and glory;
       No good thing will Yahweh withhold
       From them that walk uprightly.

12.   O Yahweh of hosts, blessed is the man
       That trusteth in thee!

The rhythm of this psalm is predominantly that of the "elegiac" style, which is common among many "Prayers of Lamentation and Supplication." This characteristic alone suggests the melancholy mood and even the pathos which also emerge from the contents. Nevertheless, as modern scholars admit, the poem belongs to the class of the hymns; it reveals throughout its development a tense anxiety, but it concludes on a note of serenity and of almost radiant assurance.

Many commentators believe that it was composed by a pilgrim on his way to Zion; however, the passion of hopeless longing for the sanctuary which permeates its lines rather indicates that the poet, who knew the Temple well, was for some unknown reason detained in a distant land. In his religious homesickness he contemplated the happiness of those who dwell in the Temple (first strophe, vss. 1-4); he then imagined the happiness of those who are able to go on the pilgrimage (second strophe, vss. 5-9); and lastly, he triumphed over his situation of exile and discovered the happiness of those who are far from Zion and yet stand in communion with "the living God" (third strophe, vss. 10-12). The key to the development of thought is provided by the three beatitudes, in vss. 4, 5 and 12.

i

"Blessed are they that dwell in thy house!"

The first strophe (vss. 1-4) begins with a prayerful exclamation: "How 'lovely and lovable' are thy dwelling places, O Yahweh of hosts!" (Vs. 1.) From the start the poet reveals himself as a mystic, for he uses the language of a lover. He is not chiefly prompted by an aesthetic emotion, as the disciple who centuries later said to Jesus, "Master, see what beautiful stones, and what magnificent edifices!" (Mk. 13:1.) He is driven by the love, not primarily of Zion, but of the God who dwells in Zion. Although he continues, "My soul longeth ('grows pale'), yea, even fainteth ('consumes itself by burning') for the courts of Yahweh" (vs. 2*a*), he indicates the true object of his yearning—"My heart and my flesh cry out for the living God!" (Vs. 2*b*.) He is not moved by an admiration of architecture or a quaint taste for ceremonial. Beyond the outward signs he looks for the inward grace, that of communing with "the living God."

As in Pss. 42 and 43 (perhaps written by the same poet), humanity is "athirst for the living God" (Ps. 42:2), because, as Tennyson put it, the object of man's longing and desire is life abundant:

> " 'Tis life, whereof our nerves are scant,
>   Oh life, not death, for which we pant;
>   More life, and fuller, that I want."

At the same time, the psalmist's religion takes hold of his total personality; not only his "soul" but also his "heart" and his "flesh" are affected by his estrangement. In heart, soul, and flesh he feels physical distress at the sensation of being removed from the God of life. One is almost tempted to discern in these lines an anticipation of the end of the psalm, when the theme of Zion is overcome by a faith which finds God in an immediate way, without the help of a sanctuary. However, the exclamation reveals only the opening phase of this spiritual adventure, when the poet is still unable clearly to distinguish between God and "his dwelling places." And Calvin's sober remark is fitting at this juncture:

> "Hence we learn that those are sadly deficient in understanding who carelessly neglect God's instituted worship, as if they were able to mount up to heaven by their own unaided efforts."

Vs. 3 is often interpreted to mean that birds nestle in the courts of Zion, *beside* the altars of God. The text does not justify this rendering. The grammatical sequence is broken, perhaps intentionally, as if the poet's emotion were too violent for the use of a correct and fluid syntax. Birds have homes of their own, but he, away from Zion, is homeless in the midst of the vast world. The creatures of nature find their resting place, but man is a stranger and a wanderer on the face of the earth. One may think of another who said, "The foxes have holes, and the birds of the air have nests; but the Son of man hath not where to lay his head" (Mt. 8:20).

The thought of homelessness aggravates the poet's nostalgia to such a pitch that, in utter destitution, he bursts forth in an incoherent cry, ". . . Thine altars!" Yet in the same breath he affirms unwittingly his closeness to the divine by expostulating, "My king, and my God!" (Vs. 3c.) The Temple is still the spiritual home for which he yearns, since those who dwell there can daily sing the praises of Yahweh of hosts. Nevertheless, his relation to God is of the most immediate and intimate kind, far from Zion though he may be. Cut off from the "church" of his time, he belongs to the company of the Most High, and he therefore exclaims, "My king, and my God!" No distance from the holy mount can separate him from the divine sovereign—a remote monarch—who is yet, in Tennyson's words, "closer [to him] than breathing, and nearer than hands and feet." At the very moment of desperate clinging to the religion of his past, the psalmist enters into the religion of his future.

ii

"Blessed is the man . . .
In whose heart are the highways to Zion!"

The second strophe (vss. 5-8), by a slight change of focus in the poet's imagination, considers the hardships and still the delights of anticipation which hinder and uphold the pilgrims "on the highways to Zion." They pass "through the valley of *Baka*" (vs. 6a); this word is often rendered by "balsam trees" (see II Sam. 5:23), which grow in arid places. As the word *baka* is closely similar to *bekeh* or *bekî,* "tears" (especially in the original Hebrew text, which did not include the writing of vowel sounds), it has been translated "weeping" in several ancient versions. Perhaps the poet intended to suggest both ideas. The pilgrims have to endure on their way the tortures of thirst, but they conquer weariness and suffering through their faith, which creates strength out of weakness and may transfigure "the vale of tears" into a place of fountains, as if the early winter rains had already covered it with green and refreshment. "They go from strength to strength" (vs. 7*a*); they receive new power when it is needed, little by little, as one victory engenders more endurance and prepares for another triumph. The goal of the journey provides for the virtue to sustain it: they know that they will "appear before God in Zion" (vs. 7*b*).

The personal prayer of vss. 8-9 seems to interrupt the development. Is it an intercession that the pilgrims expect to offer for the king as soon as they arrive at their destination, or repeat on their way as they progress through their trials? Or else, is it a supplication made on behalf of the high priest, "thine anointed"? Many interpretations have been proposed, but their diversity is in itself an indication of their improbability, and it seems best to make here a confession of ignorance.

iii

"Blessed is the man . . . that trusteth in thee!"

In the third strophe (vss. 10-12) the psalmist returns to his initial theme, the love of the God of Zion. But he adds a new note.

Not only does he contrast the joy of a single day that is spent "in thy courts" to a thousand lived elsewhere, but he also makes a dramatic choice between a seemingly difficult and unrewarding position "in the house of my God" and a tranquil dwelling "in the tents of wickedness." The traditional versions use the word "doorkeeper" in vs. 10*c* and they may be right. It has been remarked that the psalm was ascribed "to the sons of Qorach," a family of doorkeepers, attendants, and musicians of the Temple (see I Chron.

9:19; 26:1-19; II Chron. 20-19; cf. Num. 26:10-11). The Hebrew word is most difficult. It is the participle of the intensive-reflexive voice of a verb which seems to be derived from the noun meaning "threshold" or "sill," and the verse may thus be rendered:

> "I had rather stand tense and uncertain at the
> threshold of the house of my God
> Than to dwell at ease in the tents of wickedness."

Is the poet alluding to himself autobiographically? Is he making a confession of bad behavior? Not unlikely. His exile from Zion may have originated from his prodigal wandering. Perhaps he has gone to a far country, there to find worldly security and ease—at the cost of his inward peace. "In all [his] wanderings round this world of care," he has not fully forgotten the God of his youth, and now he pines for his religious home. But would he be received back in the fold? Would he deserve to be reinstated? Probably not. Still, to stand on the threshold of the house of his God, even with the agony of shame and the anxiety of doubt or the tenseness of expectation, would be infinitely more desirable than to remain in a mundane luxury, earned at the price of unfaithfulness.

Here again the interpreter must admit his ignorance, and cautiously avoid taking conjectures for demonstrated truth. Yet a fact remains. The poet in vs. 10 is reaching a new level of meditation. He not only contrasts life at the sanctuary, even for a short day, to the loneliness of the exile (vs. 10*a*), he also prefers the lowly and unsatisfying position of tense loyalty at the threshold of God's presence to the wealth and leisure of moral laxity.

The ethical note thus introduced will not be dropped. It was absent from the first two strophes, but it dominates the third. The psalmist began his meditation as a Temple mystic, and one might have thought that his religious longings were prompted only by a desire to escape from the secular world into the secluded shadow and the cloistered peace of a sanctuary. But he now understands that "Yahweh God is a sun and shield" over the whole wide earth, the true source of light and protection, of warmth and of shelter.

God makes man to live, and he also defends him against the attacks of evil. "What will you do," someone asked Luther, "if the Duke, your protector, should no longer harbor you?" He replied, "I shall take my shelter under the broad shield of Almighty God." But what about evil within? "He will give grace and glory" to those who "walk with integrity." "To walk with integrity" is a Hebrew phrase which means "to behave as if in the continuous presence of God, without any attempt at concealment, without double-mindedness." God may still be distant and remote, at first, and seem to be the *Deus Absconditus,* but time comes when, as Newman wrote,

> "To the thoughtful mind that walks with him,
> He half reveals his face."

In the meantime his grace will provide a viaticum and the reflection of his own glory will lighten the darkness.

The last beatitude sums up the discovery of personal and present salvation by faith: "Blessed is the man that trusteth in thee!" (Vs. 12.) To rely on the grace of God, to lean against his promise, to find comfort and persistent support in accepting it wholeheartedly, here and now, enables man to "live uprightly." This is an immediate and full religion which, whenever possessed, makes Zion superfluous. It may not be within everyone's reach, but, if it is given to man, its abundance becomes a sufficiency.

Far from Zion, the psalmist has accomplished a spiritual pilgrimage of his own. He may have been a distant ancestor of the Roman Catholic become Quaker. From the religion of ecclesiastic mediation he has traveled into a mystical country, without cult, without priest, without sacrament, where God alone, in a divine-human tête-à-tête, ministers unto his creature. He might have said, with St. Augustine, "I sought thee at a distance, and did not know thou wast near."

To be sure he was not aware of the momentous implications of his spiritual adventure. He did not mean to do without the religion of the Temple. In all probability he still hoped to return there, someday. His passionate longing for the sacred precincts was too deeply ingrained within the texture of his personality for him to feel or think otherwise. But his initial loss—his estrangement from Zion—became the source of his final gain, for in missing the worship of the sanctuary he discovered, wherever he was, a mode of intimacy with God. Paradoxically he composed a hymn of Zion which transcends the religion of the Temple; it was perhaps a landmark in the history of Hebrew religion. At any rate it explains how Judaism could survive the deprivation of sanctuary and pave the way for a worship of God "in spirit and in truth."

V

The psalms were gathered and edited for the worship of Yahweh in his Temple, but most of them, even the hymns of Zion, are permeated with a spirit which looks beyond the externals of cultic adoration to the prophetic dialogue between man and his maker. However, unlike some of the prophets who shouted in the name of Yahweh,

> "Take thou away from me the noise of thy songs;
> For I will not hear the melody of thy viols! . . .
> Have ye offered unto me sacrifices and offerings
> In the wilderness forty years, O house of Israel?"
> (Amos 5:23, 25; cf. Jer. 7:21-33.)

the psalmists in their hymns never tired of praising God with music and song.

Again and again they called to worship the lord of Zion.

> "Exalt Yahweh our God,
> And worship at his holy hill!" (Ps. 99:9.)

> "Serve Yahweh with gladness:
> Come into his presence with singing! . . .
> Enter his gates with thanksgiving,
> And into his courts with praise!" (Ps. 100:2, 4.)

They invited worshipers to offer sacrifices.

"Give to Yahweh the glory of his name:
    Bring an offering, and come into his courts!" (Ps. 96:8.)

"Bind the sacrifice with cords,
    Even unto the horns of the altar!" (Ps. 118:27.)

To be sure, some individual prayers transformed the meaning of the sacrificial offering and spiritualized it into the gift of "a broken and a contrite heart" (Ps. 51:16, 17; cf. Ps. 40:6 ff.), and one prophetic psalm even went so far as to place in the mouth of God the startling declaration:

"I will take no bullock out of thy house,
    Nor he-goats out of thy folds.
For every beast of the forest is mine,
    And the cattle upon a thousand hills. . . .
If I were hungry, I would not tell thee:
    For the world is mine, and the fullness thereof"
                                    (Ps. 50:9-10, 12).

Nevertheless, the same poet gladly acknowledged that,

"Out of Zion, the perfection of beauty,
    God shineth forth!" (Ps. 50:2.)

Thus, more than nature and history, Zion is the theme *par excellence* of the hymns of praise, because there God reveals his tabernacling presence.

"We have thought of thy lovingkindness, O God,
    In the midst of thy temple" (Ps. 48:9).

"In Salem also is his tabernacle,
    And his dwelling place in Zion" (Ps. 76:2).

"Yahweh loveth the gates of Zion
    More than all the dwellings of Jacob.
Glorious things are spoken of thee,
    O city of God!" (Ps. 87:2-3.)

No corporate expression of worship can excel the liturgical sequence, as it was intoned antiphonally by various singers and choirs:

> "Hallelujah!
> Praise the name of Yahweh!
> Praise him, O ye servants of Yahweh!
> Ye that stand in the house of Yahweh,
> In the courts of the house of our God! . . .
> (To the whole congregation)
> Bless Yahweh, O house of Israel!
> (To the priests)
> Bless Yahweh, O house of Aaron!
> (To the musicians)
> Bless Yahweh, O house of Levi!
> (To the laity)
> Ye that fear Yahweh, bless Yahweh!
> (*A l'unison*)
> Blessed be Yahweh out of Zion,
> Which dwelleth at Jerusalem!
> Hallelujah!" (Ps. 135:1-2, 19-21.)

The hymns of praise are filled with joy, because they sing in the name of the whole church of the saved.

> "O *come*, let *us* sing unto Yahweh:
> Let *us* make a joyful noise to the rock of our salvation!
> Let *us* come before his presence with thanksgiving,
> And make a joyful noise unto him with psalms! . . .
> For he is *our* God;
> And *we* are the people of his pasture,
> And the sheep of his hand" (Ps. 95:1-2, 7).

The hymns of praise are not concerned with the depth of individual despair and restoration, or with "the dark night of the soul," because they celebrate the power, justice, and love of God in his creation, his providence, his final triumph at the end of history, his tabernacling presence in Zion. They give to the Temple a central attention, because the Temple is the place where God meets his "church."

At first sight the hymns of Zion, by the very nature of their theme, should be more alien to Christians than the other psalms. Yet, not unlike the ancient Hebrews, Christians believe in the tabernacling presence of God on earth. "And the Word was made flesh and tabernacled among us" (John 1:14). Indeed there is a recurrent theme in the New Testament which associates the person of Christ with the Temple. "Destroy this temple, and in three days I will raise it up" (John 2:19; see Mk. 14:58; Mt. 27:40). This association is revealed in a profound way by the gospel tradition according to which, after the death of Jesus, "the veil of the temple was rent in twain from the top to the bottom" (Mk. 15:38). This association is then extended to the new community, the body of the living Christ, and in the celebration of the Eucharist—the service of praise—God eternal, creator, judge, and king of the universe perpetuates his tabernacling presence.

The hymns of Zion may therefore be appropriated by Christendom without violation of their original intent. There is between the tabernacling presence of God in Zion and the tabernacling presence of God in Christ a historical and theological continuity. If, on Christmas Day, we sing,

"This is my resting place forever;
  Here will I dwell, for I have delight therein" (Ps. 132:14),

we respect the original meaning of the poet, but we apply it to Jesus Christ. "By thus gently stretching the Psalmist's words we glorify them."[4] We do not even need to stretch the words. We sing poetry as it should be sung, poetically. No subjective interpretation is forced on the psalm. Fully aware of the passing of the centuries, we associate ourselves with the community of Israel, seeking the face of Yahweh, and we behold the glory of the incarnate Word, "full of grace and truth" (John 1:14). Admittedly we place the hymns of Zion in a new context, the world of the New Covenant. But we need them to give form, *élan*, and objective joy to our praise. On account of Christ, born in Bethlehem, the church summons,

---

[4] T. K. Cheyne, *The Christian Use of the Psalms* (New York: E. P. Dutton and Co., 1900), p. 270.

"Come to your heaven, you heavenly choirs!
  Earth hath the heaven of your desires;
  Remove your dwelling to your God,
  A stall is now His best abode;
  Sith men their homage do deny,
  Come, angels, all their fault supply."[5]

On account of Christ triumphant, the church calls the universe to sing:

"Hallelujah!
Praise ye the LORD from the heavens:
  Praise him in the height!
Praise ye him, all his angels:
  Praise ye him, all his hosts!

"Praise ye him, sun and moon:
  Praise him, all ye stars of light!
Praise him, ye heavens of heavens,
  And ye waters that be above the heavens!

"Praise the LORD from the earth,
  Ye dragons, and all deeps!
Fire and hail, snow and vapors,
  Stormy wind fulfilling his word!

"Mountains and all hills,
  Fruitful trees and all cedars,
Beasts, and all cattle,
  Creeping things, and flying fowls!

"Kings of the earth, and all people,
  Princes, and all judges of the earth,
Both young men, and maidens,
  Old men, and children!

---

[5] Robert Southwell, "Come to Your Heaven, You Heavenly Choirs!"

"Let them praise the name of the Lord,
   For his name alone is excellent;
 His glory is above the earth and heaven;
   He also exalteth the horn of his people!

"The praise of all his saints,
     Even of the children of Israel,
     A people near unto him!

       "Hallelujah!"   (Ps. 148:1-4, 7-14.)

3

Prayers in Time of Crisis

I | NATIONAL LAMENTS

FEW nations, if any, outside of Israel, have more often passed through the crucible of fire, and survived. The history of the ancient Hebrews is a long rehearsal of wars, both civil and foreign, with their accompaniment of invasion, destruction, oppression, and deportation or death. If, to this picture of woes brought about by human enemies, one adds the strokes of an adverse nature, such as locusts, floods, storms, famines, and epidemics, one may wonder how the Psalter could include any hymn of praise at all. Obviously, the joy which dominated their worship was not the manifestation of a superficial exuberance but the result of a triumphant faith. When they "rejoiced before Yahweh," they did so against the background of a long inheritance of national trials and tribulations. There were moments, however, when they could not rejoice. Faced by crisis, they turned corporately to their God and prayed for deliverance. Under the onslaught of national misery, their sense of election was sometimes shaken, but never completely shattered. It was at the time of their Exile in Babylon, when they had lost king, land, and sanctuary, that their faith rose to its summit and found in Second Isaiah and in Job its purest expression. Israel, the chosen servant of Yahweh, learned through suffering to become "a light for the nations" and the instrument of God's "salvation unto the end of the earth" (Is. 49:6). It also discovered the grace of serving God for nought (Job 1:9). Then, one may ask,

"Is it so, O Christ in heaven, that the highest suffer most, . . .
That the mark of rank in nature is capacity for pain,
That the anguish of the singer makes the sweetness of the strain?"[1]

[1] Sarah Williams, "Is It So, O Christ in Heaven?"

The "National Laments" which are preserved in the Psalter do not reach the sublimity of Second Isaiah or of Job, but they reveal the nation's sense of complete dependence on the God of the ancient covenant. Some of them, like Ps. 80, beg for salvation in the name of the love of Yahweh for his flock. Others, like Ps. 137, pledge undying loyalty to the faith of the fathers, although there is no earthly sign of hope. Still others, like Ps. 90, rise above considerations of national destiny and meditate on the situation of universal man.

I

The Shepherd of Israel
(Psalm 80)

I

1. Give ear, O Shepherd of Israel,
    Thou that leadest Joseph like a flock;
    Thou that dwellest above the cherubim, shine forth!
2.   Before Ephraim and Benjamin and Manasseh,
    Stir up thy strength,
        And come to save us!
3. *O God, restore us!*
    And lighten thy face,
        And we shall be saved!

II

4. O Yahweh, God of hosts, how long
    Wilt thou be angry against the prayer of thy people?
5. Thou feedest them with the bread of tears;
    And givest them tears to drink in great measure.
6. Thou makest us an object of derision unto our neighbors,
    And our enemies laugh among themselves.
7. *O God of hosts, restore us!*
    And lighten thy face,
        And we shall be saved!

III

8. Thou hast brought a vine out of Egypt:
    Thou hast cast out the nations and planted it.

9. Thou hast cleared [the ground] before it,
    And caused it to take deep root,
    And to fill the land.
10. The hills were covered with the shadow of it;
    And the mighty cedars with the boughs thereof.
11. It sent out its branches unto the Sea,
    And its young shoots unto the River . . .

IV

12. Why hast thou broken down its hedges,
    So that all they which pass by the way do pluck it?
13. The boar out of the forest doth ravage it,
    And the wild beast of the field doth devour it.
14. O God of hosts, return, we beseech thee,
    Look down from heaven, and behold,
  And visit this vine,
15.   And the stock which thy right hand hath planted. . . .[2]

V

16. It is burned with fire, it is cut down:
    They perish at the rebuke of thy countenance.
17. Let thy hand be upon the man of thy right hand,
    Upon the son of man [whom] thou madest strong for thyself.
18. So will not we go back from thee:
    Quicken us, and we will call upon thy name.
19. *O Yahweh, God of hosts, restore us!*
    [And] lighten thy face,
      And we shall be saved!

This psalm probably originated in the kingdom of North Israel some years before the destruction of Samaria by the Assyrians in 722 B.C. Like other "Asaph Psalms" (i.e., Pss. 77:15; 81:5), it uses the name "Joseph" for designating the nation; it ignores Judah and Jerusalem but places the northern tribes of Ephraim, Benjamin, and Manasseh at the center of its attention. North Israel suffered a long agony for about twenty-two years (*ca.* 745-722 B.C.) during which invasion and governmental hysteria disfigured the land and bled the inhabitants. It may be in answer to the appeals

---

[2] Vs. 15*b* appears to be an accidental duplication of vs. 17*b*.

of a prophet like Hosea, who lived during that age of mortal convulsions, that this prayer of national lamentation and supplication was composed.

A refrain is repeated three times in the course of the poem (vss. 3, 7, and 19) and was probably taken up by the crowd of worshipers gathered for a public fast. It is possible that the variation in the three invocations of the deity's name was strictly intentional and suggested the rising tempo of the collective passion: "O God," "O God of hosts," "O Yahweh, God of hosts."

In the first strophe (vss. 1-3), God is compared to a shepherd. This is a most moving image, because a shepherd often risks his own life for the sake of a single stray sheep. At the same time this is an acknowledgment of national stupidity and obstinacy in waywardness. When Israel is aware of being God's "people and the sheep of [his] pasture" (Ps. 79:13), it thereby confesses its utter inability to reach moral decency and civic maturity. Ancient men knew how stupid, cowardly, and irresponsible sheep could be. At the same time, the poet attributed the highest quality of endurance and self-sacrificial love to the God whom he addressed as the "shepherd of Israel." How could such a God abandon his flock? If only he would "shine forth," Israel would be "saved" (vss. 1-3).

The lines "Before Ephraim and Benjamin and Manasseh, stir up thy strength" (vs. 2) may refer to the order of march in the wilderness when, according to a certain tradition (Num. 2:18-24), those tribes journeyed immediately behind the tabernacle. Why is it then that the people's prayer does not now soothe the anger of the God of hosts? (Vss. 4-7.)

The image of the shepherd soon changes and is replaced by that of the vinegrower (vss. 8 ff.). The psalmist now appeals to the infinite tenderness and skill of a viticulturist for the vineyard of his creation. It is difficult for modern man, unless he was born in a country where the care of grapes and grapevines is a highly sophisticated art, to understand the power of the psalmist's language. Thanks to God's patient and proud nursing, Israel was once a luxurious vine, extending from the Mediterranean Sea to the Euphrates (vss. 8-11), but now, every passer-by tramples it underfoot (vss. 12-13). The sorrow of the present calamity, as Dante knew, is intensified by the memory of a pleasant past.

> *Nessun maggior dolore*
> *Che ricordarsi del tempo felice*
> *Nella miseria.*

> "There is no greater grief
> Than to remember days of joy
> When misery is at hand."

The last part of the prayer implies that Israel still considers it-self the man of God's "right hand." Is it not for the purpose of stewardship that Yahweh has made Israel strong? The sense of a unique national mission is deeply embedded in the psalmist's mind. But he knows that Israel has forfeited this signal honor on account of its own national corruption. His awareness of the peo-ple's sinfulness is discreetly revealed by the pledge which follows: "So will we not go back from thee" (vs. 18*a*). The source of Israel's plight is estrangement from God. The nation has willfully doomed its own fate.

> "Never did any public misery
> Rise of itself: God's plagues still grounded are
> On common stains of our humanity;
> And, to the flame which ruineth mankind,
> Man gives the matter, or at least gives wind."[3]

If only God would give life again to his people, and "quicken" the beat of his nation's heart, then a renewal might be possible. The psalmist, in the name of the lamenting community, begs for such an inward resurrection, but in vain. North Israel died, and its people vanished from history. In the south, Judah carried on for a while, and preserved the psalm for the Jerusalem hymnal. Then Judah's turn for expiation came also. However, the Judeans did not disintegrate throughout the world as did their northern

---

[3] Fulke Greville, *Treatie of Warres.*

brothers. Carried away into Exile, they remembered their loyalty to the God of Zion. Ps. 137 is perhaps the best example of Judean faithfulness "in a foreign land."

II

"If I Forget Thee, O Jerusalem!"
(Psalm 137)

I

1.   By the rivers of Babylon,
        There we sat down, yea, we wept,
        As we remembered Zion.
2.   Upon the willows in the midst thereof,
        We hanged our harps.
3.   For there they that carried us away captive
        Required of us a song;
     And they that wasted us, mirth, saying,
        Sing us one of the songs of Zion!

II

4.   How shall we sing the song of Yahweh
        In a strange land?
5.   If I forget thee, O Jerusalem,
        Let my right hand wither!
6.   Let my tongue cleave to the roof of my mouth
        If I do not remember thee!
     If I prefer not Jerusalem
        Above my chief joy!

III

7.   Remember, O Yahweh, the sons of Edom
        Who, in the day of Jerusalem,
     Said, Raze it! Raze it!
        Even to the foundations thereof!
8.   O daughter of Babylon, who art to be destroyed,
        Happy shall he be that rewardeth thee
        With the reward thou hast given us!
9.   Happy shall he be that taketh and dasheth
        Thy little ones against the rock!

This song of sorrow exhibits, except in its last strophe (vss. 7-9), the most exquisite feeling of grief, longing, and loyalty for the ruined city of God. "By the rivers of Babylon," the Judeans "sat," in an attitude of mourning and dejection, and wept, unashamed, bitter tears of shame (vss. 1-2). Their captors wished to be entertained by exotic music, but the exiles refused "to sing the song of Yahweh in a strange land." Still the psalmist composed a musical meditation out of the sorry scene which he witnessed "there" (vs. 1).

Modern man in western culture is sometimes made ill at ease by the cries out of the night and the almost immodest shrieks of suffering which can be heard in the Psalter. A certain nobility of character may undoubtedly be revealed in a mute acceptance of misery. We often like to repeat Schiller's words, *"Doch grosse Seelen dulden still* (Great souls suffer in silence)." On the other hand, the ancient Hebrews as well as the Mediterranean peoples in general may teach us a valuable lesson by the unhampered honesty with which they have dug into the depths of their tortured beings and transmuted their afflictions into artistic creations. Contemporary psychologists have rediscovered the therapeutic meaning of exteriorization. Has not Shakespeare also said,

> "Give sorrow words: the grief that does not speak
> Whispers the o'er-fraught heart, and bids it break?"

In a more specific way, Christians know that by giving expression to suffering in prayer, one may renew his hope or at least keep alive his faith. Thus a lament turns into a pledge of loyalty.

Many of the Judeans adapted themselves readily to the way of life they discovered in the fertile valley of Mesopotamia. But some among them refused to forget Jerusalem. The violence of the double imprecation (vss. 5-6) reveals the power of the temptation which they endured, and overcame. And notice the last verse of the second strophe: Jerusalem is still an occasion of joy. Indeed, it is "above" the singer's "chief joy."

Unfortunately, the song did not end with this solemn resolve of faithfulness. The poet suddenly broke forth into a prayer for vengeance against the Edomites, who had lent their sordid services to the Babylonian invaders "in the day of Jerusalem" (vs. 7), and he cursed "the daughter of Babylon" by declaring happy whoever would destroy her and "crush [her] little ones upon the rock" (vs. 9). The brutality of the resentment here expressed should not be minimized by any modern interpreter. Yet a question may be asked: What kind of suffering engendered such a passionate thirst for revenge? The psalmist stands very far away from Jesus, who commanded, "Love your enemies, bless them that curse you, do good to them that hate you" (Mt. 5:44), or even from the self-centered morality of the wise men who, long before St. Paul, advised,

> "If thine enemy be hungry,
>   Give him bread to eat;
> And if he be thirsty,
>   Give him water to drink:
> For thou shalt heap
>   Coals of fire upon his head,
> And Yahweh shall reward thee."
>   (Prov. 25:21-22; cf. Rom. 12:19-20.)

The poet lived in an age of violence among people whose sense of justice was exacerbated into a total blindness of hate. The prophets likewise expressed the most bitter resentment against Edom (Is. 34; Jer. 49:7-10; Ezek. 25:12-14; etc.) and Babylon (Is. 14:4-23; Jer. 25:12; 51:1 ff.; etc.), but the harshness of the times, while it helps us to understand the psalmist's passion of hatred, does not compel us to condone it. However, we should not hastily condemn it.

During the Second World War a young woman was watching her two small boys, aged three and four, who were picking flowers in an open field. An enemy airplane swooped down from the blue sky and machine-gunned the two children. There was perfect visibility and no military objective in the vicinity. Later, the mother wrote to a friend, "Yes, in the pitch of my anguish, I have hated, I have hated with all my being. Now, Christ has taken hold of me again. But I learned to understand the pathos of Ps. 137. Through the grace of the gospel, I shall continue to condemn the feelings which animated the Jews 'by the rivers of Babylon.' But I shall no longer condemn them lightly."

III

The Everlasting God
(Psalm 90)

(Invocation)

1. Lord, thou hast been for us a dwelling place
   From generation to generation.
2. Before the mountains were brought forth,
   Or ever thou hadst formed the earth and the world,
   Even from everlasting to everlasting,
   Thou art God!

I

3. Thou turnest man into dust,
   And sayest, Return, ye children of men!
4. For a thousand years in thy sight
   Are but as yesterday when it is past,
   And as a watch in the night.

5. Thou carriest them away as with a flood; they are as a sleep:
   In the morning they are like grass which groweth up;
6. In the morning it flourisheth, and groweth up;
   In the evening it is cut down, and withereth.

II

7. For we are consumed by thine anger;
   And by thy wrath we hasten away.
8. Thou hast set our iniquities before thee,
   Our secret sins in the light of thy countenance.

9. For all our days decline on account of thy fury:
   We spend our years as a sigh.

10. The days of our years are threescore years and ten,
     And if by reason of strength they be fourscore years,
     Yet is their pride but labor and sorrow;
     Yea, it is soon gone, and we fly away!

III

11. Who knoweth the power of thine anger?
     And thy wrath, according to the fear that is due unto thee?
12. So teach us to number our days,
     That we may get us a heart of wisdom.

13. Return, O Yahweh! How long?
     And have compassion for thy servants!
14. O satisfy us early with thy mercy,
     That we may rejoice and be glad all our days!
15. Make us glad according to the days wherein thou hast afflicted
     us,
     And the years wherein we have seen evil!

(Final petition)

16. Let thy work appear unto thy servants,
     And thy glory unto thy children!
17. And let the beauty of the Lord our God be upon us;
     And establish thou the work of our hands upon us:
     Yea, the work of our hands establish thou it!

By the majesty of its cadence and style, the breadth of its religious grasp, and the firmness of its faith, this psalm belongs to the masterpieces of mankind. Accustomed as we are to hearing and repeating these lines at burial services and other solemn moments of our existence, we need to make the right kind of analytical effort to penetrate beyond the familiar words and reach the truths they convey, without at the same time profaning a holy ground upon which interpreters should fear to tread.

The superscription is unique in the Psalter: "Prayer of Moses, the man of God." Perhaps the editors who incorporated it into the hymnal wished to indicate the excellence of this national lament by associating it with the historical founder of their religion. The occasion and date of its composition are obscure, but its general tone suggests that the community for whose worship it was designed had passed through grave affliction (vs. 15) and had been aware of their God's providence toward their fathers for many generations (vs. 1). Whatever his identity and age may have been, the poet was able to rise above the consideration of a particular crisis and to speak in universal terms. "The sad and stately music of this great psalm befits the dirge of a world. . . . It preaches man's mortality in immortal words."[4] Yet such a poem is not a dirge in the ordinary sense. It is a hymn of faith in the style of a lament. It preaches trust in God eternal.

The theme of human frailty and mortality is common to all poets and thinkers, since the expectation of death is shared by all men. But many and varied are the ways in which they face it. A certain psychologist of our day advises us to conquer our fears and shadows by reducing them to their proper dimensions, but when he comes to the most elemental fear of all, he abruptly reverses himself. The easy solution he recommends is to forget death altogether! Such an attitude betrays the general uneasiness of our age, which attempts to disguise "the king of horrors" under euphemistic circumlocutions and morticians' trappings.

Secular poets are more realistic but hardly more helpful. Some accept the inevitability of "the end of us all" as a natural law of growth and decay.

> "Men must endure
> Their going hence, even as their coming hither:
> Ripeness is all."[5]

Others gaze at the grave with a glance perverted by the misery of existence "under the sun," and they welcome death as a release from earth. Like an ancient Egyptian sage who intoxicated himself into musing,

> "Death is before me today
> As the fragrance of water-lilies . . .
> As returning home from a foreign war . . ."

---

[4] Alexander Maclaren, *The Psalms* in The Expositor's Bible, edited by W. R. Nicoll (New York: A. C. Armstrong and Son, 1904), *in loc.*

[5] William Shakespeare, *King Lear.*

or like Aeschylus' character who begged,

> "O Death the Healer, scorn thou not, I pray,
>   To come to me: of cureless ills thou art
>   The one physician. Pain lays not its touch
>   Upon a corpse . . . ,"

a few suffering men deliberately turn from the earthly struggle and hope that the great unknown will solve the irreducible problems or tortures of the present.

Still others do not forget death but they deny its fear and they attempt to wait for it like Browning, standing undaunted.

> "Fear death?—to feel the fog in my throat,
>   The mist in my face, . . .
> I would hate that death bandaged my eyes, and forebore,
>   And bade me creep past.
> No! let me taste the whole of it, fare like my peers,
>   The heroes of old,
> Bear the brunt, in a minute pay glad life's arrears
>   Of pain, darkness, and cold."

The psalmist is different. He does not indicate anywhere that he believes in personal immortality. Yet he neither fears nor desires death. As a member of the worshiping community of Israel, he is not concerned with the subjective fate of individuals, including himself. He adores the everlasting God. Thus he displaces the issue without dodging it.

The invocation (vss. 1-2) presents all the characteristics of a hymn of praise. It provides the proper setting for a meditation on the transience of man. How far removed we are from egocentric romanticism when we immerse ourselves in the strains of this psalm! At once we are compelled to confront, not the melancholy destiny of man, but the presence of God, who has been "for us a dwelling place . . . from generation to generation." From the start the psalmist bids the people reinstate themselves in the midst of the community of salvation which began long ago through the mediation of Moses, and which shall continue across the ages until the consummation of history. It is not an isolated son of Adam but the church which sings Isaac Watts's words:

> "O God, our help in ages past,
>   Our hope for years to come,
> Our shelter from the stormy blast,
>   And our eternal home."

To invoke a God who abides in the midst of change, to praise the creator who stood at the parturition of a world, to come before him who is "even from everlasting to everlasting," and to do so "in the communion of the saints," is the proper way to approach the theme of human mortality.

The ancient hills, symbols of stability and endurance, are mere youngsters in the eyes of the eternal godhead. Thus, in utterly unphilosophical language, but with spellbinding imagery, the poet succeeds in creating the right kind of atmosphere for his lament. God transcends the categories of time. As Shelley wrote, "The One remains, the many change and pass." Far from falling into unrelieved pessimism, the poet soars to the wind-swept high plateau of broad perspectives and infinite horizon. His faith in "the One [who] remains" allows him to meditate on the destiny of those who pass.

The first strophe (vss. 3-6) indulges in realistic observation on the contrast between the everlasting God and dying man. But death is not a part of the immutable and impersonal order of the universe. The psalm is still a prayer, not an essay on the human situation. It is a dialogue with the same God who said to Adam, lowering him to the level of the plants and the beasts, "Cursed is the ground for thy sake; in sorrow shalt thou eat of it all the days of thy life . . . ; in the sweat of thy face shalt thou eat bread, till thou return unto the ground; for out of it wast thou taken: for dust thou art, and unto dust shalt thou return" (Gen. 3:17, 19). Thus, the poet of Ps. 90 echoes sorrowfully, "Thou turnest man into dust, And sayest, Return, ye children of men!" (Vs. 3.) The reason for the divine command is stated in the second strophe (vss. 7-10): death is the universal penalty for man's iniquity. This is a hard saying, and many among us are tempted to deny its validity. But the psalmist is here at one with the entire Bible and classical Christianity. Perhaps the solidarity of the whole human race in perpetrating evil is more easily understandable in our day than in the nineteenth century. "Woe is me! for I am undone; because I am a man of unclean lips, and I dwell in the midst of a people of unclean lips." Thus cried Isaiah in the presence of God (Is. 6:5).

Not more than modern man was Israel ready to acknowledge collective and individual guilt. We dismiss too easily the Pauline phrase, "The wages of sin is death" (Rom. 6:23). The psalmist knew that death, like sin, violates the order of creation. We are unable to discover our state of sinfulness until we find ourselves in the presence of the purity of God. The Hebrew poet was able to discern the cause of man's mortality because he was intimately aware of God as the dwelling place of his "church." Only in so far as we are being saved can we discover how estranged from the divine we really are. Our conviction of sin does not necessarily depend on our deeds or secret intents of unethical behavior—some of us may be among the most "honest" of men—but it rises out of the acceptance of our salvation. We become aware of our iniquities in the measure with which God is for us a dwelling place and a home. The health he infuses within us is the revealer of our sickness. The innocence he imparts to us is the eye-opener of our criminality. The righteousness he lends to us provides the power by which we can behold ourselves as we are.

The contrast is no longer that which opposes mortal man to eternal God. It is the abyss of difference which separates the holy God from a rebellious man who always attempts to stretch the bonds of his humanity. The psalmist knows the power of God's anger precisely because he is aware of the height of man's pride. The creature forgets his creator and wishes to become a God! He dies at the very moment that he desires to live forever.

The psalmist, therefore, continues with the supplication of the third strophe (vss. 11-15). His dark interpretation of earthly existence does not lead him to despair. There lies the secret of the Bible in general and of the Psalter in particular. Many people shy away from the virile realism of the Biblical interpretation of human life under the fallacious pretext that it produces sadness and discouragement. History proves, on the contrary, that the more severely a man judges himself—when that severity is rooted upon an awareness of God's glory and care—the more actively he serves this world and the more hopefully he works for the present. The psalmist knows this truth in its fullness. God will "teach us to number our days that we get us a heart of wisdom" (vs. 12). Despondency and suicide? Nonsense! More life and more love of life. "O satisfy us in the morning with thy mercy, That we may rejoice and be glad all our days!" (Vs. 14.) This prayer reveals a state of mind which is quite different from the familiar and hopeless Eat and be merry for tomorrow we die! It is a call to enjoy this earth in the knowledge of God's eternal purpose.

The conclusion of the psalm (vss. 16-17) gives further meaning to the life of mortal man. "The work of our hands" receives its significance. Nothing is lost from the fleeting moment. In the context of God's eternity and by his grace, the deeds of the church receive the seal of approval. They are not absorbed and annihilated in the passing of time. The church becomes the tool of God and the frame of his new creation. Man is "flooded away" (vs. 5), but the community abides.

Let it be repeated. The psalmist had no conception of a heavenly existence to which some men are by divine creative power reborn after they pass through the throes of physical destruction. Here appears the mark of his ancient date. But he discerned obscurely that moment when the fullness of the divine glory would be made manifest unto God's "children."

> "Let thy work appear unto thy servants,
>   And thy glory unto thy children!
> And let the beauty of the Lord our God be upon us!"
>   (Vss. 16-17.)

The poet waited for God to show himself to men as a father. He no longer opposed the mortality of men to the eternity of God or the iniquity of men to the holiness of God. He called for the advent of this divine-human reconciliation which engulfs the guilt of the sons in the forgiveness of a father. Then, and then only, can "the work of our hands" endure.

We may read after these lines the treasure of the Christian faith. We should not forget, however, that the psalmist was unaware of it. But his was more than

> "a momentary taste
> Of *Being* from the Well amid the Waste."[6]

His faith triumphed over the seeming meaninglessness of existence. And he may have said more than he thought. His words led others to understand after him that the last breath may be the moment of a new birth.

Let us not accuse him, therefore, of being a man of his own time, for he may yet teach us a lesson that our one-sided emphasis on individual salvation causes us sorely to need. We cannot inherit eternal life alone. The resurrection of the dead makes no sense outside of the community of the saved. Ps. 90, which knows no personal rebirth to eternal life, should rebuke us by its serene trust in God's care for the continuity of the church on this earth, and by its eagerness to make man work, here and now, without any self-centered motivation of a reward in an immortal hereafter.

IV

Ps. 90 constitutes an exception. Most of the national laments plunge into a mood of questioning and even of abrupt demands which sometimes may surprise us:

"Arise, O Yahweh! Let not man prevail!" (Ps. 9:19.)

"Why standest thou afar off, O Yahweh?" (Ps. 10:1.)

"Help, Yahweh, for the godly man ceaseth from the earth!"
(Ps. 12:1.)

---

[6] Edward Fitzgerald, *The Rubáiyát of Omar Khayyám.*

"Awake! Why sleepest thou, O Yahweh?" (Ps. 44:23.)

Such prayers do not reveal an awareness of human corruption and obstinate ignorance. There are a few pleas for mercy, on the basis of a recognition of national guilt:

> "Deliver us, and purge away our sins,
> For thy name's sake!" (Ps. 79:9.)

But most of the national prayers seem to betray a sense of collective self-righteousness and fall far short of the prophets' humility. Other corporate laments, which have been preserved outside the Psalter, strike a genuinely Biblical note. For instance, the confession of Nehemiah: "Thou hast done right, but we have done wickedly" (Neh. 9:33), or the intercession of Daniel:

> "O Yahweh, to us belongeth the confusion of face,
> To our kings, to our princes, and to our fathers,
> Because we have sinned against thee" (Daniel 9:8).

It may be that the poets who composed most of the psalms of collective lamentation (Pss. 9-10; 44; 58; 60; 74; etc.) lived at times of utter dejection, and that they found themselves in a pastoral position, not unlike that of Ezekiel in Babylonia. They confronted a mood of utter desperation, and they interpreted their task as that of comforters. Thus they whipped up despondency by shouting,

> "O Yahweh, God of vengeance!
> Thou, God of vengeance, shine forth!" (Ps. 94:1.)

As in the case of Ps. 137, we shall remember the depth of national shame and religious bewilderment caused by the loss of land, king, and Temple. These men resented truthfully their misfortune as so many injuries brought against God himself.

> "O God, the heathen are come into thine inheritance:
> Thy holy temple have they defiled . . ." (Ps. 79:1).

It was for them the end of their world, and perhaps of their faith. Thus, they cried,

> "How long, O Yahweh? Wilt thou be angry forever? ...
> Wherefore should the heathen say,
> Where is their God?" (Ps. 79:5, 10.)

Perhaps, keeping in mind their suffering, we should refrain from negative criticism, even if we are compelled to regret their apparent lack of contrition and their avowed spirit of vindictiveness. Let us look at our own Christian hymnals and attempt to discover in them confessions of national guilt. There are not many.

2 | PERSONAL SUPPLICATIONS

WITH the "Prayers of the Individual" we enter into the very core of the Hebrew hymnal. Through those psalms the divine-human encounter receives in the intimate sanctuary of the soul its farthest-reaching expression. The Psalter has survived change of time, displacement of culture, and betrayal of translation for one primordial reason: it includes many "Personal Supplications" with which, age after age, lonely sufferers have been able to identify their own unspoken sorrow. Pain may unite and create a bond of fellowship—after the crisis is ended. But a man in misery is alone. We suffer only as individuals. The community is never wholly absent from the psalms of longing and misery, but their poets did not write in the name of a worshiping "church." Like Jacob who wrestled in the night at the ford of the torrent Jabbok, they were "left alone." Their suffering, whatever its direct cause and its nature, grew even deeper from the vacuum of isolation. For they felt abandoned, not only by men, but also by God himself. In their spiritual loneliness they drank the cup of bitterness to its last dregs. Thus, the accent of their suffering rings true to the worst ever endured by man, and their poems, individualized as they may be, have become typical of universal grief.

Moreover, the psalmists never stopped at a mere exteriorization of subjective pain. Their suffering was neither sterile nor useless. They invariably learned from it. Even Homer, long before them, had discovered that ". . . he who much has suffered, much will know." But what the psalmists learned through the tortures they endured was infinitely more than courage and nobility of character.

143

For their songs were not mere laments, but prayers. Even when they felt forsaken of God, they prayed, and by persistence in asking, requesting, demanding, supplicating, and begging, they ultimately received more than endurance to face the worst and power to see it through. They broke their isolation and they received their freedom. They learned fully what Aeschylus expressed in a sketchy way:

"God, whose law it is that he who learns must suffer. And even in our sleep pain that cannot forget, falls drop by drop upon the heart, and in our own despite, against our will, comes wisdom to us by the awful grace of God."

The psalmists even obtained joy in the midst of their suffering, not on account of a sophisticated form of masochism, but through the discovery of a friendly presence which lifted them out of their solitude and despair. Like Wordsworth they knew that in the end of their tribulations:

> ". . . mortal hopes defeated and o'erthrown
> Are mourned by man, and not by man alone."

More than this, they conquered their pain, because in prayer they received the power to transcend their self-centered situation.

Among the many psalms of personal supplication which have been preserved in the Hebrew hymnal, two pieces are outstanding because they contain the elements of all: Ps. 42-43, in which man rises out of spiritual despondency, and Ps. 22, where physical torment and spiritual abandon lead to victorious communion and service.

I

Thirst for the Living God
(Psalm 42-43)

I

42:1.   As the hind panteth
             After the waterbrooks,
         So panteth my soul
             After thee, O God!

2. My soul thirsteth for God,
  For the living God:
 When shall I come and appear
  In the presence of God?

3. My tears have been my meat
  Day and night,
 As people continually say unto me,
  Where is thy God?

4. I pour out my soul in me,
  As I remember these things:
 When I went with the throng,
  I led them in procession to the house of God
 With the voice of joy and praise,
  A multitude keeping the holy day ...

5. *Why art thou cast down, O my soul,*
  And why art thou disquieted in me?
 Hope thou in God, for I shall yet praise him:
  The health of "my" countenance [and] my God![1]

II

6. My soul is cast down within me:
  Therefore will I remember thee
 From the land of Jordan, and the Hermons,
  From the mountain of Mizar.

7. Deep calleth unto deep
  At the noise of thy gushing waters:
 All thy waves and thy billows
  Are gone over me.

8. In the daytime, [I say], May Yahweh
  Send his lovingkindness!
 And in the night, his song is with me,
  A prayer to the God of my life.

9. I will say unto God my rock,
  Why hast thou forgotten me?
 Why go I mourning
  Oppressed by an enemy?

---

[1] The present Hebrew text (against several ancient versions) reads "thy countenance" and places "my God" at the beginning of vs. 6; cf. vs. 11 and Ps. 43:5.

10. As if crushing my bones,
        My foes say sharp words against me,
     While they repeat daily unto me,
        Where is thy God?

11. *Why art thou cast down, O my soul,*
        And why art thou disquieted within me?
     Hope thou in God, for I shall yet praise him:
        The health of my countenance and my God!

III

43:1. Judge me, O God, and plead my cause
          Against a nation without mercy!
       Away from the deceitful and perverse man
          Bring me into security!

2. For thou art my God, my fortress:
       Why dost thou cast me off?
    Why go I mourning
       Oppressed by an enemy?

3. O send out thy light and thy truth:
       Let them lead me;
    Let them bring me unto thy holy hill
       And to thy tabernacles!

4. Then will I go unto the altar of God,
       Unto God, my delight and my joy!
    Yea, upon the harp will I praise thee,
       O God, my God!

5. *Why art thou cast down, O my soul,*
       And why art thou disquieted within me?
    Hope thou in God, for I shall yet praise him:
       The health of my countenance and my God!

There is scarcely any doubt concerning the original unity of the two poetic pieces now separated as Ps. 42 and Ps. 43. Many manuscripts present them as one poem; the same refrain appears in both (42:5, 11; 43:5); the theme, ideas, and style are homogeneous throughout and one sentence is repeated (42:9b-43:2b); lastly, Ps. 43 does not bear any title.

It is possible and even probable that this plaintive prayer comes from the same sensitive individual who wrote Ps. 84. In one as in the other we meet a man who lived far away from the Temple and longed to return there. It will also be noted that the plural noun "thy tabernacles" is used in both psalms (43:3; 84:1). However, the poem which is now before us is not a hymn but a personal supplication in the meditative mood. The psalmist was probably a Levite who belonged to the family of Qorach (see the editorial superscription in the King James version) and who had, once upon a time, taken an important part in the ceremonial of the cult. He was a musician (Ps. 43:4) and he had led the throng of worshipers in solemn procession (Ps. 42:4). The place of his exile seems to have been the mountainous and picturesque region in which the Jordan finds its sources (Ps. 42:6). There torrents of melted snow gush out in the springtime and cut their way through gullies before they merge into swollen streams. This backdrop of wild nature reflects in the poet's mind the tempests of his soul (Ps. 42:7).

In three parts, each concluded by a refrain, the will to find access toward God obtains its fruition as the poetic mood passes from the longing of desperation to an assured hope. The outward situation seems to remain unchanged, but what counts in the domain of the spirit is the secret issue of an inward drama. The psalmist has ascended the ladder of faith.

The initial line of the first strophe (vss. 1-5) at once depicts the religious yearning of the poet. In the bold similitude of the hart— or rather the hind, since the verb is in the feminine gender—the irresistible quality of the drive which impels man toward God is unforgettably portrayed. The word translated "panteth" refers to the most inordinate ardor or desire, perhaps even more intense and violent than the physical need of thirst. Such is this man's spiritual torture. His enforced separation from God's presence in the sanctuary is intolerable. The pain is even heightened by the taunts of those who surround him and who daily press him to abandon his quest. Does not his own fate offer ample evidence that God remains unconcerned or is perhaps overtly hostile? The cause of highest grief is the fear of divine enmity or at least abandon. The memory of a pleasant past (vs. 4) renders the present destitution even less bearable. With Oriental shamelessness the psalmist confesses that weeping has become his daily diet. It may be true, as Shelley wrote, that ". . . there are . . . sufferings which have no tongue," but it is equally true that "the damned don't cry" and that those who picture their despair with words have already run its course. The poet rouses himself from the discouragement and the disquietude which assail him by objectifying them as if they had already left his innermost being (vs. 5). Although God remains silent, man bids "his soul" to hope in him, and he takes the resolve to praise that God whose grace he knows to be "the health of [his] countenance." This expression refers to the salvation of his total person, the healing of his despondency as well as the deliverance from the outward cause of his religious estrangement.

The second strophe (vss. 6-11) reveals the intensity of the struggle which the psalmist wages and continues to wage within himself against the powers of doubt and despair. While the memory of the Temple from which he is now banished only stirs him to more grievous sorrow (vs. 4), the remembrance of God himself becomes a technique for spiritual endurance (vs. 6): "My soul is cast down within me: Therefore will I remember thee." To recall the past joy of ceremonial worship only sharpens the woe of present exile, but to call upon the God who knows no bond of time and space is a method of recovery. The birth and growth of faith may depend upon the externals of a "church," but direct communion with a proximate God is man's ultimate desire. "From the land of Jordan and the peaks of Hermon," this man seeks access to the sanctuary which is not made of stones. "By degrees," said Newman, "we begin to perceive that there are but two persons in the universe, our own soul, and the God who made it." The poet deliberately places the contemplation of God above the indulgences of self-pity. Nevertheless, victory is neither easily nor hastily won. As "deep calleth unto deep," one kind of distress after another harasses him. He is assailed on all sides. Anguish threatens again and again to engulf him. His enemies still hold the upper hand over him and he feels their satire as a crushing of his bones.

The third strophe (43:1-5) ushers in a prayer of decisive requests. Note the swift imperatives: "judge," "plead," "bring," "send." The mood of questioning is not yet overcome—"Why dost thou cast me off?" (43:2*b*.) But the quest is addressed to "my God, my fortress." This is no longer—in Willa Cather's words— "a solitude of atrophy, of negation, but [a solitude] of perpetual flowering." It carries within itself the seeds of growth. It prepares the climax of the prayer: "O send out thy light and thy truth: Let them lead me." Where? To the Temple. We should beware of distorting the psalmist's intention. If we separated this request from its context, we might conclude that he had discovered a religion which transcends all visible symbols and renders cultic forms superfluous. But "light" and "truth" are the guides of the pilgrim whose steps are eager for the "holy hill." Here as well as in Ps. 84, however, the words go beyond the horizon of ancient cult. God's light and truth are infinitely more powerful and beneficent than mere pilgrimage markers would be. They flood the intellectual and spiritual darkness of man with the qualities of divine lucidity and understanding. When our sorrows obscure the face of God and our faith itself is by them overshadowed, happy are we if we are able to hope. The psalmist commands us to pray as he did that the sun break through our fogs and clouds and that light illumine our path. Spiritual darkness and its consequent immobility and stagnant hopelessness result chiefly from man's own making. He stands more often than not obscured by what Thomas Hardy called "the shade from his own soul upthrown." But the light of God will enable him to face life, to take decisions, and to renew his energy for the fulfillment of the task which lies ahead of him.

The psalmist asks not for light alone but for truth as well. The truth of God, or rather his "truthfulness," appears in his light only. God is true to his own promises, and by faith regrasped man relies on them and obtains certainty. The goal of the poet's religion is still to "go to the altar of God" and there to praise him upon the harp, but now, near the sources of the Jordan, this God is already his "delight" and his "joy." In the slough of despond, or worse, under the calls and echoes of the abysses, solitary man can pray:

"the health of my countenance and my God!" He will praise him in the sanctuary someday, but his poetic creation reveals that he can praise him now, even in the wild and distant lands of the north.

Sacramental presence and corporate worship have not outlived their significance. They are the source and the *raison d'être* of the prayer which transmutes despair into hope. But the prayer can outgrow the system of worship which gave it birth.

II

From Dereliction to Fulfillment
(Psalm 22)

I

1. My God, my God, why hast thou forsaken me?
   Why art thou so far from helping me, and from the words of my roaring?
2. O my God, I cry in the daytime, but thou answerest not,
   And in the night season, but there is no rest for me.

(a)

3. Yet thou art holy, O thou that inhabitest
   The praises of Israel.
4. Our fathers trusted in thee:
   They trusted, and thou didst deliver them.
5. They cried unto thee, and were delivered:
   They trusted in thee, and were not confounded.

(b)

6. But I am a worm, and no man;
   A reproach of men, and despised of the people.
7. All they that see me laugh me to scorn;
   They shoot out the lip, they shake the head,
8. [Saying,] He committed himself unto Yahweh, let him deliver him!
   Let him save him, since he delighteth in him!

(c)

9. But thou art he that took me out of the womb:
   Thou didst make me trust upon my mother's breasts.

10. I was cast upon thee as soon as I was born,
    And from my mother's bosom thou hast been my God!
11. Be not thou far from me,
    For distress is near,
    And there is no one to help me.

II

12. Many bulls have compassed me:
    The strong bulls of Bashan have beset me round.
13. They gape upon me, their mouth wide open,
    As a ravening and a roaring lion.

(a)

14. I am poured out like water,
    And all my bones are out of joint;
    My heart is like wax;
    It is melted in the midst of my bowels.
15. My palate is parched like a potsherd,
    And my tongue cleaveth to my jaws,
    [For] thou hast brought me into the dust of death.

(b)

16. Dogs have compassed me about;
    The assembly of the wicked have enclosed me;
    They have pierced my hands and feet;
17. I may tell all my bones;
    They look and stare upon me;
18. They part my garments among them,
    And upon my vesture do they cast lots.

(c)

19. But be not thou far from me, O Yahweh!
    O thou, my strength, haste thee to help me!
20. Deliver my soul from the sword,
    My only one from the power of the dog!
21. Save me from the lion's mouth,
    And from the horns of the wild bulls "protect me!"[2]

III

22. I will declare thy name unto my brethren:
    In the midst of the congregation will I praise thee.

_____
[2] Conjectural translation. The Hebrew text reads, "thou hast answered me."

23. Ye that fear Yahweh, praise him!
    All ye the seed of Jacob, glorify him!
    And tremble in awe before him, all ye the seed of Israel!

(a)

24. For he hath not despised nor abhorred
    The affliction of the afflicted;
    Neither hath he hid his face from him;
    But when he cried unto him, he heard.
25. Thy truthfulness will I praise in the great congregation;
    My vows will I pay before them that fear him.

(b)

26. Let the humble eat and be satisfied;
    Let them that seek him praise Yahweh!
    Let their hearts live forever!
27. Let them remember and turn unto Yahweh,
    All the ends of the earth!
    And let them worship before thee
    All the families of the nations!

(c)

28. For the kingdom belongeth to Yahweh,
    And he is the governor among the nations.
29. They shall eat and worship, all they that sleep[3] in the earth;
    Before him shall bow all they that go down to the dust,
    Even he that did not keep his soul alive.
30. A seed shall serve him and will be told of the Lord;
    A generation shall come and declare his righteousness
    Unto a people yet unborn, that he hath done [this].

No personal supplication is closer to the Christian mind and heart than Ps. 22, for according to the Gospels Jesus intoned its first line upon the cross and many of its details found an echo in the various incidents of his passion. What experience, what persecution, what torture, were those of the poet who composed this psalm? We do not know. But the strains of his lament cannot fail to sound "hard and true" to the minds of sufferers everywhere; in addition, the mysterious assurance of the triumph which follows

---

[3] The Hebrew text reads, "the fat ones."

his defeat and "turns his necessity to glorious gain" may convince
men in despair that their suffering is not to be vainly endured. From
abandon to fulfillment, such is the "calvary" of this psalmist. His
prayer begins as a dirge, but it ends as a song of praise. The cry
"My God, my God, why?" leads to the last word which hails the
consummation of that same God's deed. The initial quest is resolved when posterity proclaims, "It is fulfilled."

Some commentators hold that no strophic structure appears in
this lament. They claim that grief shows itself here "in the raw"
and that a man who shouts his wounds is not concerned with poetic
form. One should not forget, however, that "poetry takes its origin
from emotion recollected in tranquillity" and that this prayer was
composed only after the physical and spiritual misery which gave
it birth had been transmuted into serenity and vision. Without doing violence to the text, one may discern a pattern which is admirably adapted to the development of the moods and ideas.

The first part (vss. 1-11) is a prayer of bewilderment which is
cast between two key expressions. It begins with the query, "why
art thou far?" (vs. 1*b*), and it ends with the plea, "Be not far!"
(Vs. 11*a*.) The initial quest should not be construed as a manifestation of revolt, perhaps not even as a sign of hopelessness. It
reveals a feeling of utter abandon, but not of complete despair.

The poet is dismayed by the silence of his God. The causes of
his sufferings remain inscrutable. The extremity of this situation
compels him to conclude that God has cast him off. Yet by addressing his query to "my God, my God," he unwittingly confesses his
faith in the very midst of his desperation. It is the memory of his
intimacy with the divine, now broken, which inspires him to ask,
"why?" The survival of his faith therefore makes his sufferings
the more shocking and the more unendurable.

The most devastating kind of torment which may beset a human
being is not physical torture or social ostracism—as the history of
martyrs shows—but spiritual loneliness due to the unaccountable
absence of a hitherto loving deity. The pains endured by a man
like Saint Paul, for instance, should certainly not be underestimated
(see II Cor. 11:23-12:8), but their sting is partly allayed by the

inner certainty revealed in the promise, "My grace is sufficient for thee: for my power is made perfect in weakness" (II Cor. 12:9). The suffering endured by the psalmist is worse than that of Saint Paul. It represents the particular kind of hell which is lived on earth by a man who has long been accustomed to the presence of God and who, in his hour of direst need, is bereft of that presence and finds the divine consolation wanting.

The poet, however, cannot resolve to believe that his God will be silent and absent forever. As a member of the "church" he contemplates the God of that "church." Here is the unique feature of his lament. An individual may be persecuted by his enemies and "rejected of men," but he still belongs to the holy company which throughout the ages serves the purpose of the lord of history. This man lies at the lowest level of dereliction, but he is still praying. He obstinately seeks the elusive object of his prayer, and for a fleeting instant his lament becomes a hymn as he sings,

> "Yet thou art holy, O thou that inhabitest
>   The praises of Israel.
> Our fathers trusted in thee . . ." (vss. 3, 4a).

Divine holiness explains divine remoteness. But God is not only holy: he also dwells in the midst of the congregation which has praised him in the past and continues to praise him in the present. The poet is no longer an individual sufferer, lost in the anonymity of a meaningless world, but a son of the promise, an heir of the covenant, and a member of the saving community. However, such a stupendous thought only makes his situation the more bewildering: "I am a worm and no man; A reproach of men, and despised of the people" (vs. 6). Like the Suffering Servant (Is. 53:3), he is mocked by the visible "church" which sarcastically interprets the silence of God as the sign of his condemnation. "Let [God] save him," they shout, "since he delighteth in him!" (Vs. 8.)

Alone against the world, the poet throws himself upon the heart of the God whom he has always known to be his "father." He does not use this word, but the idea of divine fatherhood underlies his new prayer (vss. 9-10). Ever since the time of his birth, he has felt toward this God the utmost trust that a child experiences with his human father. Indeed, it is quite remarkable that he mentions his mother, but not his progenitor. He declares that it was Yahweh who received him at birth and he refers to the Oriental gesture by which an Oriental father recognizes his paternity of a newborn infant (see Gen. 50:23). It seems, however, that the psalmist is speaking metaphorically. God has adopted him as if he were an orphan. He will not forsake him altogether.

Fortified by the memory of the help he has received from his God in the past, the sufferer is enabled to end the first part of his prayer as he began it, saying, "my God!" (Vs. 10; cf. vs. 1). But he no longer asks, "Why art thou far?" (Vs. 1.) He assumes the boldness of a son, and the regained sense of his filiality confers on him the right to cry, "Be not far from me!" (Vs. 11.)

In the second section (vss. 12-21) the poet describes his enemies (vss. 12-13) and the slow torture which they inflict on him (vss. 14-15, 16-18). He is now at the point of death, and his executioners are already dividing his clothes among themselves (vs. 18). He makes nevertheless a final plea for succor, and the lines are crowded with imperatives: "Be not far, haste thee, deliver, save!" (Vss. 19-21.) The Hebrew text reads at the end of vs. 21, "thou hast answered me!" Since this verb can hardly be constructed with the preceding words, "from the horns of the wild bulls," and in any case suggests a statement of a past fact immediately after a call for salvation, the translator would then be compelled to suppose that the sequence of thought is abruptly broken within a poetic line—a most unlikely hypothesis. The Greek version of the Septuagint reads, with almost identical letters, not a verb but a noun, and it renders the whole verse as follows,

> "Save me from the lion's mouth,
>   And 'my lowliness' from the horns of the unicorns."

The present Hebrew text is therefore uncertain. It is probable that the poet followed here as elsewhere the style of parallelism and wrote originally at the end of vs. 21*b* a verb and a pronoun, such as "protect me" or "deliver me," which provides an exact counterpart to the expression "save me" at the beginning of vs. 21*a*.

In the most startling manner the third part of the psalm (vss. 22-30) presents the intentions of the poet for the future. A complete mystery shrouds the issue of his torture. But his supplication suddenly becomes a song in which he pledges to praise his God "in the midst of the congregation" (vss. 22-23). He testifies that Yahweh is "the faithful creator" who answers prayer (vss. 24-25), and he calls all mankind to "remember" and to "turn unto Yahweh," even "all the families of the nations" (vss. 26-27). A more significant or even stupendous thought is the certainty that, when God's rule will be acknowledged over the whole earth, even the dead "shall eat and worship" and a new generation shall proclaim the divine deed "unto a people yet unborn" (vss. 28-30).

One may easily surmise that the early Christians, meditating on the prayer which soothed the agony of Jesus Christ, found in almost every sentence a prefiguration of his passion and of his redemptive work. To be sure, we should beware of artificially stretching the expressions of the psalm. There is no indication that the poet's suffering—and especially his death—brings about the conversion of mankind. Moreover, even in the third part the hero is a man of the Temple, since he promises to pay his vows before the congregation of Israel (vs. 25). But the question should still be asked: Who is he who dares to turn his gaze, right after the description of his physical and spiritual agony, on the vision of a world-wide kingdom? Who is he who embraces within the horizon of his future testimony, not only the humble of his nation, but also the foreigners and even the dead? These "shall eat" and share in a sacrifice of peace or thanksgiving. "Their hearts" shall "live forever." Who is he who boldly declares that a new generation shall witness to a new people the work of the Lord? What is this deed that God "hath done"? The very absence of a direct object at the end of the poem (vs. 30) leaves us in a mood of wonder and expectancy. Without doing violence to the text, we may apply the poem to the person and to the ministry of "the author and finisher of our faith."

We may repeat it in the spirit with which he himself borrowed its cry, saying,

> ". . . O my God, my God! why leav'st thou me,
> The Son, in whom thou dost delight to be?
> My God, my God—
>   Never was grief like mine."[4]

We may appropriate the lines which rehearse the slow death, the exposure, the thirst, the mockery:

> "A curse and an astonishment, passed by,
>   Pointed at, mocked again
> By men for whom He shed His Blood—in vain?"[5]

Through the song of a psalmist who does not confess any sinfulness, who is devoid of revolt against God or of hatred against his torturers, and who expects the advent of a universal and eternal kingdom, we may contemplate the man whose death becomes for us a birth. As sons of the "nations," may we "remember and turn" (vs. 27).

III

The "Personal Supplications" constitute the largest group of psalms belonging to one type.[6] Some of them contain striking lines, but none of them excels or even approaches the poetic beauty or theological acumen of Pss. 42-43 and 22. Their significance lies chiefly in the authentic accent which pervades their description of suffering and the obstinacy with which they beg for God's salvation.

(a)

All the poets of personal supplications write from the depth of a crisis, but their particular sufferings are due to different causes.

---

[4] George Herbert, "And They Crucified Him."
[5] Christina Rosetti, "Wednesday in Holy Week."
[6] Gunkel ascribes about forty psalms to this type.

While the author of Ps. 42-43 is helpless in the midst of a hostile community which taunts him with his apparently enforced exile from the Temple, and the poet of Ps. 22 is most probably a man condemned to death by slow torture for a charge unknown to us and perhaps to him, both of them experience persecution in the hands of human malefactors. Likewise, most of the authors of the other personal supplications suffer on account of human enmity (Pss. 3:1; 17:8-9; 59:2).

Unlike the poets of Pss. 42-43 and 22, these psalmists not only ask for deliverance, they also pray for the destruction of their enemies, sometimes on the ground that their own foes are also hostile to God himself.

> "Destroy thou them, O God!
>
> . . . .
>
> For they have rebelled against thee!" (Ps. 5:10.)

They generally couch their cries for God's avenging in the most violent terms (Pss. 55:15; 58:6; 69:23; etc.).

At least one of them even asks to be saved from death at the hands of his foes so that, as he puts it bluntly, ". . . I may requite them!" (Ps. 41:10.) Sometimes the sufferers pray God to spare the lives of their enemies, but not out of a sense of forgiveness: "Slay them not, lest my people forget!" (Ps. 59:11.)

In other supplications the cause of the crisis appears to be a mortal disease, but even in such cases the presence of human foes is lurking in the background, for a man sick unto death is the object of social rejection. Like Job, these psalmists are the butt of men's condemnation or mockery, for their physical ailments are interpreted as the evidence of a divine punishment.

> "An evil disease, say they, cleaveth fast unto him,
>   And now that he lieth he shall rise up no more.
> Yea, mine own familiar friend, in whom I trusted,
>   Which did eat of my bread, hath lifted up his heel against me"
>   (Ps. 41:8-9).

It is also probable that in some instances the sufferers attribute their pathological condition to the malevolence of human adversaries. The expression "workers of iniquity," as Mowinckel has shown, may refer to professional sorcerers who cast magical spells upon their fellow men.[7] In any case, the descriptions of illness are often concluded with a complaint about human foes.

> "Have mercy upon me, O Yahweh, for I am in trouble,
>   Mine eye is consumed with grief,
>   Yea, my soul and my belly. . . .
> For I have heard the whispers of many:
>   'Let us surround him with terror!'
> While they took counsel together against me,
>   They devised to take away my life" (Ps. 31:9, 13).

Admittedly, many of the personal supplications, like the national laments or the invectives of Jeremiah, do not make pleasant reading. Their spirit of vindictiveness must be judged in the light and spirit of the gospel. On the other hand, a therapeutic value arises from utter sincerity and honesty. These psalmists did not attempt to repress or to suppress their feelings and desires, because they found in the presence of God a complete freedom of expression and thereby obtained, no doubt, a certain psychological release. Whereas Hamlet cried, "But break, my heart,—for I must hold my tongue!" and some psalmists were compelled to write,

> "I will keep my mouth with a bridle,
>   While the wicked is before me" (Ps. 39:1),

such a restraint was not necessary before the judge of all men. In God's presence these men "poured out their heart" without shame; they showed themselves as they were, outraged by the injustice of society, baffled by the remoteness of healing or of restoration; but they did not silence the moans of their aching flesh or the anguish of their distraught minds. They found an outlet for their inward storms. They prayed and they persisted in prayer, even when submission or resignation lay beyond the reach of their will.

---

[7] Sigmund Mowinckel, *Psalmenstudien*, I, 4.

(b)

It is on account of this passionate obstinacy of request for the help of God that the authors of the personal supplications may still offer to modern Christians a spur and an example. They never tired of praying for deliverance because their faith was unshatterable. They knew centuries before Jesus that "men ought always to pray, and not to faint" (Lk. 18:1). On the surface it would seem to the modern mind that "battering the gates of heaven with storms of prayer" is a useless and undignified, even cheap, expression of man's self-centeredness and refusal to accept the limitations of his own place within the universe. Many among us are shocked by the psalmists' effrontery, and would prefer to say with Adam in *Paradise Lost,*

> "... if by prayer
> Incessant I could hope to change the will
> Of him who all things can, I would not cease
> To weary him with my assiduous cries:
> But prayer against his absolute decree
> No more avails than breath against the wind,
> Blown stifling back on him that breathes it forth:
> Therefore to his great bidding I submit."

Yet, it is paradoxically characteristic of Biblical Christianity at once to acknowledge the will of God and to persist in supplication. "In the Psalms," Calvin aptly remarks, "we may frequently observe how ... faithful men, when, almost wearied with praying, ... seemed to beat the air, and God seemed deaf to their petitions, yet [they] did not desist from praying; because the authority of the Divine word is not maintained, unless it be fully credited, notwithstanding the appearance of any circumstances to the contrary." The psalmists did not take silence for an answer. They said, although circumstances appeared unaltered and unalterable,

> "O Yahweh, God of my salvation,
>   I have cried day and night before thee....
> Thou hast laid me in the lowest pit,
>   In darkness, in the deeps" (Ps. 88:1, 6).

They charged, "Hold not thy peace, O God of my praise!" (Ps. 109:1.) They cried, "Help! Yahweh! for the godly man ceaseth, For the faithful fail among the children of men!" (Ps. 12:1.) They even commanded, "Stir up thyself, and awake to my judgment!" (Ps. 35:23.)

Some of them looked at their faith as a means of escape from the realities of horror in which they lived (Pss. 55:6-8; 143:9).

Others, on the contrary, declared to their enemies,

> "In Yahweh put I my trust;
>> How say ye to my soul,
>> Flee as a bird to the mountains?" (Ps. 11:1.)

The same psalmist knew the tragedy of existence, not only as it emerged from his own situation, but also as it appeared from his own observation of history.

> "If the foundations be destroyed,
>> What can the righteous do?" (Ps. 11:3.)

The righteous can still pray, and by their faith overcome the present.

> "For the righteous Yahweh loveth righteousness,
>> His countenance doth behold the upright" (Ps. 11:7).

And because they refused to give up, the psalmists did not pray in vain, even when their outward condition remained unchanged. In their poems is verified Emerson's plain and simple truth that "no man ever prayed heartily without learning something."

(c)

The most remarkable aspect of the personal supplications is that, although they may be called eudaemonistic prayers—that is to say, petitions for a boon or a benefit which is centered on the self-interest of the sufferers—they include almost always a self-transcending element. By praying as they did, the psalmists deepened their

religion and learned how to overcome their distress. Suffering became for them an occasion for victorious living. Because they
learned there is nothing "that's past praying for," they most irra-
tionally used what Wordsworth called "prayer, man's rational prerogative," and they forced their own destiny by transforming
themselves. In the deeply spiritual sense which is familiar to all
the anonymous saints who place themselves as prayer apprentices
at the school of the psalmists,

> "There is a tide in the affairs of men
> Which, taken at the flood, leads on to fortune;
> Omitted, all the voyage of their life
> Is bound in shallows and in miseries."[8]

The personal supplications may have remained unanswered—to
use the language of the outside world—but as Meredith wrote,
"who rises from Prayer a better man, his prayer is answered." In
those psalms, stricken men groped in the darkness for a grace
which was not forthcoming, but they received a higher grace since
they affirmed,

> "Salvation belongeth unto Yahweh!
> Thy blessing is upon thy people!" (Ps. 3:8.)

Heaven stayed closed and earth hostile, but these men sang, "My
heart shall rejoice in thy salvation" (Ps. 13:5).

No material event has yet altered the straits which prompted
the lament and yet this supplication ends in the past tense, as if the
future were already accomplished:

> "I will sing unto Yahweh,
> Because he hath dealt bountifully with me" (Ps. 13:6).

The cry reveals the hopelessness of today, but " 'tis the one path-
way from Despair." Thus, the same man who begged, "Deliver me,
O Yahweh, from the evil men!" was able to say almost at the same

---

8 Shakespeare, *Julius Caesar.*

time, "The upright shall dwell in thy presence" (Ps. 140:1, 13).
Words are not sufficient to describe the mood of delight which already seized some of the sufferers.

> "My heart is fixed, O God,
>   My heart is fixed!
> I will sing and give praise!
>   Awake up, my glory!
> Awake, psaltery and harp!
>   I will awake the dawn! ...
> Be thou exalted, O God, above the heavens!"
>   (Ps. 57:7-8, 11.)

To be sure, joy was not always unadulterated, as in the declaration, fortunately exceptional:

> "The righteous shall rejoice
>   When he seeth the vengeance:
> He shall wash his feet
>   In the blood of the wicked" (Ps. 58:10).

On the whole, however, the human expectations of the petitioners were purified by the hope of living in communion with God himself and of contemplating his "likeness."

> "As for me, I will behold thy face in righteousness,
>   I shall be satisfied, when I awake, with the contemplation
>   of thee" (Ps. 17:15).

The note of joy, even of delight, which was sounded in the very midst of agony became characteristic of Biblical and Christian spirituality. Thus, the poets of the personal supplications were the initiators of a long and yet unending lineage of sufferers who have discovered that, as Melville wrote in *Moby Dick:*

"On the starboard hand of every woe, there is a sure delight; and higher the top of that delight, than the bottom of the woe is deep. ... Delight is to him whose strong arms yet support him, when the ship of this base treacherous world has gone down beneath him. ...

Delight,—top-gallant delight is to him, who acknowledges no law or lord, but the Lord his God, and is only a patriot to heaven. Delight is to him, whom all the waves of the billows of the seas of the boisterous mob can never shake from this sure Keel of the Ages."

Such a language, of course, is foreign to the psalmists, who were no sailors; but the thought behind it is akin to the conviction which upheld their spirit. In very human ways, engrossed within a weak and weary flesh, they were, in Whittier's words:

> ". . . groping for the keys
> Of the heavenly harmonies,"

and through their persevering search they grasped by faith alone the certitude that their God, silent as he might appear to be, was granting grace and giving life.

(d)

The personal supplications may then teach modern Christians how to recover the art of request in prayer. Many among us have been misled by the philosophical concept of a noble and sublime deity whose will is immutable and beside whose glory the petitions of men appear almost like crimes of *lèse-majesté*. There is of course a wide margin of truth in Emerson's thought that "Prayer that craves a particular commodity—anything less than all good, is vicious . . . ; prayer as a means to effect a private end is theft and meanness." And the same Calvin, who recommends the example of the psalmists, is careful to add:

"Nor let us tempt God, and provoke him against us with our presumption; which is the practice of many who merely bargain with God on a certain condition, and as though he were subservient to their passions, bind him with laws of their own stipulation; with which unless he immediately complies, they give way to anger and fretfulness, to cavils, and murmurs and rage. To such persons, therefore, he frequently grants in his wrath what he denies in mercy to others."

It is easy to understand that the supplications of the Psalter may at times have been appropriated by men who devised for their own use a caricature of Biblical religion. On the other hand, by bringing their sorrows to God, without sanctimoniously masking their self-centered desires and feelings, the poets of the supplications introduced utter frankness in the realm of the inner life, and they did not try to deceive the Almighty. They threw off all pretense and they dared to appear naked before their Maker.

Some of them even consciously rose to the level of a prayer in which the final request was no longer liberation from evil men, but emancipation from evil:

> "Incline not my heart to any evil thing,
>> To practice wicked works with men that work iniquity;
>> And let me not eat of their dainties!" (Ps. 141:4.)

One or two suppliants went even so far as to request the grace of learning how to do the will of God.

> "Teach me thy way, O Yahweh!
>> I will walk in thy truth;
>> Unite my heart to fear thy name!" (Ps. 86:11.)

Such a prayer is exceptional in this type of psalm. And it is noteworthy that practically none of these sufferers was conscious of his shortcomings, failures, or guilt. Like Job discoursing with his friends, they were proud of their ethical integrity. Only a very few among them, at the point of death, dimly saw the deeper dimensions of human sin (cf. Pss. 31:10; 39:8; 41:4; 69:5), but even they failed to relate this awareness to the whole of their prayerful experience.

Some of the psalms, however, which were also composed by individuals in crisis, differ from the personal supplications precisely at this juncture. They are the "Penitential Prayers."

3 | PENITENTIAL PRAYERS

THE word "sin" is widely misunderstood in our time. Some apply it only to obvious breaches of the criminal codes, and therefore exclude it glibly from their personal vocabulary. Others vaguely connect it with sex, and thereby miss its all-inclusive implications. Theologians, however, have begun to rediscover the classical expressions of the Christian faith, including the Biblical sense of unrighteousness. Even a secular columnist writing in the New York *Times* made the following comments:

"Sin seems to have gone out of fashion as a subject of general conversation and even of pulpit discourse. Only old-style divines mention it any more, and in the field of community welfare the word is hardly known. The last public reference to it that we can recall offhand was President Coolidge's remark that his minister had preached on sin and was against it. In these new times sin is known by nicer names, such as delinquency, impropriety, indecorum, indiscretion, irregularity, laxity, and moral turpitude. A leading Methodist ecclesiastic has called for a revival of attention to sin. And high time, say we."

This is one of the reasons for which the penitential prayers of the Psalter bear an unusual significance for today. A few psalmists were not content with the condemnation of evil men who persecuted them. They searched their own souls, and by confessing before their God the crimes they had committed or by discovering an ele-

166

ment of sinfulness in the very center of their moral innocence, they developed a profound understanding of grace and forgiveness.

An awareness of sin existed at a very early date among the ancient Hebrews. While their pagan neighbors were chiefly concerned with sin as a cultic offense, they understood by the same word not only an error of ritual but also an ethical crime. In addition, even the earliest thinkers, such as the Yahwist, who lived approximately at the time of David (tenth century B.C.) and co-ordinated into a theological philosophy of history the oral traditions of the ancestors, clearly saw that sin is primarily a manifestation of man's arrogance against his creator. The story of the Garden of Eden is intended to show that man is a sinner whenever he tries to become "like gods" (Gen. 3:5). Moreover, the early Hebrews knew the process of psychological disintegration which precedes the act. "Sin lieth in wait at the threshold" (Gen. 4:7). Sinful deeds are the expression of a sinful disposition. Evil acts depend on "the imagination of the thoughts of [man's] heart" (Gen. 6:5). The perpetration of such acts is condemned not because they violate a tribal custom or the requirements of a local shrine, but because "they are evil in the sight of Yahweh." When David receives from Nathan the enlightening blow, "Thou art the man!" (II Sam. 12:7), he realizes that he has "despised" Yahweh (II Sam. 12:10) and "sinned against" God himself (II Sam. 12:13). Thus, even before the great prophets of the eighth and seventh centuries applied to the recesses of the human heart their skillful and cold scalpel, a long tradition of psychological introspection had conferred on Hebrew spirituality its unique ability to see human nature without illusory optimism.

Some psalmists possessed the sharp and incisive power of self-analysis with which the Yahwist theologian and the great prophets were endowed. Their poems, especially Ps. 51 and Ps. 130, have received a prominent place in the Christian liturgy under the respective titles of Kyrie Eleison and De Profundis (Greek and Latin of their initial words). They have become the classic examples of "confession" and "repentance."

I

Kyrie Eleison
(Psalm 51)

(Invocation)

1. Have mercy upon me, O God, according to thy lovingkindness!
   According unto the multitude of thy tender mercies blot out
   my transgressions!
2. Wash me thoroughly from mine iniquity,
   And cleanse me from my sin!

(Confession)   I

3. For I acknowledge my transgressions,
   And my sin is ever before me.
4. Against thee, thee only, have I sinned,
   And done that which is evil in thy sight,
   That thou mightest be justified when thou speakest,
   And be clear when thou judgest.

5. Behold, I was shapen in iniquity,
   And in sin did my mother conceive me.
6. Behold, thou desirest truth in the inward man,
   And in my secret being thou shalt make me know wisdom.

(Supplication)   II

7. Purge me with hyssop, and I shall be clean!
   Wash me, and I shall be whiter than snow!
8. Make me to hear joy and gladness,
   That the bones which thou hast broken may rejoice!
9. Hide thy face from my sins,
   And blot out all mine iniquities!

10. Create in me a clean heart, O God,
    And renew a steadfast spirit within me!
11. Cast me not away from thy presence,
    And take not thy holy spirit from me!
12. Restore unto me the joy of thy salvation,
    And let a spirit of good will uphold me!

(Dedication)   III

13. Then will I teach transgressors thy ways,
    And sinners shall be converted unto thee.
14. Deliver me from silence,[1] O God, thou God of my salvation!
    And my tongue shall sing aloud of thy righteousness.
15. O Lord, open thou my lips,
    And my mouth shall show forth thy praise.

16. For thou delightest not in sacrifice,
    And if I gave a burnt offering thou wouldst not be pleased.
17. The sacrifices of God are a broken spirit;
    A broken and a contrite heart, O God, thou wilt not despise.

(Addition)

18. Do good in thy good pleasure unto Zion;
    Build thou the walls of Jerusalem!
19. Then wilt thou delight in the sacrifices of righteousness,
    In burnt offering and whole burnt offering;
    Then shall they offer bullocks upon thine altar.

Psalm 51 is a prayer which originates in a purely internal and spiritual crisis, and constitutes the most profound analysis of sin and renewal to be found in the Hebrew Bible. In Martin Luther's words, it helps us to "look in the heart of all saints." Such a remark is at first glance quite startling, since the psalmist describes himself as a criminal, but as Aphra Behn's glib saying goes, "There is no sinner like a young saint." More respectful of truth, one might say, Only a saint can understand the meaning of sin. Psalm 51 opens before us the double mystery of sin consciousness and of reconciliation with God.

The *Invocation* (vss. 1-2) is a cry for mercy. At once the poet grasps the hopelessness of the human situation and the true nature of the deity. He probably could not understand the one without the other. He claims nothing for himself, but he prays to God, for he knows that the essential characteristics of the divine are "loving-

---

[1] Conjectural translation. The Hebrew word *damîm*, "bloodshed," should probably read *damôm*, "growing dumb, still, silent." Note that no correction of consonant is involved, and that for many centuries no vowel sign existed in the Hebrew manuscripts.

kindness" (vs. 1*a*) and "a mother's tenderness in abundance" (vs. 1*b*). The word *rachamîm*, "tender mercies," is derived from the Hebrew noun for "womb," and it alludes to the love of a mother for her child. One often hears that the doctrine of the fatherhood of God belongs exclusively to the New Testament. As a matter of fact, the Hebrews had a poetic understanding of God's love just as warm and all-embracing as that which is found in the Gospel. Again and again they compared their God to a father and more boldly still to a mother, so that one could maintain without courting the paradox that there is in the Old Testament an awareness not only of the fatherhood but also of the motherhood of God. Most of the Hebrew expressions used for divine love and compassion are drawn from the language which describes maternal emotions and sentiments.

It is impossible to render into English the full meaning of the initial lines of the psalm. When a young camel is weaned and taken away for the purpose of training, his mother is for a while in a state of frenzy; she refuses food and tries to loosen her bonds. In order to describe her bereavement, the Arabs use among others a verb which is a cognate of the Hebrew word for "to have grace," or "to have mercy," or again, "to yearn longingly for." This gives some idea of the powerful undertones that such a poetic metaphor, boldly applied to the deity, conveyed to the Hebrew mind. The psalmist is defenseless before his God. He is like a beaten, exhausted, guilty, wandering child, but he knows that someone is waiting for him, just as a mother is longing for the child of her womb. He cries, "Have mercy upon me, O God!" Here is utter humiliation, but also utter confidence. Human honor is lost, human desert is lacking, human right is brought to nought, human technique is of no avail. "Have mercy upon me, O God!" The poet becomes aware of his own destitution only because he knows what kind of God he is facing. In other words, complete pessimism about self is dependent on complete optimism about God. Not the man who is lost, but the man who is about to be saved can understand that he is a sinner.

Observe the three synonyms which the poet uses in quick succession in order to describe his condition. The word "transgressions" refers to acts of rebellion and of willful revolt committed against the law. "Iniquity" designates a state of distortion, bending, or twisting, which vitiates the whole outlook and therefore the subsequent behavior of a man who has committed transgressions, who experiences a growing dullness of conscience, who falls into ethical blindness and ultimately loses the will to react or the ability to discriminate between good and evil. It is the disintegration of heart and volition so graphically sketched by Burns:

> "I waive the quantum o' the sin,
> The hazard of concealing;
> But, och! it hardens a' within,
> And petrifies the feeling!"

"Sin," in Hebrew as well as in Greek, is the missing of the mark, the falling short of the goal, the incapacity to reach one's end, the failure to fulfill one's destiny. A sinner is merely a man who has never learned how to live. One can see at once that the psalmist describes a reality which has little in common with "the peccadilloes of all Piccadilly." He does not think of "sins" which may be listed in a catalogue, but he has in mind the state of "Sin" which makes men on earth feel like living dead.

Note also the three synonymous terms in which the appeal for pardon is couched. "Blot out," erase, perhaps words on a manuscript, the record of my past, the account of my deeds. "Wash me thoroughly," an intensive verb which describes the completeness of the purification needed, however severe and painful the process may be: "Wash me, beat me, tread me down, hammer me with mallets, dash me against stones, do anything with me, if only these foul stains are melted from the texture of my soul."[2] Finally, "cleanse me," an expression borrowed from the priestly ritual of purification for lepers (cf. Lev. 13:16, etc.) and lifted out of its ceremonial use. Only God himself can make this reprobate "whole."

i

After the preliminary appeal, or invocation, comes the confession (vss. 3-6). A deeply religious man is a lucid man. He knows his

---

[2] Alexander Maclaren, *The Psalms, in loc.*

transgressions and he "recognizes" or "acknowledges" them. He cannot put them out of his mind, he cannot forget. A Nemesis implacably follows him, and he exclaims in anguish, "My sin is continually before me" (vs. 3). In one of Victor Hugo's poems Cain is pursued by the eye of remorse, and after migrating into distant lands in order to escape it, he finally has a grave dug for him; there he lies down in utter darkness, hoping to be delivered from the frightful sight, but *"L'oeil était dans la tombe et regardait Cain."*[3]

The psalmist lives again the horrors of the past, or rather, the memory of the past is like an ever-recurring event which is re-enacted in the present. According to one interpretation, he realizes that however wrong he may have been in his actions against his fellow men, he has ultimately sinned against God himself. But another and more likely meaning of the text is possible. He does not confess specifically which particular law he has broken or what harm he has accomplished. He does not appear to be conscious of having hurt any man. Yet, in the presence of the thrice holy God he feels the impurity of his own nature.

Likewise, Isaiah, aware of his solidarity with society and of his own personal guilt as a human being (not a guilt of an ethical nature!), cries out after the vision of the divine:

"Woe is me! for I am undone;
    Because I am a man of unclean lips,
And I dwell in the midst of a people of unclean lips;
    For mine eyes have seen the King, Yahweh of hosts!"
                                                (Is. 6:5.)

Similarly Job, stubbornly and proudly defending his moral innocence against the false accusations of his friends, is at last compelled to confess, after his creator has addressed him from the whirlwind:

"I have heard of thee by the hearing of the ear,
    But now mine eye seeth thee.
Wherefore I sink into the abyss,
    And repent in dust and ashes" (Job 42:5-6).

---

[3] "The eye was in the tomb and looked upon Cain." Victor Hugo, *"La Conscience,"* in *La Légende des Siècles.*

Repent of what? Of ethical sins which Job has never committed? Anticipating Saint Paul, Saint Augustine, Martin Luther, Blaise Pascal, and all the noble spirits who were tortured by the consciousness of their sin in proportion to their awareness of the divine, the psalmist is in effect expostulating, "O wretched man that I am! who shall deliver me from the body of this death?" (Rom. 7:24.) This is the experience, not of a criminal who is harassed by the burden of his "sins," but of an honest man who suddenly becomes aware of divine holiness about him and therefore also of his "Sin." And thus it was that Simon Peter "fell down at Jesus' knees, saying, 'Depart from me; for I am a sinful man, O Lord!'" (Lk. 5:8.) It is probable that the experience of the psalmist belongs in some way to the same type of self-deprecation. His sense of sin is due to his sense of God. Many of us are reluctant to share in such an experience because in all likelihood we have never met God "face to face."

More difficult are the next lines (vss. 4*cd*), which are introduced by a conjunction generally indicating purpose or intent. The psalmist can hardly say that he sinned "in order that" God might justify himself by punishing sinful man. The purpose of human impurity cannot be the fulfillment of divine justice. Several uses of the same conjunction elsewhere in Biblical Hebrew point to the meaning of result or consequence rather than that of purpose. The poet is probably saying in effect, "I am a sinner against thee, so that thou wouldst be justified in punishing me and in declaring me guilty." It is in this sense that Saint Paul quotes this passage and concludes, "Our unrighteousness commendeth the righteousness of God" (Rom. 3:4-5).

The confession continues with a further recognition:

> "Behold, I was shapen in iniquity,
> And in sin did my mother conceive me" (vs. 5).

This famous verse does not suggest, as many commentators have traditionally maintained, the impurity of birth or the sin which is inherent in the act of procreation. To be sure, the priestly laws of the Pentateuch prescribe a ritual of purification after birth (Lev.

12:2; cf. Lk. 2:22 ff.). But the psalmist is obviously not concerned with the survival within Hebrew religion of such primitive
taboos. He does not say, "My birth was a crime and my conception impure." He rather acknowledges his solidarity with the whole
of the human race—"In a state of guilt was my mother when she
conceived me, and thus was I born a sinner."

In like manner Job asks,

> "Who can bring a clean thing out of an unclean one?
>   Not one" (Job 14:4),

and Eliphaz agrees with this thought:

"What is man, that he should be clean?
    And he which is born of a woman, that he should be righteous?"
                                                        (Job 15:14.)

Like other psalmists who declare,

> "The wicked are estranged from the womb,
>   They go astray as soon as they are born" (Ps. 58:3),

or Jeremiah who attempts to pierce the superficial thinking of his
contemporaries by asking,

> "Can the Ethiopian change his skin,
>   Or the leopard his spots?
>   Then, may you also do good,
>   Ye that are accustomed to do evil?" (Jer. 13:23),

the poet of Ps. 51 speaks of the depravity which pulls his total being down from the heights and at the same time of the corruption
which gnaws at his core. He is not attempting to find an excuse or
to attenuate his guilt by stating that, like all men, he was born a
sinner; he is rather acknowledging the depth of his corruption, and
this idea ushers in directly its counterpart (vs. 6). Truth is not a
commodity that man can wear on his lips or lapel and thereby become truthful. Wisdom is not a science that one can superficially

learn or borrow for public consumption. Fidelity is more than outward obedience. Faithfulness blossoms from within. Wisdom cannot be acquired unless it transforms man's inner spring of emotion
and will. What is truth, what is wisdom, if they do not change a
man at the very root of his being and power? Thus, the prayer is
now ready to move forward into its second part.

ii

The supplication (vss. 7-12) constitutes the central and turning
point of the psalm. The very structure of the strophe, with its extra
lines, suggests the amplitude of the thought and the power of the
religious desire which animates it. The petitions for cleansing, forgiving, and renewing come one on top of the other like the waves of
a rising tide. The appeal of the invocation is now reframed: its
negative and positive aspects are taken up in alternate order (vss.
7, 9, 11 and 8, 10, 12 respectively).

(a) Forgiveness means purification (or rather "un-sinning"),
and again the stringency of the penitent's condition is suggested
by the image of the branch of hyssop, which was used in the ceremonial of sprinkling after leprosy or pollution through contact with
a corpse (Lev. 14:4, 6 ff.; Num. 19:6, 18 ff.).

(b) Forgiveness means also joy, but this kind of joy is obtained
at a heavy price, since the penitent has felt the crushing of his bones,
the grinding of his whole self in contrition and sorrow.

(c) Sin is a persistent reality from which God is begged to hide
his face.

(d) A totally new creation is what is needed, a creation similar
to the ordering of chaos, formless and void, like the creation of the
world (note the use of the same verb as in Gen. 1:1). An unclean
heart may never become clean, but a new heart may be given in
the place of the old one (Jer. 24:7; Ezek. 11:19). In the midst of
his spiritual death the poet asks for a resurrection of his being. He
knows that he needs to be born anew, and he thereby anticipates

the Christian experience of the new creation (Gal. 6:15) and of the new birth (John 3:3, 6; I Pet. 1:23).

(e) To fall again would mean once more to be estranged: hence the prayer for the continuous presence of God.

(f) The final request asks not only for a renewal of the joy which flows from the certainty of present salvation but also for the transformation of the will.

It may be observed that the second clause in each of the last three petitions (vss. 10, 11, 12) contains the word "spirit": "a steadfast spirit," "thy holy spirit," and a "spirit of free will." The psalmist has already passed beyond the moment of forgiveness. He is seeking the foundation whereby a new life will be truly his. The source of life is a well-attached, firmly rooted, enduring power in man, but this in turn depends on the grace of God, the imparting of God's very own, his "holy spirit," which finally produces in man a true freedom, the will to do good, the taste for willing service, without hesitation or effort, the spirit of the authentic nobleman whose sole preoccupation is selfless dedication to a cause. All these qualities, which are indeed "more than coronets," are contained in the last expression, *ruach nedhîbhah* (vs. 12*b*), which is therefore variously translated as "a free spirit," "a willing spirit," "a spirit of free will," a "noble" or "princely spirit." When the spirit of God dwells in mortal man, it imparts in the creature some holiness of the divine; the energy of God himself transforms the unstable, fluctuating, self-centered human animal into a steadfast and willing servant, a true aristocrat, a consecrated knight, a prince and lord devoted to the welfare of his fellows. By the creative act of the creator God, man may yet emerge from the mud in which he lies prostrate and receive on this earth the title of true nobility.

This is a unique prayer. It goes far beyond the request for mercy with which it began, for it reaches and embraces all the riches of salvation: its endurance, its joy, its freedom, and its fruitfulness. But it goes further still. A reborn individual cannot be created a nobleman without becoming aware of his social responsibility. Thus, the request for a "willing spirit" introduces the last part of the psalm.

iii

The dedication (vss. 13-17) bursts open the barriers which separate the poet from the community. Saved, he will now share his wealth. Delivered from spiritual prison, he will emancipate others. Reborn from death, he will carry the good news of his quickening abroad. Recipient of life, he will help others to receive it. A new creature becomes a missionary. "Deliver me from dumbness and silent shame, O God, thou God of my salvation!" (Vs. 14.) A recurrence of the old self-centricity may still restrain the poet's zeal to testify. Immediately after his act of dedication, he is again in need of God's grace. It is God who must open man's lips; only then is human praise possible (vs. 15).

When such a level of religion is reached, what kind of sacrifice can one devise? Man will offer his own self, his *whole* self.

"The sacrifices of God are a broken spirit,
   A broken and a contrite heart, O God, thou wilt not despise."

The poet ends his penitential prayer in a hymn of consecration as he proclaims a sublime thought which is echoed in Third Isaiah:

"For thus saith the high and lofty One
   That inhabiteth eternity, whose name is Holy:
I dwell in the high and holy place,
   With him also that is of a contrite and humble spirit,
To revive the spirit of the humble,
   And to revive the heart of the contrite ones" (Is. 57:15).

The experience of the "indwelling spirit" transcends the idea of the cultic presence. Like some other psalmists who meditated on the mystery of God's sojourning in Zion, the poet of Ps. 51 is certain that the Holy One is readily to be found in man's secret sanctuary.

".. . I do not know
What lodged thee then, nor where, nor how;
But I am sure thou now dost come
Oft to a narrow, homely room,
Where thou too hast but the least part,
My God, I mean *my sinful heart*."[4]

Disapproving such a cavalier attitude toward the sacrificial system, an editor who preserved the psalm for the Temple hymnal felt compelled to add an explanatory stanza (vss. 18-19). Most modern commentators, including Jewish and Roman Catholic exegetes, agree in regarding those verses as an appendix written by an admirer of priestly ceremonies.

A study of this penitential prayer may accomplish an urgent task. The psalmist shows that a consciousness of sin, far from leading man into pessimism, despondency, and despair (as many modern humanists and psychologists maintain), is on the contrary the prerequisite for the healing of the personality and the discovery of the power to live aright.

It is of course obvious that we cannot associate ourselves easily with the feelings of this ancient penitent. Deep-rooted in the modern mind lies the idea of man's inborn freedom and goodness, and therefore we rebel at the thought of confessing our sinfulness before God. We are prone to assent when we read, for example, such a statement as this: "The thousands who had voted for Jefferson laughed aloud at John Calvin's doctrine of total depravity. How could free men believe such things? ... 'Eliza,' said one of the Eliots to her kinswoman, 'do you kneel down in church and call yourself a miserable sinner? Neither I nor any of my family will ever do that.' "[5]

This attitude, however, is not far removed from a modern pagan creed like the following: "The essence of Jewish-Christianity is sin and absolution. The essence of Nordic Paganism is blood and honor.

---

[4] Henry Vaughan, "The Dwelling Place."
[5] Catherine Drinker Bowen, *Yankee From Olympus* (Boston: An Atlantic Monthly Press Book, Little, Brown and Company, 1944).

Everlasting consciousness of sin is a symptom of racial cross-breeding and degeneration. Worried consciousness of sin is at the opposite pole from proud consciousness of race, and the two can never meet."[6] Admittedly, Christian theologians have in the past perverted the Biblical awareness of man's depravity and original sin into intellectual dogmas which were divorced from the realities of life. Events of the twentieth century, however, may compel us to rediscover that a tragic dimension of pride, stupidity, and malevolence mars human achievements and corrupts human endeavors toward good. The great poets have been more lucid in this respect than many of our social scientists. At a heavy price, we begin to realize anew the truth of Shakespeare's words:

> ". . . Man, proud man!
> Dress'd in a little brief authority,—
> Most ignorant of what he's most assured,
> His glassy essence,—like an angry ape,
> Plays such fantastic tricks before high heaven
> As make the angels weep."

Indeed, the new danger for our culture, under the pressure of modern wars, is the abrupt rediscovery of human sinfulness, without its normal predecessor, generator, and counterforce, the assurance of a loving, forgiving, and omnipotent God. All around us, men and women are searching for a cure, and they turn here and there, almost at random, to "physicians of no worth," asking them Macbeth's question:

> "Canst thou not minister to a mind diseas'd;
> Pluck from the memory a rooted sorrow;
> Raze out the written troubles of the brain;
> And with some sweet oblivious antidote
> Cleanse the stuff'd bosom of that perilous stuff
> Which weighs upon the heart?"

---

[6] Busso Loewe, *Creed of the German Pagan Movement.*

A penitential prayer like Ps. 51 is not ensconced in pessimism. It fully recognizes that evil is endemic in mankind, but it apprehends divine love in action. To be sure, its poet knows that the *sine qua non* of his salvation is, in Browning's words, "the submission of Man's nothing-perfect to God's All-complete," but he also perceives that such a submission does not end with the annihilation of the self. "Except a corn of wheat fall into the ground and die, it abideth alone: but if it die, it bringeth forth much fruit" (John 12:24). The psalmist obtains grace and freedom through self-death. Now, "grace is more than pardon, it is power, the divine power which redeems life and also uses it, rendering a man efficient for service."[7] Freedom is the emancipation from the captivity of man's own desires and selfish pursuits. This penitent is delivered from the fear of failure, from a perverse sense of inferiority or superiority, and above all, from the insidious suspicion that life is a boredom or a fruitless, insane, and sometimes sadistic adventure. Joy in reconciliation and zeal for service and praise: these are the flowers of grace and freedom. There is such a thing as the experience of salvation here and now.

The miracles of the Bible are to be found in those momentous acts of re-creation, whenever a man passes from sinfulness to sanctity, from death to life, from despair to faith. In this context, the well-known line from King Lear takes on a new meaning:

> "Nothing almost sees miracles
> But misery. . . ."

The miracle of Ps. 51 is that a man of the Old Covenant received so illuminating a vision and so penetrating a certitude. His Kyrie Eleison is almost a Nunc Dimittis.

---

[7] James Moffatt, *Grace in the New Testament* (New York: Ray Long & Richard R. Smith, Inc., 1932).

II

De Profundis
(Psalm 130)

I

1.   Out of the depths have I cried unto thee, O Yahweh!
        Lord, hear my voice!
2.   Let thine ears be attentive
        To the voice of my supplications!

II

3.   If thou shouldest mark iniquities, O Yah,
        Lord, who would stand?
4.   But there is forgiveness with thee,
        That thou mayest be feared.

III

5.   I wait for Yahweh, my soul doth wait,
        And in his word do I hope.
6.   My soul waiteth for the Lord.
        More than they that watch for the morning,
        More than they that watch for the morning.

IV

7.   Let Israel hope in Yahweh:
        For with Yahweh there is mercy,
        And with him is plenteous redemption.
8.   And it is he that shall redeem Israel
        From all her iniquities.

In a figurative and profound sense, Ps. 130 deserves to be called a "Song of Ascents,"[8] for it moves "out of the depths" to a solid hope and it broadens its horizon from a concern over personal distress to a zeal for social salvation. Its structure espouses its thought and the diction of the four strophes becomes more ample and stately

---

[8] This title is given to fifteen psalms (120-134) which were probably intoned by pilgrims on their way to the Temple of Jerusalem.

as the mood is transformed: the first two strophes are made of four lines each and the last two of five lines each (2+2; 2+2; 2+3; 3+2).

i

What are the "depths" out of which the poet cries to his God? The psalm does not offer any explicit answer. The image of the deep waters (as in Ps. 69:2, 14) points to a hopelessly evil situation. Perhaps at the gates of corporeal death, perhaps at the bottom of a spiritual abyss into which no light can penetrate, a man shouts again and again his supplications. Not "out of the depth," but "out of the depths" does his prayer upsurge. Whether the plural word refers to several occurrences and seemingly endless repetitions of the depressive state or to a single access of exorbitant proportion (the word would then be considered by Hebrew grammarians as a "plural of majesty"), one impression imposes itself: the psalmist knows the torture of abandon, loneliness, shame, helplessness, and despair. Almost beyond endurance, in Emerson's words, "under every deep a lower deep opens," and as the primeval ocean of non-being threatens to submerge him forever, he voices his agony. Inasmuch as the second strophe (vss. 3-4) reveals a most grievous sense of guilt, we may assume that he is thinking not merely or primarily of a physical distress but of the abysmal darkness of his soul. To be sure, the causes of his night are unknown. They may be related to personal circumstances, or they may spring out of the national catastrophes which have reduced Israel to nought (see the call of the last strophe, vss. 7-8). In any case, the poet has reached the moment of existence when man faces himself alone at the bottom of a pit. In the adventures of the spirit, heroic heights seem to be attained only by those who have at first descended lower and lower into the depths. At the opening of this psalm we are permitted to see the nadir of a soul.

> "My former hopes are fled,
>   My terror now begins;
>   I feel, alas! that I am dead
>   In trespasses and sins.

> Ah, whither shall I fly?
> I hear the thunder roar;
> The law proclaims destruction nigh,
> And vengeance at the door."[9]

All seems lost. But there is still prayer. An elemental cry. "Unto thee, O Yahweh."

ii

In the second strophe (vss. 3-4), the poet rises above his immediate need, to consider the situation of man in general.

> "If thou shouldest mark iniquities, O Yah,
> Lord, who would stand?"

Like the author of Psalm 51, he is aware of the common guilt which unites human kind.

> "We are soiled by a filth that we cannot clean,
>   united to supernatural vermin,
> It is not we alone, it is not the house,
>   it is not the city that is defiled,
> But the world that is wholly foul."

Some think that the severity of a poet like T. S. Eliot, as demonstrated in these lines from *Murder in the Cathedral,* is slightly unwarranted, but such a realism is shared by the whole Bible.

> "Yahweh looked down from heaven
>   Upon the children of men,
> To see if there were any that did understand. . . .
> They are all gone aside,
>   They are all together become filthy:
> There is none that doeth good; no, not one"
>   (Ps. 14:2-3; cf. Rom. 3:10-18; Lk. 11:13).

Anyone who denies the validity of this verdict is implicitly shrugging off his own share of responsibility for all the crosses of history.

---

[9] William Cowper, "My Former Hopes Are Fled."

He replies by a silent unconcern to the question which every age relentlessly asks: "Were you there when they crucified my Lord?" The Bible, however, does not attempt to convince man of sin without offering at once the warm, quickening word of redemption; and the psalmist, in the same breath in which he acknowledged the universality of sin, added, "But there is forgiveness with thee!" Only in the depth of spiritual extremity can man perceive the height, the breadth, the length, and the *depth* of the love of God. In the twinkling of an eye the singer lifts us up from "the lowest circle of hell." God is God! The will and the passion to forgive is "with" him, as an intimate friend whose benevolent counsel finds access to the very heart of a king. There is forgiveness! There is the certainty which breaks the gloom and ushers in the inward dawn, although the night lingers on.

In utterly logical fashion several commentators are disturbed by the next line, "That thou mayest be feared" (vs. 4*b*). Some try to correct the text, others suggest that this clause should be omitted (as in the Septuagint), still others interpret the idea of fear in the weakened sense of "piety" which the word obtained in later Judaism. Now, there is indeed an experience of authentic fear, of terror and of fright, which—far from being incompatible with love—arises precisely from the discovery of undeserved love. Every artist, poet, or scientist experiences such a fear at the moment of creative discovery. Every man who has truly known human love will understand this paradox. A fortiori the finite and guilty creature who receives from the creator not wrath, but love; not rejection, but welcome; not condemnation, but grace.

When man has given up hope in human devices and then becomes certain that the hand of help will be extended to him in his depths, he is ready "to serve the Lord with fear, and to rejoice with trembling" (Ps. 2:11). In forgiveness he discovers the true nature of God, whose "compassions are kindled together" (Hos. 11:8). Fearful is the love of God precisely because it forgives. That kind of love produces fear, for it constrains, compels, and conquers better than law and all its threats. Aware of the claims of divine love upon him, a forgiven man truly fears God, with a

fear that is not the opposite of love, but its fruit. A man who has
been grasped "out of the depths" knows that henceforth no compromise for him is possible, since the completeness of the gift creates
in him the completeness of the response.

> "For, though I knew His love Who followèd,
>   Yet was I sore adread
> Lest, having Him, I must have naught beside."[10]

Better than the psalmist, Christians should be able to feel the
reality of this fearful compulsion, if they truly obtain their forgiveness in the mystery of a self-sacrificing, suffering God. The
paradox of fear stemming from love is ultimately resolved in the
stumbling block of the cross.

And thus it was that Hopeful asked of Christian, in *The Pilgrim's Progress*, "How will you describe right fear?" And Christian answered, "It begetteth and continueth in the soul a great
reverence of God, his word, and ways, keeping it tender, and making it afraid to turn from them, to the right hand or to the left, to
anything that may dishonour God, break its peace, grieve the Spirit,
or cause the enemy to speak reproachfully." Thereupon Hopeful
replied, "Well said; I believe you have said the truth. Are we now
almost got past the Enchanted Ground?"

iii

With the third strophe (vss. 5-6), the poet reveals that he still
lives in the darkness of his night, but he now confidently expects
the light. He waits, tense and impatient, to be sure, more than
watchmen for the morning; but he waits in hope. He hopes for the
word of his deliverance. In the meantime his preoccupation with
his own destiny melts as in the final strophe (vss. 7-8) he remembers the church. Are not his guilt and his trial shared by Israel?
"With" Yahweh, there is mercy for the people of the promise, as
there is forgiveness for a single penitent. Turning into an evan-

---

[10] Francis Thompson, "The Hound of Heaven."

gelist, the psalmist calls upon the whole community to hope for "a plenteous redemption." His personal knowledge of the depths confers on him the ability to know the depths in which his fellow men also lie fallen. His own suffering makes it possible for him to understand the tribulations of society. His hope for a personal salvation merges into a hope for the salvation of the whole. He cannot be saved alone. "Let Israel hope in Yahweh!"

Many men, known and unknown, have learned to regain and to fortify their faith by meditating on the De Profundis. The experience of the "depths," similar in many respects to what John of the Cross called "the deep darkness of the soul," or more still to Martin Luther's *Anfechtungen,* is the hard way which leads to the apprehension of spiritual truth.

"If I were yet to live a little while," said Luther, "I should like to write a book about *Anfechtungen,* without which no man can understand either the Scriptures or the fear and love of God. No indeed, he cannot know what hope is who has never been in the midst of trials and temptations." The poet of Ps. 130 has descended far down into the chasm of anguish, and therefore, when he sings, "Let Israel hope in Yahweh," his voice has an accent of authority. No trial is ever endured in vain, and, as Newman wrote, "saints are lowered that the world may rise."

III

When asked to name the psalms which he liked best, Luther answered, "The Pauline Psalms," by which he meant the penitential prayers, particularly Pss. 51 and 130. It would be erroneous to assume, however, that these poems offer a psychological description of sin and forgiveness as profound and inclusive as those of the New Testament or of some Christian theologians, from Augustine to our day. They must be taken for what they are, not didactic treatises, but poetic testimonies. As such, they deserve to be called the forerunners of the Christian experience of salvation by faith.

Nurtured and tested by suffering, their poets discerned the intimate connection which exists between sin and anxiety. In the parturition of crisis they acquired a sharpness of self-diagnosis and a steeling of the will to live. While the outward situation which brought forth their heart-searching remained as yet unresolved, their faith lifted them out of despondency and they were reconciled with the God from whom they had been estranged. Their hope became in effect a fulfillment. In the very midst of their trials they tasted the joy of their salvation.

The other penitential prayers (Ps. 6, 32, 38, 102, 143) reflect similar travails and triumphs. The man who begged for mercy (Ps. 6:2) would also affirm, "Yahweh hath heard my supplication" (Ps. 6:9). The penitent who felt himself to be sinking under the too heavy burden of his iniquities (Ps. 38:4) would also declare his hope (Ps. 38:15). The outcast who yielded to self-pity and compared himself to "a pelican of the wilderness," "an owl of the ruins," "a bird alone on the housetop" (Ps. 102:6,7), could find in a moment the reason to proclaim:

"This shall be written for the generations to come,
    And the people which shall be created shall praise Yah,
For he hath looked down from the height of his sanctuary;
    From heaven did Yahweh behold the earth,
To hear the groaning of the prisoner,
    To loose those that are appointed to death" (Ps. 102:18-20).

Penitence is more than remorse. Attrition leads to contrition. The awareness of sin and the acceptance of pardon mean repentance, self-immolation, and surrender. Conversion must look ahead and envisage the future. The prayer of the penitent shall therefore be:

"Teach me to do thy will,
    For thou art my God!
May thy good spirit lead me
    Into the land of uprightness!" (Ps. 143:10.)

Sanctification is a never-ended undertaking. One of the penitential prayers was written after the crisis which had prompted it was dispelled. The poet looked back and said,

> "Blessed is he whose transgression is forgiven, . . .
> And in whose spirit there is no guile" (Ps. 32:1, 2),

but he also looked ahead and concluded,

> "Therefore let every one who has been shown mercy pray
>   unto thee
>   In a time when thou mayest be found:
> Surely in the floods of great waters
>   They shall not come nigh unto him" (Ps. 32:6).

After the great storms of the soul are becalmed, there is still need for watchfulness and the discipline of fidelity. There is above all a time for the return of thanks, the giving of trust, and the singing of communion. The Psalter reflects the contrasting moments of man's response to the various probings and proddings of the Eternal. Thus, besides the "Prayers in Time of Crisis," there are the "Songs of Faith."

4

*Songs of
Faith*

I | PSALMS OF THANKSGIVING

SOME years ago a distinguished scholar ventured into the realm of the philosophy of religion and attempted to demonstrate the futility of prayer.[1] None of his arguments, however, was directed against the offering of thanks. This omission may be accidental; it is in any case significant. Gratitude is the basis of worship.[2] Cicero remarked that "it is not only the greatest of all the virtues but also the parent of all the others." One may add that, if the lower religions appear to have been born out of fear, it is the return of thanks, the "eucharist," which is the beginning and the end of Biblical Christianity.

All the hymns of praise represent the response of a grateful Israel to the work and word of God in nature and history. The psalms of thanksgiving are not mere hymns of praise (although they often borrow from this type of psalmody), because they presuppose a crisis and its happy termination. Most of them were composed for the celebration of a ceremonial act, the payment of a vow made in time of distress and danger, or the sacrifice of the "thank offering," to which several allusions are found in the Psalter.

> "I will go into thy house with burnt offerings;
>   I will pay my vows
> Which my lips have uttered
>   And my mouth hath spoken when I was in trouble.
> I will offer unto thee burnt offerings of fatlings
>   With the smoke of rams;
> I will offer bullocks and goats" (Ps. 66:13-15).

[1] Kirsopp Lake, "Prayer," *The Atlantic Monthly,* August 1924.
[2] See above, pp. 20-21.

191

"I will offer to thee the sacrifice of thanksgiving,
And will call upon the name of Yahweh" (Ps. 116:17).

As Gunkel correctly noted, the poems which were originally created to accompany the sacrificial act and to confer on it an intelligible meaning came to replace that act entirely. The word *tôdhah* which at first meant the gift of thanks (literally, "the lifting of the hands") later designated "the psalm of thanksgiving," and the sacrifice itself was completely spiritualized.

"Sacrifice and offering thou didst not desire;
Mine ears hast thou opened:
Burnt offerings and sin offering hast thou not required"
(Ps. 40:6; cf. Ps. 51:16).

Was the process of spiritualization so perverting that mere liturgical symbol took the place of a sacrifice which cost dearly? Not at all. The singer gave the pledge of leading henceforth a dedicated life.

"Then said I, Lo, I come:
(In the scroll of the book written about me)
I delight to do thy will, O my God!
Yea, thy law is within my heart" (Ps. 40:7; cf. Ps. 51:17).

This attitude belongs to the prophetic type of religion (Jer. 31:33). Ethics become inseparable from a constantly renewed communion with the divine. Hence the wistful wish of Moses, which remains relevant to all ages:

"Would God that all the people of Yahweh were prophets,
And that Yahweh would put his spirit upon them!"
(Num. 11:29.)

The Psalter contains more than a score of thanksgiving songs, which reflect a wide diversity of situations and experiences. In

Ps. 124 the people of God celebrate a day of great victory. Ps. 107 appears to have been composed for the ceremony of a public and communal payment of vows which had previously been made by various pilgrims in sundry perils. With Ps. 65, Israel celebrates "Thanksgiving Day." Finally, Ps. 103 expresses the gratitude of an individual worshiper for his spiritual salvation.

I

A National Song of Victory
(Psalm 124)

I

1. If it had not been Yahweh who was on our side
    —Now may Israel say—
2. If it had not been Yahweh who was on our side,
    When men rose up against us,
3. Then, they had swallowed us up quick,
    When their wrath was kindled against us.

II

4. Then, the waters had overwhelmed us,
    The torrent had gone over our soul;
5. Then, they had gone over our soul,
    The waters of the raging flood....

III

6. Blessed be Yahweh who hath not given us
    As a prey to their teeth.
7. Our soul is escaped as a bird
    Out of the snare of the fowlers.
    The snare hath been broken,
    And as for us, we are escaped.

IV

8. Our help is in the name of Yahweh
    Who made heaven and earth.

It is not possible to identify the circumstances which have given rise to this psalm, for many times in the course of a thousand years the nation was delivered from a deathly grip. The adverse forces, in this particular occasion, appeared to be so overwhelming that the poet compared them to an irresistible flood (vss. 4-5). The people felt like a prey that a monstrous beast was about to devour alive (vs. 3). And when victory came, no self-congratulation was in order. As another poet who sang,

> "Not unto us, O Yahweh, not unto us,
>   But unto thy name give glory" (Ps. 115:1),

the psalmist ascribed the deliverance to the intervention of God, the master of nature and of history (vss. 1, 8).

To be sure, there is no suggestion of prophetic judgment. The poet was not concerned, as the great prophets were, with the moral significance or interpretation of national calamities. Nor did he intimate that Yahweh was on the side of his people on account of that people's righteousness or innocence. He did not wax lyrical, as a soldier in the day of military triumph easily might, over the achievements of Israel's armies. He did not say, for instance, as David probably did,[3] after he had been delivered from all his wars of survival,

"Yahweh rewarded me according to my righteousness,
    According to the cleanness of my hands hath he recompensed
        me" (Ps. 18:20=II Sam. 22:21).

He neither thought that God was on the side of the heavier battalions nor believed that his nation deserved to be preserved. He merely stated with gratitude that victory was God's own.

At the same time, he did not offer the national thanks with great fanfare of sentiment. David expressed his thankfulness with a tumultuous and even violent outburst of emotion:

---

[3] The core of Ps. 18 (II Sam. 22) is most likely from David, but the present form of the poem shows unmistakable evidence of later editing, probably by the Deuteronomists, who published the books of Judges, Samuel, and Kings.

"I love thee, Yahweh, my strength,
  Yahweh, my rock, my citadel, and my liberator,
My God, my cliff, in whom I take refuge,
  My shield, and the horn of my salvation, my fortress!
I cry, Praised be Yahweh!
  I am saved from mine enemies!" (Ps. 18:1-3.)

Instead of this warrior's explosive release of long pent-up fears and hardships, the poet of Ps. 124 in chastened cadence intoned:

"Blessed be Yahweh who hath not given us
  As a prey to their teeth" (vs. 6).

This sobriety does not mean, however, that the poet's gratitude was superficial. The profundity and genuineness of his feeling is betrayed by the unusual stress laid on the invitation to sing, and also by the repetition of the first line (vss. 1, 2a; cf. Ps. 129:1). The threefold use of the word "then" (vss. 3, 4, 5) in the recall of the crisis, and the recurrent image of the flooding waters also indicate the frantic state in which Israel had found itself. But the sequence of the poem is couched in "classic" severity: merely a blessing and a self-committal to the maker of the universe.

This psalm is a little masterpiece of restraint and simplicity. It expresses no feeling of bitterness against the enemy or of satisfaction over their discomfiture. Rejoicing is not in their defeat but in the nation's escape.

One should not expect to discover any profound thought in a victory song. Nevertheless, the poet's last word is a significant understatement. At first sight, any allusion to the maker of heaven and earth may appear to be a banality. But, as Thornton Wilder wrote, "there are times when it requires a high courage to speak the banal." And the recognition of a people's creatureliness is no common place. It not only enhances gratitude, it also looks forward to sober consecration. Purged of all false confidence and devoid of self-righteousness, a nation which sings this psalm on a day of victory places itself at the disposal of its maker and acknowledges the continuous providence of God. When men sincerely confess that their only help is in the creator of heaven and earth, their patriotism is in no risk of becoming, in George Jean Nathan's phrase, "an arbitrary veneration of real estate above principles." They know their proper place in the world, for they submit to the God who "hath made of one blood all nations of men" (Acts 17:26).

II

The Song of the Redeemed of the Lord
(Psalm 107)

PRELUDE

1.   O give thanks unto Yahweh, for he is good,
            For his mercy endureth forever!

2.   Let the redeemed of Yahweh say so,
            Whom he hath redeemed from adversity,

3.   And gathered out of the [distant] lands,
            From the east, and from the west,
        From the north, and from the south!

(The travelers)   I

4.   [Some] wandered in the wilderness in a solitary way:
            A track toward an inhabited city they found not.

5.   Hungry and thirsty,
            Their soul fainted in them.

6.   *Then, they cried unto Yahweh in their trouble,*
            And he delivered them from their distresses.

7.   He led them forth by the right way,
            That they might go to a city of habitation.

8.   *Oh that men would praise Yahweh for his goodness,*
            And for his wonderful works to the children of men!

9.   For he satisfieth the thirsty soul,
            And filleth the hungry soul with goodness.

(The prisoners)   II

10.   [Others] sat in darkness and in the deepest gloom,
            Being bound in affliction and iron,

11. Because they rebelled against the words of God,
    And contemned the counsel of the Most High:
12. Therefore, he brought down their heart with labor;
    They fell down, and there was none to help.

13. *Then, they cried unto Yahweh in their trouble,*
    And he saved them out of their distresses.
14. He brought them out of darkness and of the deepest gloom,
    And brake their bonds asunder.

15. *Oh that men would praise Yahweh for his goodness,*
    And for his wonderful works to the children of men!
16. For he hath broken the gates of brass,
    And cut the bars of iron asunder.

(The fools)   III
17. [Others] were fools, because of their transgressions,
    And because of their iniquities, were afflicted.
18. Their soul abhorred all manner of meat,
    And they drew near unto the gates of death.

19. *Then, they cried unto Yahweh in their trouble,*
    And he saved them out of their distresses.
20. He sent his word and healed them,
    And preserved their life from the grave.

21. *Oh that men would praise Yahweh for his goodness,*
    And for his wonderful works to the children of men!
22. Let them offer the sacrifices of thanksgiving,
    And declare his works with rejoicing!

(The sailors)   IV
23. [Others] went down to the sea in ships,
    And did business across the great waters.
24. These have seen the works of Yahweh,
    And his wonders in the deep.

25. He spoke and summoned a stormy wind,
    Which lifted up the waves thereof.
26. They mounted up to the heaven, they went down again to the
        depths:
    Their soul was melted in their anguish,

27. They reeled to and fro, and staggered like a drunken man,
    And were at their wit's end.

28. *Then, they cried unto Yahweh in their trouble,*
    And he brought them out of their distresses.
29. He made the storm a calm,
    And the waves thereof were stilled.
30. Then, they rejoiced because they were quiet,
    And he brought them into their desired haven.

31. *Oh, that men would praise Yahweh for his goodness,*
    And for his wonderful works to the children of men!
32. Let them exalt him also in the congregation of the people,
    And praise him in the assembly of the elders!

POSTLUDE

33. He turneth rivers into a wilderness,
    And the watersprings into dry ground;
34. A fruitful land into a barrenness of salt,
    For the wickedness of them that dwell therein.

35. He turneth the wilderness into an oasis,
    And dry ground into springs of waters,
36. And there he maketh the hungry to dwell,
    That they may found a city for habitation,
37. And sow the fields, and plant vineyards,
    Which may yield fruits of increase.

38. He also blesseth them, so that they are multiplied greatly,
    And he suffereth not their cattle to decrease.
39. And if they are minished and brought low,
    Through oppression, calamity, and sorrow,
40. He poureth contempt upon princes,
    And causeth them to wander through trackless wastes.

41. Yet setteth he the poor on high from their affliction,
    And multiplieth their families as a flock.
42. At their sight, the righteous shall rejoice,
    And all iniquity shall stop her mouth.

43. Whoso is wise will observe these things
    And understand the lovingkindness of Yahweh.

The opening exhortation to give thanks (vss. 1-3) is addressed to "the redeemed of Yahweh" (vs. 2), men of all walks of life who are gathered in the Temple from the four corners of the horizon. The scene evoked by the psalmist may be vividly imagined. Pilgrims have come from the vast *Diaspora* (Dispersion) to the rallying center of their faith in order to present the offerings which in their various perils they had vowed to their deliverer.

Each of the four strophes which constitute the bulk of the psalm, with its intricate double refrain (vss. 6 and 8, 13 and 15, 19 and 21, 28 and 31), is devoted to a specific class of celebrants, and the last part of the thanksgiving song (vss. 33-43) is in the form of a hymn, which may originally have been written by a poet of the wisdom school and was perhaps sung by the whole congregation.

The *first group* of pilgrims (vss. 4-9) was made of caravan travelers, who had lost their way in what Longfellow called "the sea-like, pathless, limitless waste of the desert" and had been delivered from hunger and thirst after they had prayed for their lives.

The people of the *second group* (vss. 10-16) had been prisoners, shut up in dungeons, because they had rebelled against the divine commandments (vs. 11). Brought to repentance, they had cried unto God and regained their liberty.

A *third group* (vss. 17-22) was made of "the fools" who had become sick unto death. The Hebrew view of mental and physical diseases proceeded from a dangerous generalization, for it explained illness by sin, but it contained an element of truth which the modern mind might as well recognize. The consensus of opinion was that ailments of the body and of the mind were always the result of spiritual perversion or rebellion, and the poem of Job was written partly as a protest against the falsehood of this belief. It is worth noting, however, that contemporary developments in psychosomatic medicine are not altogether far removed from the Biblical conception of the homogeneous unity of the human individual. "My son, thy sins are forgiven!" Such was the manner in which Jesus would greet many sick who obviously manifested in their various incapacities the inward disturbance of their souls. Thus, in cautiously guarded fashion and with ample provision being made for exceptions, one may read not without profit that "folly" often issues from a spiritual disorder whose cure is of a frankly religious nature. Many in our day obtain through various forms of psychotherapy a great deal of worth-while information about the hidden motivations of their behavior, but some among them, at least, will never be saved from their demonic selves until they learn the therapeutics of kneeling before God Almighty and of surrendering to his stern and loving will.

The psalmist knew about healing by faith, and he had witnessed the exultation and praise of those who, in persistent prayer, had been brought back from the edge of the grave and had been made whole. Christianity began its wildfire spread throughout the ancient world largely as a gospel of healing. The Bible affirms the unity of body and soul. This psalm testifies to the power of prayer in the preservation and rediscovery of mental and physiological health.

Finally, there were in the *fourth group* the seafaring folks (vss. 23-32), who had passed through what Byron described as

> "The hell of waters! where they howl and hiss,
>   And boil in endless torture."

The poet's sketch of the dangers incurred by those "who go down to the sea in ships" is comparable to Homer's famed lines,

> ". . . The winds aloud
> Howl o'er the masts, and sing thro' ev'ry shroud:
> Pale, trembling, tired, the sailors freeze with fears;
> And instant death on ev'ry wave appears."

But he does not write for a literary purpose. He perceives that a man at his wit's end does not speculate about the validity of prayer. As the proverb puts it, "Let him who knows not how to pray go to sea!" It may be "in the confidence of prayer" that a soul "takes hold on [God]."

Thus, this song of thanksgiving, by its selection of widely different case histories, teaches how faith is sometimes born or tested. Many come to worship God only after they have recognized through dire personal straits that he guides amid the wastes, emancipates from captivity, heals from self-inflicted wounds, and stills the tempests.

It is necessary to observe that the poet does not confront the problem of undeserved and unrelieved evil. He has no word for those who led the caravan to their intended destination and through no fault of their own never came back. He does not speak for the victims of political oppression or religious persecution who slowly rot away in their jails. He does not seem to think of those who were born, or struck early in life, with an incurable disease of body or mind. He ignores all the courageous and unsung heroes "lost at sea." But his purpose is not to inquire into the mystery of unjustified suffering. He sings on behalf of those who returned from the jaws of death. It is in this context of wonder at "merely being alive" that the psalm must be appreciated. Anyone who has faced "the king of terrors" will understand. In the course of human existence there are moments conducing to only one mood, that of grateful praise for this incredible gift—life on earth! It is not enough to say with David in Browning's "Saul,"

> "How good is man's life, the mere living! how fit to employ
> All the heart and the soul and the senses, forever in joy!"

One must also turn with newly opened eyes to the giver of the breath and say, as did Saul's mother in the Browning poem:

> " 'Let one more attest,
> I have lived, seen God's hand thro' a lifetime,
> and all was for best!' "

A man speaking thus will never take for granted his health, his freedom, or his haven. His gratitude ushers in a dedicated wisdom which in the morrow watches for, and sensitively understands, "the lovingkindness" of the Lord (vs. 43).

III

A Song for Thanksgiving Day
(Psalm 65)

I

1. Praise is fitting unto thee,
    O God, in Zion,
  And unto thee shall the vow be performed,
2.   O thou that hearest prayer!

  Unto thee shall all flesh bring
3.   The debts of iniquity.
  Our transgressions have prevailed against us,
    But thou shalt purge them away.

4. Blessed is he whom thou choosest and bringest near unto thee,
    That he may dwell in thy court.
  We shall be satisfied with the goodness of thy house,
    With the holiness of thy temple.

II

5. In righteousness dost thou answer us by terrible wonders,
    O God of our salvation!
  Thou, the confidence of all the ends of the earth,
    And of them that are afar off upon the sea!

6. Thou, who by thy strength hath set fast the mountains,
    Being girded with power,
7. Thou, who stilleth the roar of the seas,
    Even the roar of their waves.

  Nations were in tumult, [8.] and they were afraid,
    At thy tokens, they that dwell in the uttermost parts!
  The Orient and the Occident
    Thou makest to rejoice!

III

9. Thou hast visited the earth and watered it,
    Thou hast showered it with riches;
  The brook of God is full of water,
    Thou preparest the harvest of the soil. . . .[4]

10. Thou waterest the ridges thereof abundantly,
    Thou settlest the furrows thereof,
  Thou makest it soft with showers,
    Thou blessest the springing thereof.

11. Thou crownest the year with thy goodness,
    And the paths of thy chariot drip with fatness;
12. They drip upon the pastures of the wilderness,
    And the hills gird themselves with rejoicing;
  The pastures are clothed with flock;
    The valleys also are covered over with corn;
    They shout for joy, they also sing.

This psalm may well be of composite origin, for its three main parts (vss. 1-4; 5-8; 9-12) differ markedly among themselves in style as well as in theme. If such is the case, however, the editor who brought together these hitherto separate poems and was responsible for the finished song of thanksgiving has achieved a remarkable result, for he has succeeded in throwing the celebration of the harvest festivities under the floodlights of man's transgressions and of God's forgiveness. Indeed, the Hebrew farmers could not thank their God for the bounties of the soil without remembering the specifically moral relationship which bound them to the creator of nature.

i

The song opens with an obscure line which in the traditional Hebrew text means literally, "To thee praise is silent," or "is waiting." Following the Greek version of the Septuagint, most modern scholars suggest a slight transformation of the vocalic reading, and they translate, "Praise is meet unto thee." Nonetheless, the poetic rendering of the King James Version, "Praise waiteth for thee,"

---

[4] The next line, "Thus is the way thou preparest it," seems to be a marginal annotation.

may not be too far distant from the intention of the psalmist. Praise is waiting upon the bountiful Sustainer of Israel. It arises from every new manifestation of his providence. Yet, man is unworthy of access to the holy presence. Absolved of his iniquities by a sheer act of undeserved grace, he will make bold to come and dwell in the courts of Zion. Even this move on the part of the worshipers appears to be inspired and made possible by the loving power of the deity, and they discern that they come before the most high God in his temple because he has first called them and brought them near unto him (vs. 4). They find there a goodness which satisfies more profoundly than the bounties of fields and pastures. The words may suggest a richer meaning than the poet literally intended—"Man shall not live by bread alone."

ii

The God of the covenanted people is also "the confidence of all the ends of the earth" (vs. 5). This intoxicating thought reminds the celebrants of a humbling fact: they are not exclusively the objects of divine favor. All mankind stands before God with Israel. A vast universalism breathes over the assembled congregation. They contemplate the creator and master of history (vss. 6-8) while surrounded by all the inhabitants of the earth as they offer in the autumn festival (Deut. 16:13-15; Lev. 23:39-43) their sacrifice of praise. At the crowning of the year (cf. vs. 11), not only the church in Zion, but also the Orient and the Occident are made to rejoice.

iii

There is indeed cause for rejoicing: the divine husbandman has visited the earth (vs. 9)! Observe the way in which the memory of primitive magical rites of fertility have been sublimated into poetic metaphors. God's "irrigation canal" is ready for the invigoration of the fields (vs. 9); God's creaking cart drags along the country lanes and in its wheel tracks the soil sweats with the promise of sap and plenty (vs. 11). In "the teeming autumn, big with rich

increase," the worshipers look backward and forward to the cycle
of seasons, from the tilling and sowing of the soil to the reaping of
the ears and the gathering of the fruits. Through the eyes of the
poet they see, with at once a memory and a hope, "landscape
plotted and pieced—fold, fallow, and plough;"[5] they imagine the
germination of the seed, the sudden greenness which for a few
weeks transforms even the wilderness into a pasture land. Mountain slopes and hillocks are girded with bloom, the flocks adorn
the meadows as with a vestment, the fields undulate with the waves
of barley and wheat. "They shout for joy, they also sing!" (Vs.
12.) A vast symphony ascends from the earth.

Thanksgiving Day makes no petition; it proclaims the abundance with which heart and hearth are overfilled. God once more
delivers from hunger, and man in thankful wonder at the "new-old
miracle" adores and sings:

> "I walk, I lift up, I lift up heart, eyes,
>   Down all that glory in the heavens to glean our Saviour."[6]

There are moments for other moods, when the peasant in fear
and trembling asks the why of mildew, drought, or locusts. We
should not charge this psalmist with oversight or superficiality.
Like the other poets who render thanks, he captures the thrill of
gratitude, when earth answers the heavens (Hos. 2:18-23).

IV

The Thanksgiving Song of a Forgiven Man
(Psalm 103)

(God and the poet)   I
1. Bless Yahweh, O my soul,
       And all that is within me, [bless] his holy name!
2. Bless Yahweh, O my soul,
       And forget not all his benefits!

---

[5] Gerard Manley Hopkins, "Pied Beauty."
[6] *Idem,* "Hurrahing in Harvest."

3. He forgiveth all thine iniquities,
   He healeth all thy diseases,
4. He redeemeth thy life from destruction,
   He crowneth thee with lovingkindness and tender mercies,
5. He satisfieth thy desires with good things,
   So that thy youth is renewed like the eagle's.

(God and the people)   II

6. Yahweh executeth righteousness
   And judgment for all that are oppressed.
7. He made known his ways unto Moses,
   His acts unto the children of Israel.

8. Yahweh is merciful and gracious,
   Slow to anger, and plenteous in mercy.
9. He will not always chide,
   Neither will he keep his anger forever.
10. He hath not dealt with us according to our sins,
    Nor rewarded us according to our iniquities.

(The Divine Father)   III

11. For as the heaven is high above the earth,
    So great is his mercy toward them that fear him.
12. As far as the east is from the west,
    So far hath he removed our transgressions from us.

13. Like as a father pitieth his children,
    So Yahweh pitieth them that fear him.
14. For he knoweth our frame,
    He remembereth that we are dust.

(Mortal Man)   IV

15. As for man, his days are as grass;
    As the flower of the field, so he flourisheth;
16. For the wind passeth over it, and it is gone,
    And the place thereof shall know it no more.

17. But the mercy of Yahweh is from everlasting to everlasting
    Upon them that fear him,
    And his righteousness unto children's children,
18. To such as keep his covenant,
    And to those that remember his commandments to do them.

(The Heavenly King)   v

19. Yahweh hath prepared his throne in the heavens,
      And his kingdom ruleth over all.
20. Bless Yahweh, ye his angels,
      Mighty in strength, that do his commandments,
      Hearkening unto the voice of his word!

21. Bless Yahweh, all ye his hosts,
      Ye ministers of his, that do his pleasure!
22. Bless Yahweh, all his works,
      In all the places of his dominions!
      Bless Yahweh, O my soul!

This psalm is probably the best known of all the songs of thanksgiving. A recent commentator calls it "one of the purest blossoms on the tree of Biblical faith,"[7] and most interpreters agree with this judgment. Yet, the poet is not a creative thinker. He knows the literary treasures of his nation so well that his language is imbued with their thought,[8] but his originality should not be denied, for it appears in the unique structural plan within which he brings together well-tried and proved ideas.

The psalmist begins by addressing his own soul and bids it to praise God and to remember "all his benefits" (vss. 1-5), thus making of his poem an authentic song of individual thanksgiving. Soon, however, his horizon broadens to embrace much more than his own experience. He knows that he is not alone in the vast company of men whose iniquities are forgiven, diseases are healed, life is redeemed, and youth is renewed like the eagle's. He thinks of all the oppressed whose cause is upheld by a compassionate God (vs. 6), and more particularly of Israel throughout her long history of sin, retribution, and deliverance (vss. 7-10). He is no longer singing in his own name, and he becomes the mouthpiece of the covenanted people as he recalls the judgments and saving deeds of Yahweh, ruler of mankind and keeper of the elected instrument of his revelation on earth.

---

[7] Artur Weiser, *Die Psalmen, in loc.*
[8] Cf. vs. 8 with Exod. 34:6-7; vs. 9 with Is. 57:14-21; vs. 15 with Is. 40:6-7 and Job 14:1-2; vs. 16*b* with Job 7:10.

In words which shoot a glimpse of the Gospel in the Old Testament the poet achieves nothing less than an epigrammatic creed: he explains the essentials of divinity (vss. 11-12) and uncovers the supreme mystery of the godhead.

> "Like as a father pitieth his children,
>   So Yahweh pitieth them that fear him" (vs. 13).

If God is "of purer eyes than to behold evil" (Hab. 1:13), his love is greater than to abandon mortal man, whose days are grass (Ps. 103:15). Nevertheless, this love is so profound that it cannot be offered to the four corners indiscriminately. Divine mercy is from everlasting to everlasting, but it is directed only toward them that fear God, keep his covenant, and remember his commandments (vss. 16-18). From the interweaving of these two contrasting elements—the awe of man before the law of holiness and the ready answer of man to the love which will not let him go—arises the distinctive mood of gratitude in which fear of a majestic God and love of an intimate friend commingle.

Beyond Israel lies the world, and the poet now looks at the universal dominion of his King (vs. 19). Emerging from a heart-to-soul musing within himself, he opens the doors to the wind-swept spaces and for a moment communes with the music of the spheres. The invitation to praise is now issued to the whole of the heavenly court, the angels "that excel in strength" and yet obey God's word, the hosts of his ministers "that do his pleasure," and even all his works, in all the provinces of his cosmic rule (vss. 20-22*ab*).

The song of thanksgiving which began as an intimate dialogue between a man and his soul—the totality of his being—has swollen to the volume of the universe. We hear for a few instants the hymns of the celestial chorus, but the final note reminds us of the psalmist's original intent. As the sound of brass, woodwinds, and strings is subdued in a swift decrescendo, the world fades out, and the immense perspectives are focused once more on the secret sanctuary of a single, serene, forgiven man, who then calls as he initially did, *sotto voce*, "Bless Yahweh, O my soul!" (Vs. 22*c*.)

The psalmist has reverently submitted himself to the word. That is the reason for which he does not thank or praise lightly. "As our attainments in godliness in this world, whatever they may be, come far short of perfection," wrote Calvin, "there remains only one pillar on which our salvation can securely rest, and that is the goodness of God."

V

The psalmists not only expressed their gratitude for victory in warfare or for deliverance from perils and the ever-recurrent threat of famine; they also and especially returned thanks for spiritual salvation. This highest theme appears briefly at the beginning of Ps. 65; but an individual song of thanksgiving, like Ps. 103, conceived in the intimacy of private worship, is much more suitable for its expression than the solemnity and pomp of congregational hymnody. Thus, most of the songs of thanksgiving which have been preserved in the Psalter were composed by and for individuals who were eager to sing their joy over their personal experiences of forgiveness and restoration.

i

Not unlike David on his day of military triumph, a man who is victorious against himself and has overcome the tribulations of his soul is possessed by one paramount desire: to speak out the devotion which draws him toward his Saviour.

"I love Yahweh, for he hath heard . . ." (Ps. 116:1).

"I will extol thee, O Yahweh . . ." (Ps. 30:1; cf. Ps. 145:1).

"I will bless Yahweh at all times . . ." (Ps. 34:1).

"I will praise Yahweh with my whole heart . . ."
(Ps. 111:1; Ps. 138:1).

"While I live will I praise Yahweh ..." (Ps. 146:2).

The typical song of individual thanksgiving then proceeds to recall the recent crisis.

> "For thou hast delivered my soul from death,
>   Mine eyes from tears,
>   And my feet from falling ..." (Ps. 116:8).

At last, the psalmist concludes with an act of dedication.

> "I will walk before Yahweh
>   In the land of the living.
>   I believe, therefore have I spoken. ....
>   What shall I render unto Yahweh
>   For all his benefits toward me?
>   I will take the cup of salvation,
>   And call upon the name of Yahweh"
>   (Ps. 116:9-10, 12-13).

ii

The social concept is so powerfully ingrained within the religion of Israel that no joy can ever be expressed by an individual alone with his God, and the "church" is invited to share the feelings of any forgiven man.

> "Sing unto Yahweh, O ye saints of his,
>   And give thanks at the remembrance of his holiness!"
>   (Ps. 30:4.)

> "O magnify Yahweh with me,
>   And let us exalt his name together!" (Ps. 34:3.)

> "Come and hear, all ye that fear God,
>   And I will declare what he hath done for my soul"
>   (Ps. 66:16).

> "I will pay my vows now unto Yahweh
>   In the presence of all his people" (Ps. 116:14, 16).

Thus the companionship of enjoyment is the seal of sanctification. The community is never far from the inner chamber of immediate religion. The psalmists believe in "the communion of the saints."

Gratitude is the sinew of faith, and it begets a lifelong acclimatizing in humble dependence on God and confidence in his promise. A new class of psalms has its place beside the songs of thanksgiving. They are the "Psalms of Trust."

2 | PSALMS OF TRUST

THE personal laments and the songs of thanksgiving
have led us to the core of faith. As the tribulations and deliverances
of Israel are mirrored in the life of individuals, so also the faith of
the people, which endures from generation to generation, is reflected
in the faith of the ordinary man, living from day to day.

In a sense the laments intoned from the depths may well be called
"Psalms of Trust," for they would never have been composed had
their poets remained jaw-locked in sin or paralyzed in isolation and
despair. Thus, there is legitimate ground for Gunkel's classification according to which the psalms of trust are to be considered as
a subtype of the individual laments. Nevertheless, the songs of
faith differ greatly from the prayers of crisis. Although they origi-
nate without exception from men who have passed through narrow
straits, the word "lament" can in no wise adequately designate the
peculiarities of their form, the serenity of their feeling, and especially the certainty of their thought.

These psalms constitute a separate class. To be sure, they are
subtly tinged with the memories of fears gone by; they betray the
scars left by hard-won fights; they foresee the possible resumption
of "the battle! That solves every doubt;" but they reveal a resolve
to face calmly any eventual crisis. Because they come from men
who have known the gall of misery, they are devoid of arrogance.
Unlike the laments, however, they emerge from spiritual security
and abundance.

Some, like Ps. 27, stand out vividly in an atmosphere of peril
and they naturally conclude in the form of request. Others, like

Pss. 121 and 23, although they do not ignore the realities of evil, are pure hymns of praise, reduced to the miniature scale of personal intimacy with God.

I

My Light and My Salvation
(Psalm 27)

I

1. Yahweh is my light and my salvation:
       Whom shall I fear?
    Yahweh is the strength of my life:
       Of whom shall I be afraid?

2. When the wicked come upon me
       To eat up my flesh,
    Even mine enemies and my foes,
       They shall stumble and fall.

3. Though an host should encamp against me,
       My heart shall not fear;
    Though war should rise against me,
       Even then will I trust.

II

4. One thing have I desired of Yahweh,
       That will I seek after:
    That I may dwell in the house of Yahweh
       All the days of my life,
    To behold the beauty of Yahweh,
       And to meditate in his temple.

5. For he shall hide me in his pavilion
       In the day of evil;
    He shall conceal me in the secret of his tent;
       He shall set me up upon a rock.

6.   And now shall my head be lifted up
          Above mine enemies round about me;
       And I will offer in his tabernacle
          Sacrifices of joy.
          I will sing, yea, I will sing praises unto Yahweh.

                                   III

7.   Hear, O Yahweh, my voice [when] I cry;
          Have mercy also upon me and answer me!
8.   [When thou sayest,] Seek ye my face,
          My heart answers thee,
       Thy face, O Yahweh, do I seek;
9.   Hide not thy face far from me!

       Put not thy servant away in anger,
          [For] thou hast been my help!
       Leave me not, neither forsake me,
          O God of my salvation!
10.   If my father and my mother forsake me,
          Then, Yahweh will take me up.

11.   Teach me thy way, O Yahweh,
          And lead me on a level path,
          On account of my watching enemies!
12.   Deliver me not over to the will of my foes,
          For false witnesses have risen up against me,
          And such as breathe out violence.

13.   [Woe to me] if I did not believe to see
          The goodness of Yahweh in the land of the living!
14.   Wait for Yahweh! Be of good courage!
          And let thine heart be strengthened!
          Wait, I say, on Yahweh!

Most commentators of our day believe that this psalm has been artifically made of two independent pieces: a song of trust (vss. 1-6) and a prayer of supplication (vss. 7-14). However, while the contrast between praise in the first section and request in the second is obvious at a glance, a deep unity of ideas and even of style permeates the whole poem. The attitude of assured confidence which characterizes the former half is not absent from the latter, and the fearful situation which forms the background of the second half is distinctly present in the first. The admittedly marked difference, far from indicating a duality of authorship, is due to a simple and common psychological phenomenon: the transition from a state of meditation to the mood of prayer. Other psalms, like Pss. 9 and 25, and many passages of Job offer excellent parallels to this literary peculiarity.

As a matter of fact, a scrutinous analysis of the text reveals that the poem does not even divide itself in two antithetical parts (praise by a man at rest and petition by a man in distress), but falls naturally in three related groups of three strophes each (vss. 1-3; 4-6; 7-12), followed by a crowning stanza (vss. 13-14). As is usually the case, the recognition of the strophic structure offers the clue to the interpretation of the thought.

i

Here is an individual whose metal has been tested and tempered by the shock of sudden and sustained fears, the cold of long apprehensions, the heat of exerting conflicts. He knows well "whereof he speaketh" when he describes his God as "my light and my salvation, . . . the fortress of my life," and repeatedly asks "Whom shall I fear? . . . Of whom shall I be afraid?" (Vs. 1.) This accumulation of terms and this insistence at once betray the terrors of the "life situation" which confronts him.

> "What though my shrinking flesh complain,
> And murmur to contend so long?"[1]

New struggles are at hand; anguish and doubts assail him; he does not yet pray, but his meditation must sooner or later yield to his violent emotions and break forth into prayer. His faith is the only stay which keeps him safe on the edge of the precipice. The word "faith" loses its meaning unless it is projected against a back-

---

[1] Charles Wesley, "Come, O Thou Traveller Unknown."

drop of insecurity and the dizziness of height. Anything may still happen: the stings of private enemies, the devices of political oppressors, or the horrors of war. Threats can shatter his inner strength; his resistance is limited; but there is the reality of faith. "Even then will I trust" (vs. 3). Fear of men has but transient room in the spirit of one who has handed over his life to the care of an omnipotent and benevolent God. He can afford to hold in contempt his dread of the unknown as long as God is for him, as it were, a citadel erected on a high rock, a stronghold capable of braving all assaults. Indeed, the first part of the psalm has not been composed by a man at ease. Its undertones are vibrant with lurking perils, and only its dominating melody is that of triumphant trust. The psalmist has created on the individual level a vignette of Ps. 46, "A Mighty Fortress Is Our God!"

ii

As the development moves forward into the second part, we are given to witness the central character of Hebrew spirituality.[2] The psalmist's religion is never separate from worship in Zion, but it aims at a reality which lies beyond the mere externals of Temple trappings and public piety. Observe the articulation of his thought through the succession of the verbs, "desire, seek, dwell, behold, meditate." A single desire spurs his search: he wishes to inhabit the courts of the Temple, not only for a visit during the festal season or even a longer sojourn, but "all the days of [his] life" (vs. 4). A man beset on all sides, who has seen death close by, does not risk mistaking the technicalities of ecclesiastical architecture or the intricacies of liturgics for the end of his religious endeavor. He does not wish to remain for life in the Temple precincts merely to play in the sacred orchestra. The ultimate object of his desire is "to behold the beauty of Yahweh and to meditate in his temple."

In thus expressing his supreme and most constant ambition, the poet offers unwittingly a description of himself and of his inward purity. He knows that the vision of God himself is not accessible

---

[2] See above, pp. 93 ff., 117 f.

to human eyes, but he aspires to "gazing upon the delightfulness," or "the pleasantness of Yahweh," and to "contemplating." This last word is perhaps the best English rendering of the Hebrew expression, "to reflect meditatively in his temple." Contemplation is the sublime exercise of the devout spirit, the active concentration of all human energies toward a more penetrating knowledge of the purposeful goodness and graciousness of the divine toward the human. The act of contemplating—as the derivation of the word shows—is originally the privilege of a man in the "Temple," and it means for an individual not only the will to look lovingly and expectantly at the deeds and promises of God but also the desire to enjoy, in the midst of the community of other worshipers, the public services of praise and adoration; it begins with the social participation of the individual in the aesthetic rehearsal of the Word which God has revealed of himself in the history of the nations and of the chosen people. It is rooted in corporate sharing in the drama of the liturgy, but it thrusts the individual forward and leads him dynamically beyond the forms and limitations of the cult toward the most secret holy of holies until the "thou and I" encounter is consummated and man is met by God alone. To be sure, the human finiteness is never immersed and lost within the divine infinite,

> "Yet high above the limits of my seeing,
>   And folded far within the inmost heart,
>   And deep below the deeps of conscious being,
> Thy splendor shineth; there, O God, Thou art."[3]

The psalmist has experienced such moments. He longs for their renewal, because on them the solidity and constancy of his trust ultimately depend. They are not bestowed on many men, and even for the few thus enriched they remain sparse and far apart. Hence the need for a faith to fill up the long, sterile, and lonesome gaps which are familiar to all the saints. It is an obstinately sustained trust which enables the poet to survive. Quickened by one unifying

---

3 Eliza Scudder, "Who By Searching Can Find Out God?"

factor, he is freed from a dispersion of his life motives and the scattering process of conflicting ambitions; he moves ahead toward a single aim because he obeys the drive of a single desire. "One thing . . . will I seek after."

No one needs then to wonder at the inevitability of the consequences. God will hide him in the evil day, not in the Temple, as usual translations might mislead us into believing, but in his own "hut," "booth," or "pavilion," in "the secret of his tent" and the security of a high rock. The plurality and the inconsistency of these images shows that the psalmist is no longer thinking of Zion in a literal sense. He anticipates the shelter which God provides even "now" (vs. 6). The certainty of his future deliverance from eventual dangers is so concrete that he imagines in advance his acts of gratitude: the offering of a sacrifice of thanksgiving and a song of praise. His faith, like that of Israel in its hymns of history, stands above the categories of past, present and future. Through trust in Yahweh he conquers not only his fears but even "cunning time" and his ignorance of the morrow.

iii

Soliloquy is no longer an adequate mode of expression when man is thrilled with the hope of God's help in trouble. In his exultation the psalmist does not forget that he can do nothing by himself, that he is wholly dependent on the power of God, and that his faith is not the work of his own hands but the result of utter reliance on the divine will. Thus prayer bursts forth from the mood of meditation (vss. 7-12). The unity which binds the psalm into a homogeneous whole from its inception to its completion appears in some remarkable parallels of ideas and even of expressions which are found between the preceding sections and the third part of the development.

"Thy face, O Yahweh, do I seek" (vs. 8) corresponds to "One thing . . . will I seek" (vs. 4); likewise, the search for the face of Yahweh (vs. 8) answers the wish to behold his "delightful beauty" (vs. 4); moreover, all the declarations contained in the first part (vss. 1-3) are echoed and summed up in the statement of the third, "Thou hast been my help" (vs. 9); and, finally, the supplication is only an acknowledgment of God's initial invitation (vs. 8). The poet prays because he responds to the call, "Seek ye my face!" While the style is elliptical, the sense is not doubtful. Besides, such an experience has been duplicated and indeed verified by countless mystics of all ages who heard their God say, "Thou wouldst not seek me, had I not already found thee,"[4] and who replied, "It sufficed that I was found of thee."[5]

A rigid dogmatist may ask the poet, "Canst thou by searching find out God?" (Job 11:7.) Yet the church of Israel read in its own history the patient protest of that same God: "I said not unto the seed of Jacob, Seek ye me in vain" (Is. 45:19). So also, when we turn toward him, it is he who allures us, and we merely heed his call and reply, Amen. His love is greater than the highest among men, that of a father and of a mother (vs. 9; cf. Is. 49:15). To such a God man may confidently speak in the words of Horatius Bonar:

> "Thy way, not mine, O Lord,
> However dark it be!
> Lead me by thine own hand,
> Choose out the path for me."

Not necessarily the smooth and easy route, but the plain course, "a level path," i.e., "a path of uprightness," "on account of my watching enemies" (vs. 11). To be sure, the psalmist prays for a safe road, but his petition is not devoid of ethical meaning. "He who thus desires to commit himself to the safeguard and protection of God, must first renounce crafty and wicked devices," wrote Calvin. "We must not expect that God, who promises to grant a happy issue only to the single in heart, and those who trust in his faithfulness, will bless crooked and wicked counsels."

---

[4] Paraphrasing the familiar words of Augustine and Pascal.
[5] Edward Dowden, "Seeking God."

A final strophe brings this song of trust to its culmination (vss. 13-14). The prayer is now ended, but again the perception of proximate threats is so harrowing that common sense alone would yield to despair. Faith is the poet's only means of survival.

> "If I did not believe to see
>   The goodness of Yahweh in the land of the living . . ."

The sentence remains unfinished, for the prospect is too horrible for verbal formulation. Moreover, there is no faith so well rooted that it is immune to doubt. Turning therefore from God to himself, the poet admonishes his own will in a twofold, complementary way. "Wait for Yahweh," or as the older version of the Anglican Prayer Book had it, "O tarry thou the Lord's leisure!" This self-injunction, which is repeated emphatically in the final line, is not tantamount to passive or static quietism; it is an active, even an intensive, although patient, form of waiting, comparable to that proposed to the prophet Habakkuk (2:3). In short, a composed and willful expectancy. And the first *mot d'ordre* is continued and qualified by the second: "Be of good courage!" Or, as the Greek translation of the Septuagint rendered it, "Be manly!" "Act as a man!" These are the mottoes of the psalmist. His faith relies on hopeful waiting. But it loses thereby nothing of its virility.

Songs of trust are not inspired by "dew-pearled hilltops." They grow in a world of bewilderment very much like our own.

II

"Whence Cometh My Help?"
(Psalm 121)

I

1.   I lift up mine eyes unto the hills:
          Whence cometh my help?
2.   My help [cometh] from Yahweh,
          Which made heaven and earth.

II

3. He will not suffer thy foot to be moved;
 He that keepeth thee will not slumber.
4. Behold, he shall neither slumber nor sleep,
 That keepeth Israel.

III

5. Yahweh is thy keeper;
 Yahweh is thy shade upon thy right hand.
6. By day the sun shall not smite thee,
 Nor the moon by night.

IV

7. Yahweh shall preserve thee from all evil,
 He shall preserve thy soul.
8. Yahweh shall preserve thy going out and thy coming in,
 From this time forth, and even forevermore.

This gem of Hebrew psalmody elicits a unanimity of admiration but not of interpretation. As a song of ascents it was used during the postexilic period by pilgrims who were on their way to Zion for the celebration of festivals; was it specifically composed for this purpose? Why did the poet look up to the hills? What did the hills mean to him? Scholars are sharply divided among themselves as they try to answer these apparently simple questions.

i

One detail of importance rallies the opinion of all. In spite of the traditional renderings, including that of the King James Version, it is impossible to consider the opening verse as forming a single sentence and to translate:

  "I will lift up mine eyes unto the hills,
   From whence cometh my help."

The Hebrew word which introduces the second clause is not a relative, but an interrogative adverb of location, and we are compelled to construe this verse as forming two independent phrases:

"I lift up mine eyes unto the hills:
Whence cometh my help?"

In addition, the context which follows (vs. 2) shows that this help
does not come from the hills, but originates, far beyond them, from
Yahweh alone, who is not only their creator but also "the maker
of heaven and earth."

The question may still legitimately be asked, Was it the sight
of the hills which caused the poet to feel the need of help, or was
it rather on account of a previous state of fear that he raised his
eyes toward them?

Many scholars suppose that the psalmist was a sixth-century
exile who lived perforce in the fertile but flat land of Babylonia
and turned toward the barren hills yonder (which his eyes could
not even see) because they symbolized for him the religion of his
fathers. He found a ready help in the faith that Yahweh, "who
made heaven and earth," was taking care of his own, even though
Zion had been laid waste and the people decimated or dispersed.
This interpretation disregards the context, as the whole poem suggests beyond doubt a scene of travel by day and night toward a
distant goal (see vss. 3-7).

One exegete has recently suggested that the sight of the hills was
for the poet a source, not of comfort or inspiration, but on the contrary of dismay and anguish: as he started on his journey he remembered the many dangers threatening a caravan and even more ˘
a lonely traveler in a mountainous region; the paths are rocky and
narrow, leading man and beast along precipitous slopes, and brig-
ands lie in wait behind boulders, cliffs, and defiles. In his distress
the pilgrim cried, "Whence cometh my help?" And he received the
answer of his faith.

Against this down-to-earth and attractive explanation, there is
a strong argument. In Biblical Hebrew the expression "to lift up
the eyes unto" has a favorable meaning and suggests a mood of
pleasure, desire, hope, and even love and adoration (cf. Gen. 39:7;
Ps. 123:1; Deut. 3:27; 4:19; Ezek. 8:5; Is. 51:6; etc.). In other
words, the psalmist most probably looked up toward the mountains

"whose sunbright summit mingles with the sky" because he was moved by a feeling of longing and expectancy. Moreover, perils which confront travelers do not lurk in the heights but are hidden in the dark recesses of canyons, gorges, and glens toward which no one needs to "lift up his eyes" in order to see them. Most likely the psalmist was a pilgrim going up to a hilltop shrine in order to find God there.

A further question remains: where? Following Ehrlich and Gunkel, many contemporary students believe that the poet was bewildered by the multiplicity of the "high places," those ancient sanctuaries of Palestine which had been taken over from the Canaanites and were still considered by the populace as the abodes of some divine beings. In his religious confusion the poet looked up, first to one mountain, then to another, and he asked in effect, "To which one of these sacred crests shall I ascend and bring my adoration?" The answer was not delayed: "No help is to come from any of those hills; thy help cometh from Yahweh, who made the whole of them!" This interpretation, attractive as it may be, is hardly possible, for the remainder of the poem shows that the psalmist was never tempted by any lingering survival of polytheistic belief. His conception of God was so universalistic that no room whatever was left in his mind for the existence of other deities.

Pursuing this general line of thought, however, a smiliar hypothesis in a modified form might still be considered. The "high places" had indeed been adapted from paganism to the cult of Yahweh, but they still sheltered many superstitious practices which were incompatible with the true religion of Israel. Because these shrines fostered a self-centered piety rather than a selfless devotion to the will of God, they were strongly denounced by the prophets of the eighth and seventh centuries (Amos 7:9; Hos. 10:8; II Kings 16:4; Jer. 17:3; etc.) and finally destroyed by King Josiah (621 B.C.) in his effort to implement the Deuteronomic law on centralization of worship in Jerusalem (Deut. 12:2 ff.; cf. II Kings 23:5 ff.). Nevertheless, the ancient shrines on the hilltops, where generations had worshiped Yahweh, were still dear to the hearts of many peasants and village dwellers. Perhaps the psalmist was one of them, and as he set foot on his lawful pilgrimage he could not refrain from remembering with wistfulness the solemnity of revered and hallowed rites which were no more. Respect for old forms and family traditions, especially in spiritual matters, has deep virtue. Many in later life have returned to a sane outlook and a wholesome conduct simply by remembering "the decent church that topped the neighbouring hill."

On the other hand, mere faithfulness to the religion of the past does not represent the spirit of Biblical Christianity. The great prophets and Jesus clearly and courageously saw that new wine could not be kept in old skins. As Voltaire wrote, "the more ancient the abuse, the more sacred it is," and the more pernicious it becomes. What was right, perhaps, at a certain moment of history, may be wrong in a new age.

> "The old order changeth, yielding place to new,
> And God fulfils Himself in many ways,
> Lest one good custom should corrupt the world."[6]

Casting a longing glance upon the hills where his ancestors had prayed and adored for centuries, the poet indulged in a bit of misgiving and regret; he may even have questioned the wisdom of Josiah's reform; but, swiftly bracing himself, he threw away his doubts by declaring in an intimate dialogue:

> "My help [cometh] from Yahweh,
> Which made heaven and earth!"

Because of a total lack of evidence, it seems preferable, on the whole, to reject all these conjectures, and to understand the "hills" as referring to Zion. The use of the plural number constitutes no valid argument against this identification. Although the Temple of Jerusalem was built on a single height, it was customary to speak of "the hills of Zion" (Pss. 87:1; 133:3; cf. 125:2). If we follow this view, we may discover in this psalm a profound message.

---

[6] Alfred, Lord Tennyson, "Morte d'Arthur."

ii

The poet was a pilgrim on his way to the Temple, and he looked up eagerly to the holy mountains, or at least to the ranges which led to Jerusalem. At the same time, he understood that his true succor came from above and beyond those summits. Like his fellow singers who composed hymns in honor of the Lord of Zion, he was devoutly cognizant of the sanctity of the Temple, but the eyes of his faith reached farther than "the ramparts of a Godhead's dwelling," to the very God who transcends nature, history, *and* Zion.

This ancient traveler should not be "caricatured" as a modern alpinist whose aesthetic and religious sensitivity is stimulated by the majesty of snowy peaks. (In any case, the Palestinian range is not comparable to the Alps.) No doubt, like other Hebrew poets, he felt in a deep way the beauty of nature, and he must have been at once attracted, sobered, and inspired by the sight of the "everlasting hills," and more especially by the vision of the Temple ceremonial which they suggested to his mind. Yet he did not confuse the end with the means of attaining it. His was a religion of immediacy in faith.

Coleridge, waiting before sunrise in the Valley of Chamonix, began by addressing the Mont Blanc, saying:

> "... Thou, most awful Form!
> Risest from forth thy silent sea of pines,
> How silently! Around thee and above
> Deep is the air and dark, substantial, black,
> An ebon mass: methinks thou piercest it,
> As with a wedge! But when I look again,
> It is thine own calm home, thy crystal shrine,
> Thy habitation from eternity!"[7]

Nevertheless, he continued with this significant shift of stress:

---

[7] Samuel Taylor Coleridge, "Hymn Before Sunrise in the Vale of Chamouni."

> "O dread and silent Mount! I gazed upon thee,
>   Till thou, still present to the bodily sense,
>   Didst vanish from my thought: entranced in prayer
> I worshiped the Invisible alone."[8]

Centuries before him, the Hebrew singer had known how to distinguish between love of beauty in nature or sanctuary, and faith in God, awesome, invisible, eternal, and present. Majestic scenes of nature, events of history, and all the Zions, may exhibit God to man only when man already knows God in personal and secret trust.

iii

Like all the other songs of faith this psalm was born in an atmosphere of insecurity and distress. But as the lines follow each other with repetition of key words according to the poetic device of concatenation, or staircase progression ("help," "slumbereth not," "keepeth," or "preserveth" which in the Hebrew text is the same verb used six times), the feeling of anguish gradually disappears and is swallowed up in certainty. Observe the change which takes place already between vs. 3 and vs. 4. In the former the poet formulates a wish, and the text should be translated:

> "May he not suffer thy foot to stumble!
>   May thy keeper not slumber!" (Vs. 3.)

But in the latter, the same idea is expressed as a simple affirmation of faith, as if the wish implied a doubt which is now eradicated:

> "Behold, he neither slumbereth nor sleepeth,
>   The keeper of Israel!" (Vs. 4.)

Several critics have been disturbed by the mention of Israel at this place. On the contrary, the reader ought to rejoice at this

---
[8] *Ibid.*

typically Biblical trait. The individual believer is never detached from the body of the church to which he belongs. His assurance teaches us that in our desire to receive God's gracious care and protection we must always begin with the promises he has made to his whole people. There are moments in the history of the church as well as in the history of individuals when our guardian appears to slumber, but our trust in his watchful providence should never be obscured by our limited or hasty observations of the passing moment. We, as creatures, are a part of the vast design of salvation which is unfolding from generation to generation on this earth. The psalmist holds fast to the testimony of the fathers (Gen. 28:13-15), and he is no longer lost in an impersonal stream of events. He feels at the right place in the universe, for his keeper is the keeper of Israel. He goes forward without fear of stumbling (vs. 3), of being struck by the heat of the sun or by the malignant impact of "moonstrokes" (vss. 5-6). This ancient belief in the pernicious influence of the moon may very well belong to the realm not of superstition but of practical experience; as modern chemists are well aware, the shades of dyed textiles will fade much faster when they are exposed to the light of a full moon rather than to the rays of the sun.

In any case, with a few examples the poet disposes of the fears most likely to assail a pilgrim. Laid open to common discomforts and perils, like any other earthly being, the man of God will proceed, not undisturbed; he will be ashamed of his recurrent anxieties, but not paralyzed by the risks encountered on the road. Committing his life to the will of the ruler and overruler of all men and events, he will return home as he went abroad. In all circumstances of his existence he will rely only on the power and the grace of the lord of the "church." His "going out" and his "coming in" (an expression which referred to the whole of human existence: cf. II Sam. 3:25; Is. 37:28) will take him toward his ultimate destination.

Beyond the hills, above all that is majestic and excellent in the world, lies the object of man's trust against perils. This psalm, with its extremely simple and yet almost inaccessible lesson, leads us in our daily living from our fears and our false confidences to the acceptance of salvation by faith alone.

III

"The Lord Is My Shepherd"
(Psalm 23)

I

1. Yahweh is my shepherd:
        I shall not want.
2. He maketh me to lie down in green pastures;
        He leadeth me beside the still waters;
3.   He restoreth my soul.

II

He leadeth me in the paths of righteousness
    For his name's sake.
4. Yea, though I walk through the valley of the shadow of death,
        I fear no evil,
        For thou art with me.
    Thy rod and thy staff,
        They comfort me.

III

5. Thou preparest a table before me
        In the presence of mine enemies;
    Thou anointest my head with oil;
        My cup runneth over.
6. Only goodness and mercy shall pursue me
        All the days of my life,
    And I will dwell in the house of Yahweh
        For the length of [my] days.

When we read this best known and most beloved of all psalms,
we are face to face with an art as simple and great as the religion
which it clothes. Before a true masterpiece, should not the interpreter step aside and vanish? The poem shines forth and speaks to
any reader who will come toward it with the freshness and expectancy of a child. We must sing it with the spirit, but we must sing
it "with the understanding also" (I Cor. 14:15).

Let us first of all ask whether we are justified in calling this psalm "The Shepherd Song." Most commentators believe that the image of the shepherd is used only in the first two strophes (vss. 1-3*a;* 3 *bc*-4) and is abruptly replaced in the third (vss. 5-6) by the similitude of the gracious host who, in his desert tent, offers asylum to a fugitive, an outlaw, or a runaway slave. Some critics have even suggested that the psalm actually contains three distinct images: the shepherd in the first strophe (vss. 1-3*a*); the caravan leader in the second (vss. 3*bc*-4), and the Bedouin host in the third (vss. 5-6). In all probability, though not with demonstrable certainty, the pastoral scene of the first verses is continued throughout the psalm, which then presents a complete homogeneity in its artistic treatment as well as in its religious intention.[9]

The ancient Hebrews were nomads who drove flocks over large pastures for centuries before they finally settled in Palestine and learned the arts of husbandry. Even during the Biblical period the Israelites were shepherds as well as farmers, and they well knew the infinite amount of care, patience, skill, and sometimes self-sacrificing heroism required of the pastoral vocation. Therefore, no description of divine love and care for man could be more eloquent in their minds than the comparison of God to a shepherd. As it was natural for a closely knit society, conscious above all of its corporate unity, this pregnant image was used more often in relation to the people as a whole than to the individual man of faith. Yahweh was truly "the shepherd of Israel" (Gen. 49:24; cf. Ps. 80:1). For the prophets who saluted the dawn of a new age, Yahweh would "shepherd" the people "like a lamb in a large place" (Hos. 4:16). During the Babylonian Exile, when the Judeans felt lost "as sheep that have not a shepherd" (I Kings 22:17), their faith was rekindled with the hope that God would "search" them and "seek them out . . . , as a shepherd seeketh out his flock . . . ,

---

[9] This view was proposed almost half a century ago by Faddul Moghabghab, a Christian Arab. In an attractive study, *Four Psalms, XXIII, XXXVI, LII, CXXI, Interpreted for Practical Use* (London: Hodder and Stoughton, 1896), George Adam Smith attempted likewise to safeguard the unity of the poem by suggesting that the host was also the shepherd, but he admitted that man was compared first to a sheep, then to a human fugitive, thereby falling back on the traditional interpretation.

out of all places where they have been scattered, in the cloudy and dark day" (Ezek. 34:11 ff.). Likewise, Second Isaiah preached the good news and sang:

> "He shall feed his flock as a shepherd;
>> He shall gather the lambs in his arms;
> He shall carry them in his bosom;
>> He shall gently lead those that are with young"
>>> (Is. 40:11; cf. 49:9; 63:14).

The psalmists also rejoiced and thanked God in the thought that they belonged to "the people of his pasture" and were "the sheep of his hand" (Pss. 95:7; 100:3; cf. 28:9; 79:13). The relationship of the individual to his God was even depicted with the same image at an early date. According to the traditions recorded in the Elohist strand of the Hexateuch (ninth or eighth centuries B.C.), Jacob spoke of "the God which shepherded me all my life long [literally, "from my youth"] unto this day . . ." (Gen. 48:15). Thus, the psalmist knew that he would sound deep echoes in the memory of his fellows when he simply said:

> "The Lord is my shepherd:
> I shall not want" (vs. 1).

The whole of faith is contained in this first line. It constitutes in itself a complete, all-inclusive creed, which is thereafter illustrated in three different scenes of pastoral existence.

i

At the grazing ground (vss. 1-3*a*), the skillful shepherd knows the places where the grass is fresh, thick, and green. After the sheep have eaten their fill, he does not immediately lead them to drink; otherwise, some of them might bloat to death. Then he takes them to quiet streams, not torrents where the current is treacherous or the water icy, but to cool pools of stillness where all can safely find refreshment and life again. God provides for all the needs of man, and he knows which diet and schedule are appropriate for man's well-being. As grazing requires walking over an extensive area, sheep are often exhausted, since they literally have "worked for their living"; but a shepherd's foresight and considerate planning bring them back to life: "He restoreth my soul" (vs. 3). This expression refers primarily to the physical release from thirst, but the poetic mind of an Oriental does not establish any clear distinction between the material and the spiritual realms of existence. Without imposing an artificial method of allegorical interpretation, we may find here a confession of gratitude after an experience of total rebirth and quickening.

ii

As a flock migrates from one meadow to another (vss. 3*bc*-4), dangers constantly arise along the way. The shepherd, however, knows the right track. For the honor of his name, he selects the best route; he does not mislead his sheep. Yet, narrow vales may not always be avoided. Although the Hebrew word *tsalmûth* means "deep shadow" and should not be read as *tsal maweth*, "the shadow of death," traditional translations are faithful to the intention of the poet, for death indeed awaits sheep in precipices and caves. As the poet now remembers vividly some experience of a narrow escape, his emotion of fear comes abruptly to the fore of his consciousness and transforms the mood of quiet meditation into that of prayer.

> "I fear no evil,
> For thou art with me" (vs. 4).

It is the proximate and real presence of the shepherd which calms the frets of sheep and man. Not only "thy rod," this sturdy club for which jackals, wolves, and other wild beasts have developed a healthy respect, but also "thy staff," this long stick which thou art sometimes compelled to use upon me, dumb and obstinate sheep that I am, *"they* comfort me." The psalmist acknowledges man's unwillingness to follow in the paths of righteousness. He is well aware of his stupid rebelliousness. As a sheep is tempted, even in the "glen of gloom," to go astray or to stay behind for some attractive grass on a rocky slope, likewise man in spite of his best judgment or sometimes out of plain imbecility will flirt with peril while seeking self-interest. He needs the strokes of correction. He may even at length learn to expect them and thereby find comfort in God's watchful and stern discipline. There is solace in the teaching of sorrow. A true leader not only shows the right way but also commands, calls, warns, and—whenever necessary—scolds and chastens. Suffering is not always the consequence or the evidence of sin, but, as Browning wrote:

> "In the eye of God
> Pain may have purpose and be justified."

iii

It is against this background of naked realism and in this atmosphere of evil on earth that the third strophe must be understood, and thus it bestows on the poem a climactic significance (vss. 5-6). Several critics among those who think that the image of the shepherd now gives way to that of the welcoming host are uneasy about the mention of the "enemies." Why should God, they ask, prepare a table for his guest in the presence of the foes? Is it in order to taunt them in their impotence? The implication is rather unfortunate, these scholars continue, for the line conveys a suggestion of boasting on the part of the poet, thereby marring the limpidity and serenity of the thought. This difficulty disappears when the third strophe is interpreted as maintaining the image of the shepherd. The expression "prepare a table" does not necessarily refer to a scene of human hospitality in a sheik's tent. The verb *arakh*, which came to mean "to prepare," originally referred to the "setting in order" of the battleground. The noun *shulchan*, which in a sedentary community came to mean "table," referred originally to "the spreading" of a cloak or leather skin on the ground. Now the primary task of a shepherd in the Near East is to *prepare* the pasture *ahead* of his flock. He carefully surveys the grazing area, and as he goes he uproots noxious weeds that sheep never learn to avoid (even today some unskilled or negligent shepherds lose many sheep through accidental poisoning), he cuts off thorny thistles or cacti which would otherwise scratch the ears, eyes, nostrils, lips, tongue, legs, and other sensitive parts of the grazing animals. He also uncovers the nests of snakes and scorpions, destroys them with various devices and thus, sometimes through actual struggle, "prepares before" the sheep a decent, pleasant, and safe pasture ground "in the presence of" the sheep's multitudinous enemies.

Nevertheless, accidents still happen. At eventide, when the flock is gathered to the fold, the shepherd examines his sheep one by one as they file in. Bruised and bloody heads are anointed with oil, and the animals which are sick with fatigue and fright receive in an actual earthen "cup" a medicinal potion made usually of fermented hemp or barley mixed with honey and therapeutic herbs. It must be noted that the phrase "My cup runneth over" in all probability should be translated "my cup is intoxicating" (cf. several uses of the verb from which the word *rewayah* is derived: Prov. 5:19; 17: 18; Is. 34:5).

In other words, while the similitude of the gracious host is not impossible, the image of the shepherd, if maintained in the third strophe, carries a powerfully religious significance. God is a shepherd who painstakingly and tenderly nurses the wounds and ailments of my existence. He is not only my feeder and my leader; he is also the healer of my diseases: a deft and devoted physician.

The experience of the poet is complete. Instead of the traditional foes which harass the sheep,

> "Only goodness and mercy shall pursue me
> All the days of my life" (vs. 6).

The verb "pursue" (rather than the weak "follow") is a final allusion to the evil realities of this earth. The man of God is exposed to the *pursuit* of divine love and affection. "Fear wist not to evade,

as Love wist to pursue."[10] He will then "dwell in the house of Yahweh," literally, "for a length of days." This difficult expression
seems to allude to "old age" (cf. Deut. 30:20; Job 12:12; Ps. 91:
16; Prov. 3:2) or "a long time" (Pss. 21:4; 93:5; Prov. 3:16;
Lam. 5:20). It is therefore most improbable that the original poet
had in mind the idea of life everlasting. Yet, as his psalm became
the property of later Judaism and Christianity, readers have rightly
found in those words the symbol of their hope for an eternal dwelling in the house of their Lord. What could have been the meaning
intended by the psalmist? In the event that he was a Temple singer,
then he probably meant that he would live till the end of his earthly
life in the precincts of the sanctuary. Obviously, however, he was
a professional shepherd, a man of the vast outdoors, trekking along
the ranges of the mountains and breathing the air of the open
spaces. He may have been bold enough to suggest that, for him,
life under the care of his true pastor was like a continuous dwelling
in the temple.

This supreme psalm of trust is not a pastoral idyl. Its poet, far
from being sheltered and protected from historical reality, has
passed through grim experiences. Yet his faith has made him triumph, not only over his fears, but also over sadness. There is no
doubt that he was endowed with the grace of serenity in joyful
communion with a personally known God. His psalm breathes a
happiness that "the world cannot give." As we too easily forget
our provider when we enjoy peace and comfort, we may receive
from this song, first of all, an elementary lesson in quiet gratitude,
and a curiosity for seeking in our lives the tokens of divine benediction.

Notice, however, that the poet fears neither want (vs. 1) nor
peril (vs. 4) only because he recognizes the closeness of God in
his existence. "Thou art with me." Evil is not ignored, nor even
minimized, and foes are still in pursuit, but God-bronzed will power
enables him to look, not at his enemies, but at his real pursuers,
"goodness and mercy." Moreover, the tenses of the verbs clearly

---

[10] Francis Thompson, "The Hound of Heaven."

suggest that the past experience of evil may be repeated at any time. *"Whenever* I walk in the valley of the shadow of death . . ."" Such is the probable translation. Any new crisis is calmly envisaged. Thus, the psalmist unconsciously gives us a lesson in realism and in consecrated courage. He binds together the past and the future, and his faith intertwines his experience with his hope.

Nevertheless, he has not apparently descended into the lowest depths of misery, "Adown titanic glooms of chasmed fears."[11] Unlike Job or the poets of Pss. 22 and 130, he probably has never emptied the goblet of wormwood, and although he has been exposed to death, he has not tasted total sorrow, for he has not felt abandoned by men *and* God. This may explain why his acceptance of the divine gifts is slightly passive—not smug, to be sure, but facile and quietistic. This fact may account for the lack of the social dimension in his religious grasping. Unless he meant by "dwelling in the house of Yahweh" the fellowship of the "church," he was not seemingly aware of the blessings and of the responsibilities of corporate solidarity within the community of believers.

The absence of this element in his religion is the more astonishing when one thinks of the possibilities that the image of the flock might have suggested to his poetic mind. After all, the Hebrew word for "neighbor" and "friend" is derived from the term "grazer," "fellow sheep." The poet might have at least thought of his lost comrades:

> "For on the hill are many strayed,
> Some held in thickets plunge and cry,"[12]

and he might have brought the idea of their salvation within the realm of his religious happiness. We would, however, deal him an injustice, were we to condemn him for not being as profound a thinker as the poet of Job, Second Isaiah, and a few of the other psalmists. For his purpose was to sing trust in God and to deliver a glad witness, not to ponder on the mystery of injustice and perdition.

---

[11] *Ibid.*
[12] Ruth Pitter, "Help, Good Shepherd."

Finally, he taught in an unwitting way the virtue of true humility. Although he has not indicated that the reality of sin always impairs in some degree the harmony which may exist between God and man, even the greatest saints, he subtly suggested that the staff of his shepherd has a disciplinary connotation. It is never easy to follow the leader "on the right track." Whenever we repeat this line, we should lucidly and soberly pray to God, saying,

> *"I shall in all my best obey you . . .*
>   Only
> We have these dreams!
>   Only—
>   the old have announced us the
>   Irremediable woe, the ill
>   Long done, lost in the times before memory."[13]

When the psalmist used the image of the shepherd, he was not only describing God as a provider, guide, guardian, defender, healer, and even pursuer. He was also intimating that man, after all, is nothing but a dumb creature, for, as Aristotle observed long ago, sheep are "the most silly and foolish animals." Surely this psalm should not be a favorite among contemporary humanists. If man is compared to a sheep, then he is naturally moved by gregarious and selfish drives, not by control of his instincts, mastery of his greed, and lucidity of reflection. In order to live at all, he must rely entirely on the grace of one infinitely greater and wiser than he, completely surrender his discernment and conduct to the light and will of God, have a sense of his own weakness, poverty, and even destitution. In brief, he must live by trust in God alone, not by calculations or idolatry—of self or of others. He must consent to be led in plain and straight paths. That is the hard way. The psalmist preached no other.

In the end his humility sends us back to his understanding of the deity. His trust—and therefore the stifling of his pride—became possible because he was aware of the qualities of his shepherd. He

---

[13] Archibald MacLeish, *The Hamlet of A. MacLeish* (Boston: Houghton Mifflin Co., 1928). Quoted by permission of the publisher.

perceived in a dim and limited fashion that his pastor, like young David with the flock of Jesse (I Sam. 17:34-35; cf. Amos 3:12), would not spare his efforts, but would risk even his own safety for the sake of saving his sheep. Centuries afterward, a handful of men discerned this central element of the godhead: "A good shepherd layeth down his life for the sheep" (John 10:15).

This is the supreme reason for which men and women across the ages have found and still find in the Twenty-third Psalm, better perhaps than anywhere else, strength in temptation, peace in sorrow, and comfort in agony. At the elemental moments of their lives, they borrow its words as they commit themselves and their all to "the undiscouraged God."

IV

Trust is the motif which underlines the whole Psalter. It also characterizes the response of man to God's urgings and proddings throughout the Bible. Luther and the other reformers were true to Scripture when they stressed salvation by faith.

An ancient tradition recalls how Abraham "believed," that is to say, "leaned or relied firmly upon" God's word of promise, and his trust was "counted to him for righteousness" (Gen. 15:6). Likewise, the prophets well knew the intimate connection which exists between "faith" and "staith," a condition of firmness and stability that no exterior catastrophe or interior bewilderment can alter (Is. 7:9; cf. 28:16; 30:15). So also, in trusting, the psalmists received a quietude and a "peace of mind" which overcame the vicissitudes and even the tragedy of their existence (Pss. 62:1-2; 131:2).

> "He that dwelleth in the secret place of the Most High
> Shall abide under the shadow of the Almighty.
> He will say of Yahweh, He is my refuge and my fortress!
> My God! In him will I trust" (Ps. 91:1-2).

A few singers of faith went a step further than the others and told of the "delights" they experienced in God's continuous pres-

ence. The deity they adored was indeed the transcendent and holy
king of the universe:

> "Thy mercy, O Yahweh, is in the heavens,
>   And thy faithfulness reacheth unto the clouds;
> Thy righteousness is like the great mountains;
>   Thy judgments are like the great abyss!" (Ps. 36:5-6.)

But they not only glorified God, they also fully enjoyed him forever:

> "How excellent is thy lovingkindness, O God!
>   The sons of man take refuge under the shadow of thy wings;
> They drink to their fill the abundance of thy house;
>   Thou satisfiest them with the river of thy delights" (Ps. 36:7-8).

In using the word "delight" *(edhen)*, this poet was probably
alluding to paradise *(edhen)*, and he suggested that even now a
union with the divine was possible; the streams of grace watered
his soul and transmuted his whole being into a luxuriant garden.
He could then conclude, speaking on behalf of the community of
believers:

> "For with thee is the fountain of life;
>   In thy light shall we see light" (Ps. 36:9).

Lest, however, such holy pleasures be short-lived, he prayed:

> "O continue thy lovingkindness unto them that know thee,
>   And thy righteousness to the upright in heart" (Ps. 36:10).

Ethical accent and social sense are thus never absent from what
may be called "Biblical mysticism." Faith is not a blossom without fruit. Trust produces standards of behavior. Moreover the
man who in sheer faith makes the total commitment is not forever
left without the enchantment of God's companionship. Side by
side with the songs of trust, there are the "Psalms of 'Wisdom' and
Communion."

3 | PSALMS OF "WISDOM" AND COMMUNION

IT IS A NOTEWORTHY and somewhat startling fact that the highest expressions of fellowship with God in the Psalter emanate from men influenced by the schools of wisdom.

For centuries before the dawn of Hebrew religion the wise men or sages of Babylonia, Edom, and Egypt meditated on the meaning of human life. Most of them concluded that virtue or crime always finds its proper retribution. Hebrew sages, likewise, whose teachings are preserved mainly in the book of Proverbs (chs. 1-29), equated righteousness or "the fear of Yahweh" with prosperity, and ill-behavior or "folly" with misfortune and sudden death. A number of psalms which have been composed in the didactic style of the wisdom literature set forth this dogma of moralistic optimism: they hold that morality always reaps its reward (see particularly, in full or in part, Pss. 1, 14[53], 34, 94, 111, 112, 119, 127, 128, 144). Indeed, this note now dominates the Psalter as a whole, since the present edition of the anthology begins with a beatitude of the "wisdom" type:

"Blessed is the man
   That walketh not in the counsel of the ungodly,
   Nor standeth in the way of sinners,
   Nor sitteth in the seat of the scornful!
But his delight is in the law of Yahweh,
   And in his law doth he meditate day and night" (Ps. 1:1-2).

James Moffatt, the well-known translator of the Bible, once said, "I like the 'wisdom-psalms.' Some people think that they are not

239

as inspiring as the great cries of distress and deliverance which one finds in such pieces as Pss. 51 and 130, but we cannot breathe every day the rarefied air of the high mountains. We must come down to the plains, with their soft lines and lights, with the homely sights of trifles around us; and, after all, these meditations of the pious sages do not deal with trifles." Indeed, a quiet certainty animates their poetry, and a simple joy radiates from their words. Moreover, "blessedness" in Hebrew does not suggest a state of "beatific" aloofness, a splendid isolation comparable to the impassiveness of the Hellenistic gods, or a self-satisfied detachment from "the turbulence and terrors of this world." The Hebrew word *ashrê,* usually rendered "blessed" or "happy," probably derives from a root meaning "to go forth," "to advance" and, in one of its forms, "to lead the way." The happiness of the Bible is not motionless but dynamic, and it has social implications. It goes somewhere, it has a purpose, and it opens a path to others.

> "Oh, the happiness of the man that feareth Yahweh,
>   That delighteth greatly in his commandments! . . .
>   He is gracious and full of compassion . . . " (Ps. 112:1, 4).

We cannot disregard the sunny lesson of the wisdom psalms without impoverishing ourselves.

Nonetheless, some sages applied at an early age a critical eye to the shocking mystery of injustice on the earth: the apparently undeserved suffering of the righteous and the prosperity of evil men who go unpunished. In Babylonia and Egypt some wise men fell into pessimism as they examined with honesty the scandal of the seemingly good man who suffers. "Does it pay to be religious?" In Israel the poem of Job was conceived partly as an attempt to solve this riddle. Job is the supreme figure of the man "who serves God for nought" (Job 1:9). Through bafflement over the problem of injustice he learned the meaning of pure religion.

Two wisdom meditations, Ps. 139 and Ps. 73, were written by men who belonged to the same school of thinking as that which produced the masterpiece of Job. With directness they faced the

enigma of evil, but they overcame their doubts by an experience
of companionship with a righteous and loving deity.

I

God Searches Man

(Psalm 139)

I

1. O Yahweh, thou hast searched me, and known me.
2. Thou knowest my downsitting and mine uprising,
    Thou understandest my thought afar off.
3. Thou winnowest my path and my lying down,
    And art acquainted with all my ways.
4. For there is not a word in my tongue,
    But, lo, O Yahweh, thou knowest it altogether.

5. Thou hast beset me behind and before,
    And laid thine hand upon me.
6. Such knowledge is too wonderful for me;
    It is high; I cannot attain it.

II

7. Whither shall I go from thy spirit?
    Or whither shall I flee from thy presence?
8. If I ascend up into heaven, thou art there;
    If I make my bed in hell, behold, thou!
9. If I take the wings of the morning,
    And dwell in the uttermost parts of the sea,
10. Even there shall thy hand lead me,
    And thy right hand shall hold me.

11. If I say, Surely the darkness shall cover me,
    And night shall encompass me about,[1]
12. Even the darkness darkeneth not from thee,
    But the night shineth as the day:
    The darkness and the light are both alike to thee.

---

[1] Hebrew text uncertain.

III

13. Yea, it is thou that possessed my reins;
     Thou didst weave me in my mother's womb.
14. I will praise thee, for I am fearfully and wonderfully made;
     Marvelous are thy works,
     And that my soul knoweth right well.
15. My frame was not hid from thee
     When I was made in secret,
     And curiously wrought in the lowest parts of the earth.
16. Thine eyes did see my substance, yet being imperfect;
     And in thy book, all of these were written,
     My days were being ordained,
     When as yet there was none of them.[2]

17. How precious are thy thoughts unto me, O God!
     How great is the sum of them!
18. If I should count them, they are more in number than the sand;
     When I awake, I am still with thee.

IV

19. Surely thou wilt slay the wicked, O God!
     Depart from me, therefore, ye bloody men!
20. For they speak against thee wickedly,
     And thine enemies take thy name in vain.
21. Do I not hate them, O Yahweh, that hate thee?
     And am I not grieved with those that rise up against thee?
22. I hate them with perfect hatred;
     I count them mine own enemies.

23. Search me, O God, and know my heart;
     Try me, and know my doubts;
24. And see if there be any wicked way in me,
     And lead me in the way everlasting!

A dry résumé fails to convey the noble sweep of the poetry, the depth of the sentiment, or the scope of the thought. In the first three strophes the psalmist contemplates God's omniscience (vss. 1-6), omnipresence (vss. 7-12), omnipotence (vss. 13-18), and in the fourth strophe he declares his abhorrence of evil men (vss. 19-

---

2 Hebrew text uncertain.

22) and makes a final plea for inner purification and guidance (vss. 23-24). The poet is not a theologian describing the attributes of the deity. With the spiritual look of faith and the warmth of conviction he gazes on the infinite person who searches him, finite creature that he is, and he speaks of the divine perfections, not in general and abstract terms, but in the vivid and personal tone of testimony. Thus, instead of merely speaking of "omniscience," he says that God knows *him;* instead of simply referring to "omnipresence," he declares that God is so close to *him* that he cannot anywhere escape the divine hand; instead of examining "omnipotence," he wonders at the power of a God who personally created *him* before his birth.

We are brought into the Biblical method of concreteness. The psalmist does not cultivate a cold dogmatism. He is not a doctrinarian. His monotheism means something to him only in so far as it affects the very beat of his heart. He feels almost through a sixth sensory organ the intimacy, the inescapability, and the creativity of God. His religion is so intense that he turns from his solitary tête-à-tête with God in prayer to an outburst of passion against evil men. But he finally rallies to a sober sense of his own inadequacy and brings the psalm to a close by laying open his very doubts before the God who knows and can do all things. He begs in the end for illumination, cleansing, and the divulgence of the way everlasting.

i

From the initial line (vs. 1), we are introduced to the crystal-like transparency of the poet's soul. God knows him through and through, because he had probed his mind, scrutinized his motivations, sifted the intricacies of his character, fathomed his most obscure instincts, sounded his reactions under stress, measured his tempers, explored the dark recesses of his subconscious, dug into the very core of his being. Here is a man who, after having undergone a long—and always painful—process of test and trial, perceives the impossibility of deceiving God, and thus learns the possibility of not deceiving himself. He acquires psychological lucidity through religious candidness. He develops the rare art of self-analysis by surrendering to God's probing scalpel. Far more than the details of his external activities are known to the Almighty. His very thoughts, or, rather, his secret and intimate intentions are discerned and comprehended before he has carried them into effect or even formulated them in his mind. The word *rea*, "thought," means specifically "desire," "disposition," "longing," and refers to inclinations, propensities, or appetites which are entertained in imagination or which seek to gain admittance at the threshold of consciousness in relation to a private aim and purpose. So minutely is my inner intent investigated that my unborn wish is embraced by the foreknowledge of God (vss. 2b, 4). However afar off I may be from God, he is never aloof; he never indulges in a state of lofty unconcern. He is "thoroughly familiar with all my ways" (vs. 3); he surrounds me on every side; his hand is on my shoulder (vs. 5); such a divine science is utterly beyond my comprehension (vs. 6) and it overwhelms me.

ii

The presence of God is indeed so crushing that the poet desperately attempts to escape it. "Whither shall I go from thy spirit?" (Vs. 7a.) What a contrast with the psalms of trust! Some among us may feel that they are not trying to flee from God. They are rather stiffening their muscles and hardening their efforts in order to find him. In our homelessness we long for his shelter. In our solitude we yearn for his companionship. Often we pray, in the words of Charles Wesley:

> "Other refuge have I none;
>   Hangs my helpless soul on Thee;
> Leave, ah! leave me not alone,
>   Still support and comfort me!
> All my trust on Thee is stayed,
>   All my help from Thee I bring;
> Cover my defenseless head
>   With the shadow of Thy wing."

On the contrary, the psalmist cries, "Whither shall I flee from thy presence?" (Vs. 7*b*.) Why did he want to run away from God? Is it, peradventure, that like Adam, the type of mankind, he wished to hide himself from the presence of the Lord God because he was afraid? (Gen. 3:8-10.) And why should he be afraid were he not an offender? It is a matter of general and personal experience that each man, at one time or another during his existence, has tried unavailingly to conceal his nakedness among the trees of the garden as he heard the voice of God, his pursuer, saying, "Man, where art thou?" (Gen. 3:9.) The presence of God may not always be a blessing; to the man caught in the pride of his achievements or the shame of his revolt, it is a curse! If God be truly God,[3] we cannot endure the glare of his piercing glance. "And the Lord turned, and looked upon Peter. And Peter ... went out, and wept bitterly" (Lk. 22:61, 62). But what about the man who cannot go out?

The psalmist has tried every subterfuge for eluding the eye of the "God all-seeing" (Gen. 16:13).

> "O whither shall I fly? what path untrod
> Shall I seek out to 'scape the flaming rod
> Of my offended, of my angry God?"[4]

To be sure, by "heaven" and "hell" (vs. 8) or "the uttermost parts of the sea" (vs. 9) the poet perhaps meant nothing more than the exceedingly distant sections of the universe which, in his cosmogony, lay outside man's habitat. But inasmuch as it was physically impossible for him to enter these inaccessible regions, we have the right to read in those lines a confession of his ludicrous endeavors to do without God, whose presence he could not stand. He wanted a heaven of his own making, and so do we, whenever we substitute for the God who disturbs us a philosophically satisfying, artistically attractive, and morally pleasing deity. There can be a profound

---

[3] See the remarkably challenging sermon of Paul Tillich, "The Escape From God," in *The Shaking of the Foundations* (New York: Charles Scribner's Sons, 1948), pp. 38 ff.

[4] Francis Quarles, "O Whither Shall I Fly?"

truth in the atheist's ironical statement, "An honest God is the noblest work of man."[5] If we worship our man-made *ideal* of beauty and justice, we suddenly discover, beside this magnificent *idol,* the true God whom we cannot ignore. "If I ascend up into heaven, thou art there!"

On the other hand, the desire to dodge the responsibilities and sorrows of our existence, or the wish to escape the consequences of our guilt, prompts us more than once in our life to call for death. In order to shun God's notice, shall we then go "to deadmen's unde-lightsome stay?"[6] Shall we court the grave, seek the oblivion of the endless night, give up the fight of the "here and now," and beg for the long repose at last? Like Job, cursing his day, we may have cast an envious look on death, saying,

> "For now should I have lain still and been quiet,
>   I should have slept; then had I been at rest,
> With kings and counselors of the earth,
>   Which built pyramids for themselves . . ." (Job 3:13-14).

But who knows whether death is final? Suppose that, like the fallen angel in *Paradise Lost,* we find ourselves still facing our-selves?

> "Me miserable! which way shall I fly
> Infinite wrath, and infinite despair?
> Which way I fly is Hell; myself am Hell;
> And in the lowest deep a lower deep
> Still threatening to devour me opens wide,
> To which the Hell I suffer seems a Heaven."

Is not cowardice before life the ultimate rebellion? But even then we must face the Inescapable One: "If I make my bed in hell, be-hold, thou!"

Again, some might prefer to "take the wings of the morning" and, like the beams of the rising sun, flash in an instant to "the utter-most parts of the sea," but the lure of the west or the constant push-

---

[5] R. G. Ingersoll, *Gods, and Other Lectures.*
[6] Mary Herbert, Countess of Pembroke, "Psalm 139."

ing away of the "last" frontier, either on the surface of this planet
or in the realm of scientific acquisition, does not heal the ancient
ills, nor does it provide man with his salvation.

> "Even led to west he would me catch,
>   Nor should I lurk with western things."[7]

Then darkness is perhaps the answer (vs. 11). "The fool saith
in his heart, There is no God" (Ps. 14:1), so that in the intellectual
void he thinks he can make, he may go undisturbed, like robbers or
beasts in the forest, to the pursuit of his deeds (Ps. 10:2-11).

> "Do thou thy best, O secret night,
>   In sable veil to cover me. . . ."[8]

Is it not because God is "the eternal torment of men" that we seek
so laboriously to shoo him out of his world? Is it not for unethical
reasons that we attempt in various ways to negate his existence—or
his influence?

> "There is no reason to flee a god who is the perfect picture of
> everything that is good in man. . . . There is no reason to flee from
> a god who is nothing more than a benevolent father, a father who
> guarantees our immortality and final happiness. Why try to escape
> from someone who serves us so well?"[9]

The psalmist knows that God judges and condemns. The divine
presence oppresses him because it is a damning presence. He does
not make an elaborate confession of his sinfulness. He does much
more than that; he describes the inherent evil which clings like
mud to his limbs by telling his insane adventures in the spheres or
in the nether land of escapism. He cannot escape from himself because he cannot shut God out of his existence. We draw the lines
which have remained unexpressed. We transpose his language to
our situation. It is as if we could say, with Gerard Manley Hopkins:

---

[7] *Ibid.*
[8] *Ibid.*
[9] Tillich, *op. cit.*, p. 42.

"I am gall, I am heartburn. God's most deep decree
Bitter would have me taste: my taste was me;
Bones built in me, flesh filled, blood brimmed the curse.
   Selfyeast of spirit a dull dough sours. I see
The lost are like this, and their scourge to be
As I am mine, their sweating selves; but worse."

The psalmist, like this penitent, is already saved. The last lines
of the second strophe anticipate the enlightenment of the third.
The hand that holds him is the hand that made him.

" 'Tis vain to flee; 'tis neither here nor there
   Can escape that hand, until that hand forbear; . . .
'Tis vain to flee, till gentle mercy show
   Her better eye. . . ."[10]

iii

There is a deep connection between the poet's contemplation of
omnipresence and his meditation on omnipotence. In the third
strophe (vss. 13-18) he regains confidence by turning his concen-
trative attention to the wonder of his birth (vss. 13-16) and of his
destiny (vss. 17-18). God created *me* in a marvelous way, and my
days have a purpose. I have an end to fulfill.

As an ancient sage, the poet was acquainted with primitive no-
tions concerning human conception and embryology. We should
not therefore be disturbed by his mythological allusions (vss. 13-
15). In a language which is strongly reminiscent of Job (10:9-12)
he acknowledged with gratitude and wonder that he came from the
hand of God. He represented the creator of the universe, wrote
Calvin, "as sitting King in the very reins of man, as the center of
his jurisdiction." At the beginning of his existence the "innermost
energies" of his body were "possessed" or "created" by the deity
who then "wove" him together and "wrought like embroidery" his
yet shapeless substance. The idea of his "divine" origin made him
break into a song of thanksgiving: "I will praise thee, for I am

---

10 Francis Quarles, *op. cit.*

fearfully and wonderfully made!" The very God from whom, in a futile attempt, he wished to flee is the "craftsman" who with inconceivable skill formed the intricate marvels of his body and lovingly gave him the breath of life.

More than this, the poet declares that his unborn days were "all of them" written in the divine book "when as yet there was none of them." A great many rash statements have been made for or against "predestination," "election," "foreordination," and related doctrines. The Bible knows them from beginning to end, but not as weapons of judgment to be brandished by men against their fellow men. Predestination is not a dogma to be taught, but a spiritual experience of a man alone with his God. It is an awareness, intimate, fearful, and sublime, of belonging completely to the creator of all. "In him we live, and move, and have our being; . . . for we are also his offspring" (Acts 17:28). Predestination is the expression of a certainty, neither modest nor arrogant, of having been brought into existence for a mission which fits into God's grand design.

Jeremiah expressed this conviction in the form of his prophetic call: "The word of Yahweh came unto me, saying, Before I formed thee in thy mother's womb, and before thou camest forth to birth, I sanctified thee, and I ordained thee a prophet unto the nations" (Jer. 1:5; cf. Rom. 8:28-29). The psalmist found comfort in the knowledge that his life was not the result of an accident and that his days were not dependent on the meeting of impersonal forces. He was no longer staggered by the inescapability of God's presence when he remembered that he had come into the world by the fiat of the ruler of the world and that the compass of his years was embraced by the God who stands above the human categories of past, present, and future.

The sense of being chosen does not in itself mean anything. The reality of election depends on the type of God one worships. Thinking of the ancient Egyptians—and probably also of modern pagans among us—Thomas Mann writes, "There are some chosen ones full of doubt, humility, and self-reproach, unable to believe in their own election. . . . And there are others . . . consciously favored of the gods, not at all surprised at whatever elevation and consummation come their way." On the contrary, the Biblical awareness of destiny saves at once from self-deprecation and self-satisfaction; it produces neither a timorous state of irresolution nor a delusion of greatness; it stands above humility and pride; it delivers both from dejection and megalomania; it merely makes one delight in the will of God at the right place and at the right moment.

The psalmist beheld God's hand in the course and goal of his life as well as in the inception thereof. His existence, limited and imperfect, perhaps even burdened by guilt, had a divine meaning. He no longer merely existed; he lived for a purpose. Others may add, with Wordsworth, in the light of Christ's dispensation:

> "My heart was full: I made no vows, but vows
> Were made for me; bond, unknown to me
> Was given that I should be, else, sinning greatly,
> A dedicated spirit. . . ."

The psalmist, while no Christian poet, yet heralded the awesome and joyful mystery which causes man to endure, resist, persist, overcome, and live fully. The thoughts of God are now for him "precious" and "excellent." No longer does he strive to shun the "designer infinite." "When I awake, I am still with thee" (vs. 18*b*).

After his moments of absorption and perhaps suprasensual ecstasy, this man is not "lost in the divine." He may be a mystic; but his mysticism is not of the kind in which finite man is identified with the infinity of God. Communion is a state of daily occurrence, not a passing rapture, not a coalescence or a merging into a divine-human oneness. It is an "ordinary" reality whereby God is still holy God, and man remains in his humanity. But man is no longer alone, nor does he wish to be so. "I am still with thee, in thy company, before thy face, in the light of thy countenance."

iv

Without any transition or warning the fourth strophe begins with an outburst against the wicked (vss. 19-22). Many interpreters would agree with T. Witton Davies' statement, "If we remove this section altogether, the rest of the Psalm makes a complete and charming poem." Even without this passage, however, the poem is not exactly "charming." Where is the charm of a poet who is so desperate that he wishes to lie down in hell?

One scholar—Moses Buttenwieser—imagines that, inasmuch as vss. 19-22 "mar the poetic unity of the poem," they belonged originally elsewhere; namely, vss. 19-20 after Ps. 140:12 and vss. 21-22 after Ps. 141:4. Accidentally omitted from these contexts, they were inserted by a scribe in the margin of the scroll, and a later copyist transcribed them to the wrong place, after Ps. 139:18. This is an ingenious, even brilliant, but irresponsible example of Biblical criticism. Such a conjecture, aside from its lack of manuscript evidence, disregards the strophic structure of Ps. 139 and also the fact that most, if not all, psalms of communion are similarly "marred" by allusions to evil and evil men. Indeed, it would seem that the closer the psalmists came to God, the more violently they expressed their aversion for the wicked.

Let us try to understand the mentality of this poet. His conception of the divine person was unusually vivid and vigorous. He felt completely dedicated to the glory of God. The ties which bound him to his creator were close and unbreakable. Suddenly he thought of other men. Is it conceivable that some people deliberately rise against their maker, as ancient giants usurping their freedom? The poet would not commune with them. He would rather, in the words of Calvin, "renounce all earthly friendships than falsely pander with flattery to the favour of those who do everything to draw down upon themselves the divine displeasure." Loyalty and zeal for the cause of God should indeed incite us to exercise the strictest caution and to avoid any compromise with the designs of wily men. Unfortunately, the poet was not able to distinguish between repugnance for evil deeds and hatred of their perpetrators. Calvin himself was uneasy about this text. "The hatred of which the Psalmist speaks," he wrote, "is directed to the sins rather than the persons of the wicked." And with a commendable restraint which belies the Reformer's reputation, he concluded, "We are, so far as lies in us, to study peace with all men; we are to seek the good of all, and if possible, they are to be reclaimed by kindness and good offices: only so far as they are enemies to God we must strenuously confront their resentment."

Still, the psalmist said,

> "I hate them with perfect hatred;
> I count them mine enemies."

This may very well be Oriental hyperbole. As Christians, however, we must dissociate ourselves from this language. Here lies the seed of theological intolerance and fanaticism which has corrupted the history of most "Christian" churches. Even when the apostle Paul advises, "Rejoice in the Lord. . . . Beware of the dogs" (Phil. 3:1-2), we must penitently ask to what extent we, as finite and sinful creatures, can dare to erect ourselves as judges of our fellows.

The psalmist declared God's enemies to be his own, but how can any man attribute to himself the right of deciding whether or not his neighbor is God's enemy? Such an attitude reveals the kind of arrogance which crucified Christ and then in his name sent "heretics" to the stake. Intolerance is par excellence the sin of religion. To be sure, our own lack of zeal also prevents us from condemning the zealots. Nevertheless, in so far as we are committed to the Gospel, we may not condone the psalmist's malignity.

Strikingly enough, he obscurely discerned that he was not right. Immediately after his display of indignation, he prayed,

> "Search me, O God, and know my heart;
> Try me, and know my doubts" (vs. 23).

He had already been "searched" by God (vs. 1), but he now begged for further painful testing. He needed again and again to be hammered under fire or "tried" in order to be disentangled from his dross and at last to emerge as pure gold. He would not seek any more to avoid the crucible of trial. The usual translation, "know my thoughts," fails to convey the strength of the Hebrew original. The word used here is not *rea,* "intimate thought," as in vss. 2

and 17, but *sarappim*, "disquieting thoughts" (cf. Job 4:13; 20:2; and especially Ps. 94:19), a term derived from the idea of "cleavage," "branching out in two different directions." Elijah used a cognate when he asked, "How long will ye go limping on two divided opinions?" (I Kings 18:21.) Likewise, a psalmist spoke of the "half-hearted ones," or "doubters" (Ps. 119:113). The poet of Ps. 139 is actually confessing a state of confusion in his own mind when he prays, "Know my doubts!" Did he realize that by giving vent to his theological odium he had acted as a god, or at least as an equal to God? We are unable to tell. Nevertheless, his final prayer reveals that he relented from his insolent pride. He was *disquieted;* perhaps he *doubted* the righteousness of his position.

"See if there be any wicked way in me," or, rather, "any oppressive, harmful and hurtful tendency in me," or possibly even, "any idolatrous sin in me." This request to a certain degree redeems the arrogance of the preceding lines. At the same time the genuineness of his faith is shown in the very consciousness of his doubt. He needs the continuous enlightenment and guidance of God. "Lead me in the way everlasting," bring me to the land of permanence, show me the path toward the good which abides.

> "If not to thee, where, whither shall I go? . . .

> Then work thy will; if passion bid me flee,
> My reason shall obey; my wings shall be
> Stretch'd out no further than from thee to thee."[11]

Like Job, the psalmist had felt stifled by the searching of God. He had asked in effect,

> "How long wilt thou not depart from me,
> Nor let me alone till I swallow down my spittle?"
> (Job 7:19.)

Now, the solitude which he had vainly sought is transmuted into

---

[11] Francis Quarles, *op. cit.*

the confidence of a son in his father. Life is no longer a bane but a benediction.

This is in some respects the greatest prayer of the psalter. Yet Ps. 73 takes us one step further.

II

God Upholds Man
(Psalm 73)

I

1. Truly God is good to the upright,[12]
   Even to such as are of a clean heart.
2. But as for me, my feet were almost gone;
   My steps had well nigh slipped.

3. For I was envious at the arrogant,
   When I saw the prosperity of the wicked.
4. For they have no pangs,[12]
   Their body is sound and plump;
5. They are not in trouble as other mortals,
   Neither are they plagued as other men;
6. Therefore they wear their pride as a necklace,
   And violence as a vestment.

7. Their iniquity protrudes from their fatness,[12]
   They have more than heart could wish.
8. They scoff, and utter wickedness,
   They speak loftily of oppression.
9. They set their mouth against the heavens,
   And their tongue walketh through the earth.
10. Therefore the people turn after them,[12]
    And find no blemish in them.[12]

11. And they say, How doth God know?
    And is there knowledge in the Most High?
12. Behold, these are the ungodly;
    Always at ease, they increase their riches.

---

[12] The Hebrew text is uncertain.

13. Verily I have in vain cleansed my heart
       And washed my hands in innocency.
14. For all the day long have I been plagued,
       And chastened every morning.

II

15. If I had said, I will speak thus;
       Behold, I had betrayed the generation of thy children.
16. But when I thought how I might grasp this,
       It was too hard for me,
17. Until I went to the sanctuary of God,
       And considered their latter end.
18. Surely thou settest them in slippery places,
       Thou castest them down into destruction.

19. How are they brought into desolation, as in a moment!
       They are utterly consumed with terrors.
20. As a dream when one awaketh, they are gone,[13]
       As a nightmare despised on awaking.[14]
21. Thus, my heart was embittered,
       And I was pricked in my reins.
22. So brutish was I, and ignorant:
       I was as a beast in thy presence.

23. Nevertheless, I am continually with thee;
       Thou hast holden me by my right hand;
24. Thou shalt guide me with thy counsel,
       And afterward receive me to glory.
25. Whom have I in heaven but thee?
       And there is none upon earth that I desire beside thee.
26. My flesh and my heart faileth:
       But God is the strength of my heart,
       And my portion forever.

27. For, lo, they that are far from thee shall perish:
       Thou hast destroyed all them that go a-whoring from thee.
28. But for me it is good to draw near to God:
       I have put my trust in the Lord Yahweh,
       That I may declare all thy works.

---

[13] The Hebrew text is uncertain.
[14] Literally, "On awaking, their image thou shalt despise."

For men who believe in the justice of God's rule over the world, the prosperity of the godless as well as the suffering of the pious constitute a shocking spectacle. Like Job, the author of Ps. 73 perceived in his own flesh the incongruity of physical torment (vs. 14). In the form of a meditative prayer in two parts he recounted his peregrinations through the seas of skepticism (vss. 3-14) until he reached the haven of grace (vss. 15-26). The opening strophe (vss. 1-2) states the problem, and the closing stanza (vss. 27-28) indicates why the poem was composed.

i

Looking back on his experience, the psalmist begins by affirming his faith in divine goodness (vs. 1). That is precisely the cause of his doubts (vs. 2). Since the godless appear to live unchecked and even blessed in spite of their iniquity (vss. 3-6; 7-10), as they openly flout Israel's conviction in God's righteousness and power (vss. 11-12), what is the use of religious and moral standards? "Verily I have in vain cleansed my heart" (vs. 13).

Like many wise men, past and present, the poet conceived religion as a method of obtaining success and a happy life. When the technique seemed to fail, he almost yielded to despair. We must take seriously the quests and the protests of those who say, with Gerard Manley Hopkins:

> "Thou art indeed just, Lord, if I contend
> With thee; but, sir, so what I plead is just.
> Why do sinners' ways prosper? and why must
> Disappointment all I endeavour end?"

The acuteness of the scandal caused the psalmist to falter but not to fall. He learned the meaning of selfless dedication, and thereby, unexpectedly, the secrets of a higher happiness.

ii

Under the strokes of physical pain and moral sorrow, man reacts usually in prostration or revolt; he retreats within his own world away from society and sometimes cultivates complacency in suffering. Here the true evil lies in developing suspicion against the universe of God and men. Tenderness for ourselves warps our intellects and we end by loving our grief. The psalmist was saved from the trap of isolation because he had the sense of his responsibility toward the church.

"If I had said, I will speak thus;
    Behold, I had betrayed the generation of thy children" (vs. 15).

By giving up faith, and by spreading abroad his unbelief, he would have lost not only himself, but also drawn into his ruin the men whose wavering uncertainty would have fed on his defeat. His consideration for the weak and for the meek—people who perhaps suffered more than he did—prevented him from airing his perplexities. Still, his silent attempt at resolving alone the enigma of injustice proved too hard for him (vs. 16) "until [he] went into the sanctuary of God" (vs. 17) and poured out his anguish before the divine face. A monologue leads a philosophical query to a dead end; only a dialogue with the infinite goodness can break man's isolation. Even a pagan poet, Aeschylus, discerned a bit of this truth: "Long tarries destiny, but comes to those who pray."

To be sure, our petitions are often answered in the unforeseen and perhaps undesired way. As Elizabeth Barrett Browning wrote,

"God answers sharp and sudden on some prayers,
    And thrusts the thing we have prayed for in our face,
    A gauntlet with a gift in 't."

The man who is determined to pray is already out of the pit. "Tormented by torturing doubts, August Hermann Francke resolved to call upon God, a God in whom he did not believe, or rather in whom he believed that he did not believe, imploring Him to take pity upon him, . . . if perchance He really existed." Thus wrote Miguel de Unamuno, who had said in his own "Atheist's Prayer,"

"Sufro yo a tu costa,
Dios no existiente, pues si tú existieras
existiería yo también de veras."

"Thou art the cause of my suffering,
O non-existing God, for if Thou didst exist,
Then should I also really exist."

The psalmist never doubted the existence of God, but he questioned whether the God in whom he had believed was also the God whom he could trust. Then, at the shadow of Zion, the visible and tangible center of Israel's life, he was thrown into the real presence of God, and a holy communion with that God rendered the obstacles evanescent. "Nevertheless, I am continually with thee" (vs. 23). The word "nevertheless," absent in the Hebrew text, correctly conveys the change of atmosphere. It is the symbol of faith at all cost, the *"Dennoch"* or the *"Quand même"* of all martyrs. Daniel before the fiery furnace uttered a similar word when he said, "Our God . . . will deliver us out of thine hand, O king. *But if not,* be it known unto thee, O king, that we will not serve thy god . . . " (Dan. 3:17-18).

The tyrants may seem to triumph, but they will some day be forgotten as a dream (vss. 19-20). They will vanish in the Saint Helenas of oblivion or upon the pyres of self-destruction. Only God remains.

In all probability, the poet still faced a hostile world. The outward circumstances of his life remained unchanged. Nothing is told of a material salvation, a healing from disease, a restitution of honor or riches. He may be just as poor now as he ever was, but he has grown into a wealth which compares with no earthly or heavenly possessions. He has received in the delights of God's companionship the grace which sufficeth (II Cor. 12:9).

Looking back on his previous haste and folly, he now discovers that he has acted with God as if he had been a behemoth, the Egyptian *pe-eh-mw* or water ox, perhaps the hippopotamus (Job 40:15), a plump colossus of flesh, the symbol of plain stupidity (vs. 22). Nothing really matters now, outside of the new certainty: "Thou hast holden me by my right hand" (vs. 23*b*). I am given a lift out of the mire where my bitterness and apathy kept me stagnant; a sense of direction and the vision of a distant goal animate my progress; thou shalt precede me on my path, "And afterward receive me to glory" (vs. 24*b*).

In all probability, these words mean that life with God may not be broken or interrupted by death. Like Enoch of the distant ages, of whom it had been written that he "walked with God, and he was not, for God *received* him" (Gen. 5:24), the author of Ps. 73 is certain that his communion with the lord of life shall last forever.[15] The centuries-old repugnance of Hebraism against speculations concerning the afterdeath is overcome. The psalmist does not believe in the natural immortality of the soul, nor does he formulate a faith in a reward beyond the grave in order to redress the injustices of the present. Such considerations do not even enter his mind. His approach is entirely on another plane. His intimacy with the divine person is such that it cannot be at the mercy of death. It possesses the quality of permanence—nay, of eternity. What else then could be asked for? (Vs. 25.) In the words of Martin Luther:

> "The whole wide world delights me not,
> For heaven and earth, Lord, care I not,
> If I may be with thee."

Flesh and heart may fail. This is incidental. God is the "rock of my heart" and "my portion forever" (vss. 26*b* and 26*c*); that is to say, not only the solid basis of my thought and will, but also the only desire of my affection.

Here is a destitute troubadour of the Eternal. Landless, homeless, defenseless, he has now a share, a portion, a lot, an acreage, a garden enclosed and luxuriant, a field which ripens to harvest, an orchard, a grove of olive trees, a vineyard, a home. The dream of the wandering nomad, without the sordid enslavement of the peasant to the soil, is transposed into the spiritual realm.

---

[15] Many scholars interpret vs. 24*b* as referring only to restoration on earth, but they ignore thereby the climactic significance of the adverb "afterward" and the full meaning of the verb "receive."

Distant from God, a man exists as if he were already dead (vs. 27). Close to God, the psalmist wishes to draw nearer still.

> "Thou art my way; I wander if thou fly:
> Thou art my light; if hid, how blind am I!
> Thou art my life; if thou withdraw, I die."[16]

The reality of God's presence constitutes the poet's supreme good, his only good. The psalm was composed in order to declare God's deeds. The poet is a witness of God's works. Like many another psalmist, the doubter has become an Evangelist; the skeptic, a bearer of "good news."

No philosophical solution to the problem of evil is offered here, or anywhere else in the Bible. But the psalmist has displaced the question and made it thereby unimportant.

"In his fellowship with God he has found that nothing matters in comparison with that fellowship. He had been perplexed that the ungodly should prosper, and almost thought of throwing in his lot with them. But now he knows that, however great their possessions, they are truly destitute, while the man who has found fellowship with God is rich though he possesses nothing. That is the real solution—not an answer to the riddle, but the attainment of a state of mind in which there is no desire to ask it."[17]

Because he has routed phantoms and clung "to Faith beyond the forms of Faith," the psalmist has been given to taste the ineffable joy. His union with the Lord God invalidates even the curse of mortality. Death recedes from his horizon, demoted and utterly inconsequential. Rather is it transfigured as a threshold to new joy: a full welcome within the glory of God. The poet's mysticism—if the word may be used—is, as always in the Bible, of a peculiarly Hebraic brand: instead of blurring, it intensifies man's duty toward his fellows. More than ever aware of his solidarity with the "church," the psalmist will publish, not his faith, but all

---

[16] Francis Quarles, "Why Dost Thou Shade Thy Lovely Face?"
[17] William Temple, *Nature, Man and God* (London: Macmillan, 1934), p. 43.

of God's "accomplishments." Gratitude has become the motive of
poetic creation.

III

Other "wisdom meditations" of the Psalter surveyed the earthly
triumphs of evil men in the calm perspective of God's time. The
psalmists, as well as the prophets, took the long view of history.

i

For example, the author of Ps. 37 had benefited from the wisdom of a mature tradition and enlightened experience when he
remarked:

"I have seen the wicked in great power,
    And spreading himself like a green bay tree.
Yet, I passed by, and lo, he was not.
    Yea, I sought him, but he could not be found" (vss. 35-36).

Unlike the poets of Ps. 73 and Job, however, he oversimplified the
realities of existence and even closed his eyes to tragedy when he
said:

"I have been young, and now am old;
    Yet have I not seen the righteous forsaken,
    Nor his seed begging bread" (vs. 25).

Still, the true solution of which he caught a glimpse was not dependent on an unrealistic reaffirmation of the belief in individual
and "this worldly" retribution. Like the poets of Ps. 73 and Job,
he resolved the tension which opposes morality and peace by ex-
tolling the joy he obtained in divine communion.

"Find thy delights in Yahweh,
    And he shall give thee the desires of thine heart" (vs. 4).

The problem of evil loses its undermining power when the affections of man are attuned to the wishes of his creator, and faith itself leads to the "exquisite delights" of the love of God.

ii

The poet of Ps. 49 was unique among the "wisdom" psalmists in this respect: he did not associate moral evil with the mere possession of riches, nor did he equate the wealthy with the tyrants. But he knew there are things which money cannot buy. "Those who trust in their wealth" are not able to give to God a ransom for their life; the multitude of their riches will not enable them to live forever (vss. 6-9); in the end, "Death shall shepherd them" (vs. 14). By contrast, the psalmist entertained for himself a momentous hope:

> "Surely, God will redeem my life
> From the power of the grave,
> For he shall receive me" (vs. 15).

Does the poet signify by these words that he will never die? Certainly not. Then, does he mean that he will now be redeemed from mortal danger and preserved from a premature death, but that of course he will die someday at a ripe old age? Commentators are not agreed on an answer. Taken at their face value, all the words which are used here point toward the same direction: the psalmist opposes his own faith to the vain hopes of those who desire to live forever; he is looking neither for deathlessness nor for the natural immortality of the spiritual aspect of his being, but for a "reception," at his death, within the heart of God himself. Any concrete formulation of this prospect is beyond his capacity, to be sure. The assurance of God's own welcome is sufficient. "He shall receive me." As in Ps. 73, where the same verb is used in a parallel context (vs. 24*b*), the theme of life everlasting emerges from that of fellowship with God. Eternal delight is not a reality which depends on the normal endowments of man. It may be con-

templated only in the light of divine grace. It derives solely from
the gift of present communion.

iii

Although not a "wisdom" meditation, one prayer of trust is
closely related to Ps. 73 in ideas as well as in words, and it also
breaks through the veil and the horror of death.

"I have set Yahweh always before me. . . .
  Therefore my heart is glad, and I rejoice;
    Yea, my flesh shall dwell in hope,
For thou wilt not abandon my life to the grave,
    Neither wilt thou suffer thine holy one to see the pit.
Thou wilt show me the path of life:
    In thy presence is fullness of joy,
    At thy right hand are pleasures forevermore" (Ps. 16:8-11).

Whereas most of the psalmists, like most men of the Old Covenant, conceived Sheol or the sojourn of the dead as a place where
there is neither praise nor even remembrance of God (see, for instance, Pss. 6:5; 88:5, 12; 115:17), a few among them lived in so
close a union with God that death ceased to frighten or even to
concern them. The very prospect of a separation from the omnipotent and merciful Father became for them an utter impossibility.
They stepped onto the threshold of a new world in which the presence of God created not only deliverance from evil but also entrance
into life eternal.

"... Thou, our God, art gracious and true,
Long-suffering, and in mercy ordering all things.
For even if we sin, we are thine, knowing thy dominion.
But we shall not sin, knowing that we are accounted thine:
For to know thee is perfect righteousness;
Yea, to know thy dominion is the root of immortality"
              (Book of Wisdom, 15:1-3).

This assurance, however, is never based on a right acquired by
man. It is never a cocksure certainty.

"Delight is to him, whom all the waves of the billows of the seas of the boisterous mob can never shake from this sure Keel of Ages. And eternal delight and deliciousness will be his, who coming to lay him down, can say with his final breath—O Father!—chiefly known to me by Thy rod—mortal or immortal, here I die. I have striven to be Thine, more than to be this world's, or mine own. Yet this is nothing; I leave eternity to Thee; for what is man that he should live out the lifetime of his God?"[18]

God remains sovereign, and man respects the freedom of God.

It was with the full and fresh awareness of their salvation in unity with the risen Christ that the early Christians applied the hope of the psalmists to the new era of the New Covenant (Acts 2:29-33). They, too, grounded both their triumph over suffering and their expectation of eternity on their present appurtenance to God's own family. "We know that in every thing God worketh for good with them that love him . . ." (Rom. 8:28). "Now are we the sons of God, and it doth not yet appear what we shall be" (I John 3:2), but we are fully "persuaded that neither death, nor life, nor angels, nor principalities, nor powers, nor things present, nor things to come, nor height, nor depth, nor any other creatures, shall be able to separate us from the love of God, which is in Christ Jesus our Lord" (Rom. 8:38-39).

---

18 Herman Melville, *Moby Dick.*

5

Their Meaning
for Today

THEIR MEANING FOR TODAY

INTELLECTUAL honesty compels the modern Christian to admit that some of the poetry of the Psalter is aged and outdated. Several psalms contain lines which are coarse from both an artistic and a religious standpoint. Here is for instance a colorful clause, which is placed in the mouth of God himself:

"Moab is my washpot,
    Over Edom will I cast out my shoe" (Pss. 60:8; 108:9).

No one may deny that its imagery belongs to other canons of aesthetics than ours, or that its theology is enclosed within historical peculiarities which, to say the least, are not directly relevant to our time. Let us recognize frankly and boldly the limitations of some of the psalms. We shall then be in a better position for straining the wine from the dregs and preserving the permanent from the ephemeral.

I

First of all, a few prayers are imbued with the feeling of *Schadenfreude* or "malignant joy," an emotion more akin to paganism than to the gospel of Jesus. Indeed, it sometimes goes beyond the passion of vindictiveness which mars Ps. 137 or the fanaticism which animates a part of Ps. 139. For example:

"The righteous shall rejoice when he seeth vengeance;
    He shall wash his feet in the blood of the wicked"
                                        (Ps. 58:10).

To be sure, outbursts of this kind must be viewed against the

267

background of untold oppression and tyranny, and they are partly allayed by the awareness that "Verily, there is a God that judgeth in the earth" (Ps. 58:11). Nonetheless, the bitterness needs to be softened and even overcome, as Alexander Maclaren has written, "by some effluence from the spirit of Him who wept over Jerusalem, and yet pronounced its doom."

In the second place, several of these poets fail to see that the men whom they are pleased to call "the righteous" are often, if not always, gnawed within themselves by the worm of complacency, and pride. As soon as a man declares,

> "I am like a green olive tree
>   In the house of God" (Ps. 52:8*a*),

he displays the spirit of "separateness" (the literal meaning of "Pharisaism") by which a morally decent citizen prays thus within himself, "God, I thank thee that I am not as other men are" (Lk. 18:11).

Again, most of the psalmists were poor, and while economic poverty creates spiritual receptivity and produces a sensitiveness to social justice, it also tends to warp a man's outlook on life, embitter his relationships with "successful men," and blind his understanding of those who have the responsibilities of civic or international power. The psalms are filled with references to "the poor," "the afflicted," "the needy," "the weak," "the meek," "the humble," "the lowly," and "the pious." Through their sufferings these men learned the meaning of pure religion; they were beaten into repentance, they were tempered into fidelity, and some of them were even whipped into the heroism of endurance without reward. Too often, however, we cannot help discerning a certain element of one-sidedness in their judgments. While we must always respond to their cries—as to those of the hungry and oppressed everywhere—and pay heed to their critique of material and political corruption, we should also beware of the "defense mechanism" inherent in persecuted minorities and the "martyrdom complex" of courageous men who have testified under stress, have survived martyrdom, and thus claim to have earned access to unerring truth. Jesus did not call himself righteous, nor even "good" (Lk. 18:19). In the third place, the psalmists shared the prescientific world view of their age. Their language was influenced by various myth patterns common to the Egyptians and the ancient Semites. It is also probable that they attributed some of their ills to the practice of witchcraft. They spoke of "the gods" as if they believed in their existence (although they never worshiped them), and they pictured Yahweh as "riding upon the cherub" or "sweeping along the wings of the wind" (Ps. 18:10). At this point, however, we must take great care not to dismiss their message on the ground that it is entangled with mythological and otherwise "primitive" expressions. Contrary to the popular belief of our day, contemporary theologians begin to recognize that a myth is by no means untrue. It is rather the poetic, and sometimes the only possible, expression of a truth which escapes rational formulation. In spite of archaisms of language and other limitations, the Psalter offers to the modern Christian a lyrical channel of unique beauty and power for the parturition of his prayer and the offering of his praise.

II

Alone in the Bible, the psalmists have succeeded in unifying the prophetic and the priestly approaches to religion. The prophets preached the will of a stern God who said, "This is the way: walk ye in it." The priests had at their disposal the whole apparatus of traditional ritualism—the sacred word and the sacred act which hit a man "below the neck" and often conquer his subconscious while failing to reach his mind—and they dispensed the sacramental grace of absolution, forgiveness, and consecration to a worshiper who might easily—and often did—separate his ethical behavior from the deeds and decisions of his piety.

More humanely than the prophets and more rigidly than the priests, the psalmists understood man's inability to win his own salvation by obedience to a law or the use of a hallowed technique.

They offered the pastoral consolations of the priests without neglecting the moral demands of the prophets for righteousness in living. They spoke the harsh word of God's judgment without producing despair, and they conveyed the soothing benefits of religion without inducing indolence or self-arrogance.

Luther rightly called the Psalter "a Bible in miniature." Indeed, the psalms occupy in the Scripture as well as in the church a situation of uniqueness, for they mirror the faith of Israel as a whole, and they provide a bridge between moralism, which too easily condemns, and sacramentalism, which too easily condones. Their poets did not emphasize ethical conduct at the expense of fidelity to the forms of devotion, nor did they stress man's freedom to choose between good and evil at the cost of God's power to judge the sins and to heal the wounds of man. They impregnated the quietism of saints, sheltered from the storms of the street, with the leaven, the seed, and the salt of the prophetic *"do and don't."* They maintained a balance between the welcoming embrace of an open church *(ecclesia)* and the strict obedience of a closed sect *(ecclesiola).* They kept in tension the equilibrium which must always be maintained between a militant church on earth and a triumphant kingdom at the end of history.

Their faith unwittingly translated itself into theological certainties, and while they wrote only hymns and prayers, and not treatises of beliefs, they substantiated that faith into a creed on God, man, and salvation, which is that of the entire Bible, not excluding the New Testament. While poets, they were profound theologians. And that is the reason for which their hymnal remains a living book for today.

III

As poets of worship, the psalmists gathered the whole created realm into their act of adoration. To the glory of God they offered all: the universe of nature, the world of history, and the microcosm of glory and shame which lay within themselves.

i

They interpreted the voice of nature as the response of transient things and animals to the benevolence of an eternal creator. They saw the traces of God's hand in the heavens above and in the fields below, and they summoned the elements together in a cosmic symphony of praise. Yet, had they said,

> ". . . Earth's crammed with heaven,
> And every common bush afire with God,"

they would have added, as did Elizabeth Barrett Browning in *Aurora Leigh:*

> "But only he who sees, takes off his shoes—
> The rest sit round it and pluck blackberries,
> And daub their natural faces unaware
> More and more from the first similitude."

Creation obtains a meaning only in so far as it is subservient to the dominion of God, whose faithful steward and responsible plenipotentiary over nature is man. But is man faithful and responsible?

ii

They heard the voice of history and saw the theater where God metes out his judgment upon the nations and reveals at once his justice and his mercy. A cynic like Voltaire may be shortsighted enough to remark that "the history of the great events of this world is hardly more than the history of crimes," but the psalmists discovered beneath and above them the righteous purpose of a creator who brings about the fulfillment of his creation. Living in tragic times not altogether different from ours, they did not yield to a cyclical, deterministic, and therefore meaningless, view of history, saying,

> "There is the moral of all human tales;
> 'Tis but the same rehearsal of the past,
> First freedom, and then glory—when that fails,
> Wealth, vice, corruption—barbarism at last."[1]

While they acknowledged that barbarism is the fruit of corruption, they did not believe that the future is "the same rehearsal of the past," for they discerned a line of salvation cutting across the generations of men. Yet they did not commit the opposite error common to all humanists, according to which man's conquest of the forces of nature follows a pattern of inevitable progress. They waited for the advent of the kingdom, not of man, but of God. They expected an age of universal peace based on brotherhood, not through man's scientific achievements, but by God's redemptive grace. As they gathered in the temple for the celebration of the cultic drama, they lived ahead of their age and gazed at the end or goal of history as a liturgical present. Thus they could sing, "The Lord hath become King!"

Although at times they ambiguously associated Zion with the center of God's kingdom, they dimly but surely beheld the vision of a purified Israel, servant of the Lord and light of the nations. One of the psalmists—the poet of Ps. 22—used words which went even further in that direction: he pictured an individual incarnation of true Israel, "despised and rejected of men, . . . smitten of God and afflicted"—the instrumentality of salvation for a people yet unborn, the co-ordinating apex of history. "Now let the isles rejoice!" Commenting on this verse, John Donne rightly declared of the psalms:

> "They show us islanders our joy, our king;
> They tell us *why*, and teach us *how* to sing."

Quite naturally, the early Christians read the "royal" hymns in the light of their own faith, and they gave to many poems of the Psalter a messianic interpretation.

---

[1] George Gordon Byron, *Childe Harold*.

iii

The psalmists listened to the word of God spoken in the silence of their secret selves. They searched for the presence of the Holy God in the Temple and they found it there. Yet a few of them carried their search farther, and their faith transcended the reality of Zion. While the mystery of the cultic act and the fellowship of the community were the channel of mediation whereby they found entry into the world of worship and learned the true name of Zion— *Yahweh-Shammah*, "The Lord-is-There" (Ez. 48:35)—they ultimately encountered God in a realm which lay beyond Zion. Like the men of old, Abraham, Moses, and Elijah, of whom it was said that they talked with God face to face, some poets of the psalms, mortal, finite, and sinful creatures, were ushered into a Holy of Holies which was not made by man. They gained admittance into an intimate tête-à-tête with infinite holiness, infinite glory, infinite justice, and what Gerard Manly Hopkins called "God's better beauty, grace."

Hurt by other men or by their own sins, they experienced the power of the depths. In the presence of the Holy God they gasped at greater depths still. They lay naked before the sun and they communed with darkness. They learned the unavailing, useless, ineffectual character of their deeds, of their achievements, of their morality, of their piety. Faith alone kept them at the edge of the abyss. Faith, *emûnah*—a word which is akin to *amen*—was for them a fence, a stay, the only protection against a fall into nothingness. They "trusted" *(batach)* or "relied" on a God whose will is love, and only then did they find "security" *(betach)*.

> "I trusted in thee, O Yahweh;
> I said, Thou art my God!
> My times are in thy hand" (Ps. 31:14, 15*a*).

It was their immediate knowledge of God which made them look at themselves as they really were, but it was also the awareness of their destitution which enabled them to discover the fullness of

God. Those who knew him best were those who knew themselves without a veil. Here lies perhaps supremely the "Christian" significance of the psalms: the need for a death and for a re-creation.

> "Create in me a clean heart, O God, . . .
> Take not thy holy spirit from me" (Ps. 51:10, 11).

To be sure, even the poet of this prayer lacked a perception of his own death in God. He could not say, like John Donne:

> "I am a little world made cunningly
> Of elements and an angelic sprite,
> But black sin hath betray'd to endless night
> My world's both parts, and O, both parts must die."

Whenever we speak of the "Christian" significance of the psalmists, we must beware of making them speak as reborn men of the New Covenant. They wanted the light which is shed only by the contemplation of a self-offering God, of a God who shows his love for man, and to this end accepts to suffer for man in the form of a mere man. They did not see, and they could not see, that divine love needs

> "The heel on the finishing blade of grass,
> The self-confidence of the falling root,
> Needs death, death of the grain, our death."[2]

In other words, we must admit that the psalmists did not live under the sign of the Incarnation and in the new world of the Resurrection. They were totally unable to pray, like David in Browning's "Saul,"

> " 'Tis the weakness in strength, that I cry for! my flesh, that I seek
> In the Godhead! I seek and I find it. O . . . [soul], it shall be
> A Face like my face that receives thee, a Man like to me,
> Thou shalt love and be loved by, forever: a Hand like this hand
> Shall throw open the gates of new life to thee! See the Christ
>   stand!"

---

2 W. H. Auden, "1929," in *The Collected Poetry of W. H. Auden* (New York: Random House, 1945). Quoted by permission.

In a sense, therefore, the psalmists are greater than "Christian" poets, for, although without Christ, they grasped the profundity of their own unworthiness, and they pinned their faith on a forgiveness which we, who breathe the air of the Gospel, negate by the sterility of our lives.

IV

As Christians, we must feed on the hymns and the lonely prayers of the Psalter, for they anticipate the Christian characteristic par excellence, namely: the evangelistic zeal, the will to share divine riches with other men, the sense of the corporateness of the invisible church. As John Wesley wrote, "The Bible knows nothing of solitary religion." Those nameless worshipers of the Jerusalem Temple who were moved to become poets and thus wrote the psalms obeyed this peculiarly Hebraic sense of social solidarity. They sang as witnesses. Because they stood alone before God, with only their sin and his grace, they turned outside toward the people. The more intense their private life, the more social their religion became. They would have understood the cry of the apostle, "Woe is unto me, if I preach not the gospel!" (I Cor. 9:16.)

Finally, a handful of the psalmists seemed to have looked beyond the grave. United to God on earth, they felt united to him forever. The fear of annihilation had lost its sting. Had they lived a few generations later, they would have joined in the Christian certitude which above reason declares, in the words of John Donne, "I shall rise from the dead, from the dark station, from the prosternation of death, and never miss the sun, which shall then be put out, for I shall see the Son of God, the Sun of glory, and shine myself, as that sun shines."

It is legitimate that, for the Christian reader of today, all the psalms, the hymns of praise, the laments, the confessions, the songs of trust and communion, be received in the spirit of Christ.

Suggested Readings

Barnes, W. E., *The Psalms*, 2 vols., New York and London, 1931.
Gunkel, H., *Die Psalmen*, Göttingen, 1926.
Gunkel, H., und Begrich, J., *Einleitung in die Psalmen*, Göttingen, 1933.
James, F., *Thirty Psalmists*, New York, 1938.
Leslie, E. A., *The Psalms*, New York and Nashville, 1949.
Oesterley, W. O. E., *A Fresh Approach to the Psalms*, New York, 1937.
Oesterley, W. O. E., *The Psalms*, 2 vols., London, 1939.
Paterson, J., *The Praises of Israel*, New York, 1950.
Snaith, N., *Hymns of the Temple* [Pss. 42-43, 44, 46, 50, 73], London, 1951.
Weiser, A., *Die Psalmen*, Göttingen, 1950.

INDEX TO PSALM REFERENCES

The Psalms which have been studied at length are indicated by an asterisk (*).